ESSAYS ON CREATIVITY IN THE SCIENCES

ESSAYS ON
Creativity
in the Sciences

BY ASSOCIATES OF THE

CREATIVE SCIENCE SEMINAR

DIVISION OF GENERAL EDUCATION

NEW YORK UNIVERSITY

EDITED BY *Myron A. Coler*

FOREWORD BY *Paul A. McGhee*

NEW YORK UNIVERSITY PRESS

1963

CONTRIBUTORS

ELLIS BLADE, *Industrial Scientist and Consultant, Markite Corporation.*

MARY-FRANCES BLADE, *Professor of Mechanical Engineering, The Cooper Union, New York.*

MYRON A. COLER, *Director, Creative Science Program and Adjunct Professor, Division of General Education and Extension Services, New York University, New York; President, Markite Corporation.*

H. HERBERT FOX, *Vice-President, Cyclo Chemical Corporation, Los Angeles.*

NICHOLAS E. GOLOVIN, *Technical Adviser, Space Science and Technology, Office of Science and Technology, Executive Office of the President, Washington.*

HAROLD K. HUGHES, *Professor of Physics, Indiana State College, Terre Haute, Indiana.*

HAROLD W. MOHRMAN, *Director of Research, Overseas Division, Monsanto Chemical Company, St. Louis.*

ANNE ROE, *Professor of Education and Director, Center for Research in Careers, Harvard University, Cambridge.*

SIDNEY G. ROTH, *Director, Office of Research Services and Professor of Mathematics, New York University; Special Assistant to Director, Office of Grants and Research Contracts, National Aeronautics and Space Administration, Washington.*

RUSSELL F. W. SMITH, *Professor of Adult Education and Associate Dean, Division of General Education and Extension Services, New York University, New York.*

MORTON I. TEICHER, *Dean, Wurzweiler School of Social Work, Yeshiva University, New York.*

FOREWORD

THE DIRECTOR of the Creative Science Program and its Seminars, who was the program's originator and continues to be its energizing and unifying force, has indicated in the preface that follows the nature of the sessions held by this unusual group during its brief history. The same essay provides far more than a bare introduction to the symposium that follows, as it dispels many of the hazy and romantic suppositions with which consideration of the subject of creativity has frequently been beclouded.

It may be of some interest to comment on the auspices that encouraged the organization of the Creative Science Seminar and are currently helping to sustain it. In fact, to do so may even be pertinent to the subject under discussion, since such comment leads to the related question of whether the administration of a complex institution such as a university can in itself be said to be creative; or, if this suggestion seems extravagant, whether it can truly be supportive of efforts and programs that give promise of being "creative." Professor Sidney G. Roth deals directly with this aspect of the matter in his essay "Creativity in an Academic Atmosphere" and other contributors to the present volume touch upon it. Within the proper limits of a foreword I will make only one additional comment.

There may be some advantage, in a university, in having an autonomous school or division freely committed to the purposes and possibilities of continuing higher education, wherever this may lead. Such is, at any rate, the present status and role of the Division of General Education and Extension Services of New York University, within which the Creative Science Seminar was administratively nurtured. This free pursuit of interests and needs in the area of continuing education represents in some measure an elaboration of, if not a departure from, the usual conception of the role of the extension division in a university. Traditionally, this role as usually stated has been "to extend the resources of the university and place them at the service of the community."

As far as it goes, there can be no quarrel with this statement of purpose. When it is an expression of a genuine institutional commitment and is carried out with energy and imagination, it is a task of large dimensions indeed, capable of engaging the highest levels of intelligence and administrative talent. Moreover, it is obvious that as a constituent member of the family of schools within the university, the extension division will seek first of all to represent and reflect the subject-matter strengths and authority figures of its parent, the university; these are the primary assets and resources of any extension division. Yet if the extension division can "extend" only the resources that presently exist in a university, and is permitted to represent only the subject-matter authority figures currently on its full-time faculty, its agenda must inevitably be limited.

The charter for university extension must now be rewritten. There are on every side so many needs in the broad area of continuing education that the idea of "extending the resources that currently exist within the university," even if it could easily be done, is no longer adequate. In today's world, the task of the staff of university extension must be to identify and organize the resources of the community to meet the interests and needs of continuing higher education.

Obviously, the possibilities for implementing such a revised view of the role of extension are in large measure a function of the resources of the community in which the university is located. (Sometimes, too, these possibilities derive from a university's view of its "community.") If a university is located in a rural area, the most important authority figures may well be all on campus or else, at the other extreme, in sections of the state too remote to make involvement easily possible. But in large cities, in areas of industrial concentration, and in centers of corporate management and finance, there may be in many subject areas more authority figures and frontier thinkers outside the university walls than are employed inside. Surely it is the path of wisdom to involve these outside specialists in serving the university's purposes in continuing education. There may be risks, as when no competent appraisal of an outside specialist can be secured within the academic community. But the intense new interests and pressing needs of society are not to be adjourned because of the accidental factor that a university has no department containing expertise with respect to a particular need.

The call for a new interpretation of the role of university extension may seem far removed from the ideas about creativity contained in the essays that follow. Yet the discussion appears not unrelated to the nature of the Creative Science Seminar. The Seminar members are not colleagues or associates from the same department, school, or college. They represent different institutions and different disciplines. And they came to the Seminar sessions in New York City each month, some flying in from distant parts of the country. They were investigating a subject in which no school or department has hegemony, in which expertise is where you find it. It is in such a context that the contemporary extension division or school should be prepared to work. In his preface, Dr. Coler has written of the importance of environment favorable to creative efforts. It may be in a school primarily committed to the purposes, avenues, and byways of continuing education that such a group will often find its most supportive environment.

Some of the broad purposes of the university are well served by a school committed not to a particular integration of related topics and problems (such as law, engineering, or business) but freely committed to the needs of continuing higher education, wherever they may lead, and to the organization of community resources to serve these needs. Such, in our view, is the new role of university extension. When it is accepted and effectively fulfilled, hopefully it will provide an environment not only favorable to the study of creativity but supportive of many creative efforts that now have no appropriate home within the academic community.

PAUL A. McGHEE
DEAN, DIVISION OF GENERAL EDUCA-
TION AND EXTENSION SERVICES
NEW YORK UNIVERSITY

CONTENTS

PREFACE

THE CREATIVE SCIENCE PROGRAM under the Division of General Education and Extension Services of New York University has as one of its most important activities the Creative Science Seminar. The overall program is dedicated to the belief that the conservation, cultivation, and implementation of creative talent are among our most important national needs and responsibilities. A tacit but basic initial premise is that the scientific method can be applied to scientific creativity itself.

It may be interesting to note in passing that the program was initiated before the advent of Sputnik.

From the outset it was considered essential that the seminar be of a truly interdisciplinary nature. There have been too many unsatisfactory conferences on creativity at which psychologists have harangued psychologists, engineers have addressed engineers, and so forth. There are also some rather naïve ideas extant regarding the requirements for true interdisciplinary activity. Inviting a sprinkling of outsiders to an otherwise homogeneous group can at best be characterized as only a step in the right direction. If the group is too small, an insufficient number of disciplines may be represented; if it is too large, many of the participants may become mere listeners. A person does not necessarily have the interest or temperament to become a useful member of an interdisciplinary group simply because his professional credentials are impressive. Many are seemingly immune to thoughts and knowledge not originating in the area of their own specific disciplines. At the opposite extreme an interdisciplinary group can degenerate to a "committee" in the worst sense of the word.

Finally, real time is required to properly transmit, receive, and indulge in feedback and processing of views and information. A meeting of distinguished scholars with great aptitude for interdisciplinary communication may fall far short of its potential if there is time only for reading a string of papers at each other without adequate time for interaction.

The Creative Science Seminar has been convening one full Saturday each month of the academic year for some five years. In addition, there have been special meetings. A week-long conference held at Cooper Union's Green Engineering Camp gave particular attention to material forming the basis of these essays, and each associate had a chance to function as a sort of editor-at-large. Many of our Seminar associates have also participated in the Conference on Education for Creativity in the Sciences at New York University. The closed sessions of the seminar have been covered by some two hundred hours of tape recordings.

In the course of the seminars, each associate has formally presented at least two diverse papers to the other associates. The presentations have been exposed to extended discussion as well as to written comment. As a result, the authors have often revised their views as well as their presentations.

An interesting experimental device has consisted of deliberately staggering the agenda so that no major presentation and discussion is completed in a single meeting. Although this device causes some repetitiveness and discontinuity, I believe that on the whole it has worked out well. The redundancy favors more discriminating emphasis and improved communication. The spreading over time encourages a certain amount of maturing and evolution of the material beyond that which normally takes place when there are sharp cutoffs and no return engagements.

Each associate was asked to select his or her paper of choice as a basis for this collection of *Essays on Creativity in the Sciences*. The volume is therefore manifestly not intended to be a definitive treatise, a handbook, a text, or even a systematic account of the work of the Seminar. (In fact, the work originally conceived for the Seminar and its successors has really just begun to evolve.) In view of the manner in which some essays have been developed, it is natural not only that they should display diverse personal interests and approaches but also that in a number of instances they exhibit varying degrees of direct conflict in interpretation and philosophy.

Conversely, in observing the evolution of the material over the years, I have been fascinated by the extent to which even those holding highly disparate views have knowingly or unknowingly borrowed from each other, usually to synergistic advantage. I believe that one of the more durable values of this collection lies in future appreciation of these "borrowing" patterns. Such patterns are, of course, easily obscured by the diversity of topics and the superficial differences in style and writing ability which are characteristic of most collections and compilations.

In serving as editor I have tried to avoid acting as a master of ceremonies, since I do not believe that these essays lend themselves to pat introductions or light recappings. I have tried even harder to avoid playing the censor with respect to either substance or form of expression. This restraint does not arise from a laissez-faire philosophy on my part but rather from a sincere respect for the abilities and accomplishments of the Seminar associates as individuals. They have all done or directed creative work in their fields of specialization. In addition, as participants and leaders of other professional and study groups, they have brought to the Seminar and their essays the benefits of much more than their own personal knowledge.

Many of the essays, although devoted to major topics, are specialized in viewpoint and personal in form. Accordingly, they are not directed to a uniform audience. The subject of "creativity" is truly complex and the field embryonic from the standpoint of systematic interdisciplinary studies. Before proceeding to the individual essays, it might be helpful to review some of the facts and fallacies associated with "creativity" and to indicate some of the considerations entering into our approach.

Man's irresistible desire not only to "explain" things but to expound in detail on those things which he does not understand has led to a world of conjecture running the gamut from brilliant scientific hypotheses through charming fairy tales and mythology to plain nonsense.

The words "creativity" and "creativeness," together with their many derivatives and equivalents, are now applied to an enormous collection of endeavors varying from sound scholarship to what might be charitably characterized as dubious "thinkmanship" and complete preoccupation with trivia.

The significant goal is not to come up with an airtight definition, nor to poke fun at approaches that are shallow but well intentioned. We shall certainly not attempt to offer still another set of rules for personal creativity.

For some strange reason, most people seem to feel that creativity is wrapped in goodness, virtue, and dedication. However, unless we read moral values into the definition, we are compelled to admit that the "works" of Torquemada, de Sade, and Hitler were creative in their own pathological ways. The products of creativity in the sciences are certainly amoral: a newly created drug may prolong the life of a parasitic criminal as well as that of a worthy citizen.

Although productivity is often incorrectly confused with creativity, there is perhaps some justification for this error. One cannot have creativity without productivity. Productivity is often used as a measure of creativity. For example, the total number of technical papers published by a scientist and the number of paintings exhibited by an artist are often mentioned in this sense. Sometimes, with prevailing limited knowledge, there may appear to be no better measure. The passage of time may change the evaluation. A van Gogh may not have been appreciated until after his death; an extremely prolific novelist whose success stemmed solely from riding a fad may be deservedly forgotten within a single generation. Insofar as productivity is a measure of drive and motivation—and highly creative people are, almost by definition, highly motivated—there is a further basis of correlation. Yet, in the final analysis, productivity is not creativity. It appears to be a necessary but insufficient condition. Abundant works permit and even favor but cannot guarantee creativity.

The relation of creativity to novelty and originality is again one of necessity rather than sufficiency. To rewrite this preface, translating alternate words into a foreign language, would be a novel and perhaps original act, but it would not be creative because it would be dead-ended, an act apparently having neither immediate nor future meaningful implications. A vivid imagination is certainly a valuable if not indispensable aid in suggesting and recognizing worthwhile possibilities, but, without discipline, it may conjure up much that is worthless and deluding.

One might be tempted to cut this discussion short by taking refuge in the dictionary or otherwise demanding a tidy definition of creativity. To borrow a phrase from patent technology, "in the present state of the art" this is not constructively possible. I believe that creativity as a subject may be as difficult to deal with in words alone as mathematics and chemistry would be without their distinctive symbols.

There is a tendency to talk of creativity as if it were an absolute personal endowment or possession, like the color of one's eyes or the weight of one's brain. We often hear of a man referred to as "a highly creative person." Without further qualification, such phrases might be quite misleading. Overemphasis on the personal-success-story type of approach has also led to many delightful anecdotes and a sense of understanding of creativity which is unfortunately often not valid or useful. Relatively few highly creative people in the sciences have been articulate about their methods; some with complete sincerity appear to have been creative in spite of rather than because of their alleged methods. Some imply that their creative contributions were preceded by dramatic "flashes of insight"—often conveniently overlooking the fact that their duds and blind-alley ventures were similarly preceded by dramatic flashes.

Research on creativity has been overly confined to the study of creative individuals, not in social situations but in isolation. We are now, by way of analogy, more or less at the stage of Tycho Brahe's investigation of planetary motion. We need more Brahes to collect information about creativity, then the Keplers to organize this information into probable, useful patterns, paving the way for future Newtons to offer hypotheses that will really encompass our observations and, what is more important, lead to fertile predictions. Beyond that we may expect future Einsteins to build upon, alter, and expand upon the foundations established by the Newtons.

Creativity, like sound, cannot exist in a vacuum. To focus on the creative individual without considering his environment or cultural background is almost a sure way of guaranteeing an incomplete and probably incorrect theory of creativity. What would have been the creative contribution of a Rembrandt born into a tribe of illiterate headhunters? Would Archimedes have pioneered the airplane instead of the lever if he had been a contemporary of the Wright brothers? A few such rhetorical questions are enough to point up the inevitable dependence of the creative event on the environment as well as the individual.

Historical periods like the Renaissance, during which an extraordinary amount of creative activity went on, seem to offer strong indications that something in the environment during such periods promotes this activity. To understand the nature of an environment we have to understand the people who influence it.

There are some people for whom the ability to create an environment in which others can function well seems to be in itself a special talent—as though environment were a medium or material in which they can express their particular creative abilities more effectively than by their direct performance in the arts or sciences. For example, the impresario Diaghilev, whose talented protégés recalled him with mixed feelings, was apparently not personally distinguished as a painter, composer, or dancer. Nevertheless, he seems to have stimulated and advanced many individuals directly talented in these areas, such as Picasso and Nijinsky.

Although we have dealt with creativity as if it had a certain constancy, this too can be misleading. Despite the fact that we may speak of creative artists, writers, and scientists in the same breath, there is no strong evidence that we are necessarily dealing with precisely the same phenomena. In fact, there are major differences. Thus, for example, mathematics and the natural sciences and technology are cumulative, so that all prior work must be considered, at least in principle. A contemporary creative writer may ignore or may not even be familiar with the works of Sophocles; a scientist cannot even complete his elementary education without utilizing the contributions of Euclid and Archimedes. Again, although science is much more subjective and influenced by emotional and aesthetic factors than is commonly realized, the explicitly dominant role played by feelings, form of expression, and style in the arts results in widely different bases of evaluation and preference. Brahms could have said, "I do not like contemporary Japanese music" without the need for further qualifying remarks. If Fermi had said, "I do not like contemporary Japanese physics," an explanation would have been expected, since the work of Yukawa and others cannot be properly dismissed just on the basis of personal taste. These fundamental differences result in turn in differences in the types of personalities that are attracted to the several fields of endeavor.

We selected the sciences as our first area of exploration, not because we think them necessarily more important than the arts, but because scientific achievements, being less complicated by aesthetic and personal considerations, are more subject to verification. We felt that we could make a better start by trying to delineate patterns of creativity in scientific work, where achievement is more directly measurable. However, if we do succeed in tracing patterns of creativity in scientific fields, we believe that the knowledge gained should have meaning and value in other areas as well.

MYRON A. COLER

ACKNOWLEDGMENTS

I should like to acknowledge the early and sustained interest and encouragement received from Dean Paul A. McGhee and Professor Sidney G. Roth with respect to the entire Creative Science Program.

As indicated, the other Seminar associates have not only provided their individual contributions but have also served in a way as editors-at-large in continuous substantive reviews of the Seminar presentations and essays. Morris I. Stein, Professor of Psychology and Director of the Research Center for Human Relations of New York University, became a Seminar associate subsequent to our commitment to this collection of essays and hence is not included among the authors. However, he contributed actively to the reviews and Seminar program.

The work of the Seminar has been enriched and advanced by the presence and presentations of friends and distinguished guest participants. A number of the essays in this volume have benefited specifically from their participation.

I should like to thank the publishers of *Pleasures in Learning* and *Teaching and Learning* for permission to quote, with modifications, from my articles "What Creativity Is Not" and "Creators of Environment."

Mrs. Marjorie M. Roth, Mrs. Shirley M. Herman, and associates at the Markite Corporation have supplied essential assistance in connection with the preparation of manuscripts and in other related tasks.

MYRON A. COLER

CULTURE AND CREATIVITY

Morton I. Teicher

ANTHROPOLOGY IS THE STUDY of the whole man. It deals with
man's biological makeup, man's historical development, his many
forms of government, family systems, religions, literature, music—
all that man acquires and transmits from generation to generation
as a member of society. The task of the anthropologist is to seek
understanding of man and his works by means of systematic
comparison of the vast experiment in survival which has been
and is being conducted throughout the world's time and space by
all mankind and by the forerunners of man.

The study of anthropology yields an understanding of all
cultures, including our own. It develops a respect for the rights
and beliefs of others; it provides a scientific basis for consideration
of races. From anthropology one can derive knowledge of personality in culture and an understanding of social institutions. The
anthropologist is concerned with physical and behavioral similarities and differences as they are found among all the past and
present peoples of the globe.

Creativity is one significant aspect of human behavior. In
view of the anthropologist's broad range of interest in human behavior, it would appear that he ought to have a contribution to
make to a consideration of creativity.

This contribution falls into two broad categories. First,
the anthropologist can furnish a background against which creativity can be considered. Second, the anthropologist can offer

1

evidence with respect to creativity as an aspect of cultural change and cultural variation.

Let us first consider the nature of the background provided by anthropology. By and large, this is contained within the seminal contribution of anthropology—the concept of culture.

Culture is the matrix and the context for creativity; indeed, it is the matrix and context for all human behavior. It is the foundation on which creativity is built. It is the stored knowledge of man which provides the basis for creative acts.

In the sense in which culture is being used here, it is not the common notion of a special interest in music, art, and literature. It is not the kind of culture that describes the practice of horticulture and agriculture. It is not the medium used in a laboratory to grow bacteria.

Culture, as used by anthropologists, includes all of these but is in fact much more than these. It is the artificial environment; it is that part of the environment which is created by man. Culture is the total lifeway of a people. It is the social legacy which an individual acquires from the group, starting with his family as the primary source. Culture is the design for living characteristic of a particular society. It is the way of mankind. It includes all that men have done as men in their science, their philosophy, their art, their literature, their technology, their music, their social organization, their politics, their religion, their poetry, their morals, their ethics. It is all of that which makes it possible for us to deal with our experiences, our sorrows, our joys, our problems, and with each other. It is all of that which represents the sum total of our answers to the universal questions of man. These questions, asked by all men through all time and space include: What is our relationship to each other? What is our relationship to nature? What is our relationship to supernatural forces? The answers to these questions make up our culture; they make us human. Through these answers, provided through our common heritage, we are enabled to relate things and people to each other. We are enabled to see the relevance of one to another.

Culture is all of that which we take for granted in our daily lives. It is that which we need not explain. It is that which we rely on and which makes it possible for us to live with each other, knowing that we can count on each other to behave in generally predictable fashion. Culture provides us with, and is made up of, the great themes which run through our society. It is that which we come back to and recognize. It is that which we share with each other and which we communicate to each other from generation to generation.

In this sense, then, every human being is a cultured individual, for no man can live without culture. An individual without culture is simply not a member of the human species.

The concept of culture implies that man is conditioned and molded by his culture. However, a piece of behavior such as creativity takes place not in culture but in the people who are creatures, carriers, and creators of culture. People who are members of the same culture tend to be more or less like each other. They are never quite the same, since each is subject to his own conditioning, his own place in the social structure, and his own biological structure. Because of this, we need to think in terms of an interpenetrating relationship between personality and culture. We cannot think of one without the other. Just as we cannot understand man and his creative acts without understanding culture, so can we not understand culture without understanding man. Neither exists without the other.

Our culture, elaborated and developed, makes creativity possible, and, in turn, is enriched by creativity. The relationship between culture and creativity is a reciprocal relationship of interdependence.

This relationship suggests that an individual is creative only if the necessary and sufficient conditions exist in his culture to allow for the expression of his creativity. A Stone Age Eskimo could not be expected to place a satellite in the sky. Moreover, if one limits the concern with creativity to that which is found in science and technology, one can say that the reciprocal relationship between culture and creativity is such that a creative product is not really an invention unless it is socially accepted. The creative product has to operate within the culture; it has to work and it has to be accepted. If it does not work, then it is a failure as an invention. It may exist individually or mechanically, but it only becomes an actuality when it is socially accepted. The fate of a creative product is dependent on the culture into which it is introduced. Any creative product always encounters existing cultural conditions and these conditions determine whether, when, how, and in what form it gets adopted.

The implication for the creative individual and for society

of this interdependent relationship between creativity and culture is that congenital creative capacity will only be realized and manifest if the culture permits it. Had Einstein been born an Eskimo, he could hardly have been expected to develop the theory of relativity. Favorable cultural circumstances are essential for the expression of the creative potential in any given individual. Similarly, the existence of a particular level of cultural development calls forth certain inventions and discoveries. This view is substantiated by the history of science and technology, replete as it is with instances of simultaneous inventions. One can almost argue that cultural conditions are so basic for creative acts that inventions are culturally determined. At the very least, it appears clear that there exists a fundamental connection between the conditions of a given culture and the creation of a particular invention. The creative individual uses his talent and makes his discovery within the limited range permitted by his culture.

The range is further limited by the fact that despite increases in education and communication, no single individual today can encompass the sum total of his culture. Each of us possesses but a small piece of our culture, and as the consequences of our scientific and technological creativity expand and extend the already inexhaustible store of culture, the proportion we possess individually grows ever smaller.

While the accumulation of things and ideas in a given culture sets limits to creativity, it is ultimately the range of knowledge possessed by an individual which must be taken into account. For this reason, any barrier to communication or to the dissemination of knowledge operates to inhibit creativity. The culture provides the ingredients for new ideas. Since the magnitude of these ingredients grows ever greater, an inevitable problem exists in selectively concentrating a sufficient number of these ingredients in the mind of the individual, who is ultimately the creator. While the very range of information in itself creates a problem, it is important not to complicate matters even further by blocking access to appropriate ingredients through artificially erected cultural devices which get in the way of free and open interchange.

Negative attitudes toward cooperation represent an illustration of a cultural condition which can impede creativity. The existence of cooperation as a value as contrasted with competition as a value is not haphazard. It derives from deep-rooted attitudes which are related to the ways in which the culture answers the question of how man is related to his fellowman. Cooperation may be valued or deplored. Both attitudes may exist simultaneously, giving rise to a dilemma when a particular line of behavior has to be determined. The attitude varies in time within one culture, and it certainly varies from one culture to another.

Our culture has institutionalized a variety of methods to foster cooperation. We have professional associations, learned societies, conferences, international meetings, journals, books, symposia, workshops, institutes, and many other devices to promote cooperation. When hostility and suspicion prevent people from attending international meetings or from exchanging books and journals, they bar cooperation and impede creativity.

The attitude toward cooperation is one illustration of a cultural influence on creativity. A further illustration is the attitude held within a culture toward change. If the standardized attitude toward change is favorable, then the culture will be receptive to creativity. If, on the other hand, the culture is negatively disposed toward change, then new products resulting from creativity will be unwelcome disturbers of the *status quo*.

In some cultures, such as the Zuñi of New Mexico or the pre-Communist Chinese, change was neither anticipated nor desired. The new idea was a discordant intrusion, undesired and unsought. By contrast, modern Americans welcome new developments and innovations. The newest gadget and the latest fashion is considered to be good simply by virtue of its newness. We believe that change is inevitable and natural. We have faith in progress; we believe that things are getting better all the time and that change will take us along the unending road to perfection.

Our attitude toward change clearly provides a more favorable condition for creativity than that of the Zuñi. While this is true in general, it should be noted that our positive attitude is not uniformly held in all bearers of the culture. The aged, for example, typically deplore the rapidity of changes which overturn the values of their youth. It may well be that new attitudes toward change will have to be developed if there is to be any expectation of creative innovations from older people.

The culturally defined relationship to authority offers yet another example of how culture provides the background for creativity. Reverence for the patriarchs and the old ways, accompanied by filial piety, defines a dependent relationship to authority which is not particularly conducive to freedom of inquiry. As specialized knowledge in the culture becomes more highly elaborated, we tend to rely more heavily on the authoritative expert for everything from fixing our cars to rearing our children. And yet we are so suspicious of authority that we are often wary of the expert.

It would appear that dependence on authority as the source and definition of what is good produces a cultural condition less favorable to creativity than one in which dissent is valued. The essential problem here is one of developing and maintaining a social system in which dissent can be cultivated without cultivating anarchy.

Attitudes toward authority, toward change, and toward cooperation exemplify ways in which the belief system of a culture influences and affects creativity. Understanding these and other aspects of culture, as well as the concept of culture itself, provides a background which the anthropologist can contribute to our understanding of creativity.

A further contribution which may be derived from anthropology grows out of its interest in cultural change—in the processes of cultural variation through time and space. The anthropologist has been interested in analyzing the processes of cultural variation, especially since such processes occur in all societies, even though the rates and the magnitudes differ. Of particular interest has been the question as to whether cultural change comes about as a result of creative acts within a culture or as a result of taking over new ideas and things from another culture. Such analyses are essential for adequate comprehension of culture.

The issue has been phrased in terms of independent invention or diffusion. It turns on the question of man's creativeness. When similar institutions, artifacts, or ideas are found in different cultures, were they independently created or was there a single creation followed by diffusion to the various regions of the world in which the phenomenon may be observed?

The general finding among anthropologists is that elements which have been taken over are more commonly found than those which are independently created. It is apparently easier to take over what someone else has devised than to originate an independent solution to a problem. In any given culture, however, there is always a mixture of both kinds of elements. Resourcefulness and creativity are found in all cultures. From a broad cultural perspective, man is far more creative than he is ordinarily given credit for. There is a kind of ceaseless manipulation of culture that is reflected in the continuous process of change characterizing all cultures, despite the variations in rate. Human creativity is widely distributed among many cultures. Nevertheless, there are clearly enormous differences in technology, and the question legitimately arises as to whether or not nonliterate man is less creative or possesses less capacity than modern man. Put differently, the problem is one of accounting for the differences in technology which are so patent and obvious as we study different cultures.

The problem becomes even more intriguing when we realize that genus *Homo sapiens* is basically the same biological organism all over the world and that he has remained the same biologically for thousands of years. Man's biological sameness all over the world is demonstrated by his ability to breed with other races of man throughout the world. We have the same organism and brain, the same capacity to think, to discover, to dream, to create. For thousands of years we have neither lost nor gained anything of biological significance. The basic biological attributes which are essential for creativity are found in man all over the world. All men have hands with opposable thumbs; all men have stereoscopic vision; all men have the nervous system which makes learning possible; all men have acute sensory perception and discrimination; all men have memory; all men have the capacity to abstract and to symbolize; all men can see relationships among events and relationships through and to time; all men have language, and every language has equal relative capacity to transmit the knowledge and understanding of its speakers.

Despite these fundamental similarities and capacities, there are obvious differences in technology. Does this make nonliterate man less creative than we are?

If one were to measure creativity solely by intentional, planned invention, then one would have to assert that nonliterate man was not creative, since inventions of this order were rare. Few cultures were characterized by the elaborate division of labor which enables people in our culture to devote themselves to finding new solutions to established problems with all kinds of incentives for success.

We do know, however, that nonliterate man, whose history fills 98 percent of the human time record, was many-sided. This is demonstrated over and over again by his arts, his languages, his technologies, and his social institutions. Nonliterate man was continuously creative, and while his creativity went into technology, it went still more into social discovery and social arrangements. He created a variety of social structures designed to free the individual in order to function. He possessed great creative powers, and while most of his inventions and discoveries were accidental rather than intentional, the creative feature was inevitably present. The inventions and discoveries of nonliterate man required creative insight; they required a creative mental image which saw the possibility of new relationships, without the ability to record these new relationships.

It seems quite reasonable to assume that certain individuals in prehistoric times recognized that certain occurrences that they observed had some application to human needs. For example, one of the first great discoveries in human history was that one could use a stone as a tool. It seems reasonable to speculate that this discovery was preceded by the observation that a falling stone crushes things. The leap from this observation to the visualization of a stone as a hammer to break bones or crack nuts was a great creative act, even though it seems commonplace to us.

Another great discovery was the use of fire. Although fire occurs in nature as a result of lightning or volcanic eruptions, there was surely no artificially created fire at first. Some creative genius probably observed that animals burned in a natural fire were good to eat. Some other creative genius observed that a smoldering fire was a source of warmth. Still another noted that fire could be used for purposes of light. It was these observations which undoubtedly led to efforts to preserve and control fires. Many nonliterate peoples have permanent fires which are kept glowing. The step from preserving fire to starting a new one was a further act of great creativity. When the observation that friction produces fire led to the idea that one could artificially produce fire, this discovery of how to produce fire was harnessed in a process of creativity which represents one of the most important steps ever taken by man.

We marvel today at the gadgetry and technology which are literally taking man out of this world. One cannot deprecate the genius and creativity involved in this magnificent achievement. Neither can one forget, however, that for its time and place, in relationship to the then existing level of complexity, the control of fire and the use of a stone as a tool were acts of incalculable genius and creativity. Indeed, there is a long, unbroken chain of creativity which inextricably binds tomorrow's astronaut in a dependent relationship to yesterday's caveman.

Antecedents are essential to almost every creative act. Culture changes by a slow process of increments and accumulation. The sheer bulk of things and ideas has accumulated enormously through time. This accretion provides for us today a great variety of antecedents on which to base our creative acts. The sparseness of the base in early times highlights and magnifies the creativity of early man. Every creative product today can be traced to its antecedents. The bringing together of these antecedents in some new combination is the essence of creativity.

So important is the matter of antecedents that it is often difficult to determine reliably just when a particular invention took place. The more an invention is analyzed, the more important do the antecedents seem. By comparison, the new step or the new combination appears to be less significant.

There is little substance to the frequently encountered popular view that creativity is a single dramatic act by one individual. The creative act, on the contrary, involves a complex, lengthy, and often tedious process. The talent and genius of the creative individual would amount to nothing without a long chain of antecedents. The creative product is the result of a cumulative series of increments passed on through many hands and minds— often for many years—and finally subjected to some new increment. This belies the romantic notion of a creative genius making a completely new invention at one stroke—out of nothing. Most inventions are not single acts of one mind; they are cumulative results. They are, in fact, cultural events, and they are, therefore, gradual events.

The importance of antecedents highlights the achievements of nonliterate man in using a stone as a tool or in preserving and making fire. These acts of creativity lacked antecedents; they were consequently notable beyond measure.

Most of the other great discoveries and inventions on which our culture rests occurred early in history, when culture was sparse and the antecedents few. Let us cite a few illustrations:

1. The relationship between a seed and a plant.
2. Domestication of animals.
3. Making of pottery.
4. Preserving of food.
5. Use of intoxicating drinks.
6. Medicinal properties of plants.
7. Preparation of skins.
8. Basketmaking.
9. Spinning and weaving.
10. Working of metals.
11. Use of traps.
12. Building of houses.
13. Wearing of clothing.
14. Use of animals for transportation.
15. Sailing.
16. Writing.
17. Counting.
18. Religion.
19. Government.
20. Use of the wheel.

While lists of basic inventions and discoveries prepared by different people would vary, the foregoing list indicates some of the creative acts which occurred in prehistoric times. Their significance is so fundamental as to offer potent evidence in support of the contention here advanced that nonliterate man was creative in a very high degree.

More specific illustrations of nonliterate man's creativity can be derived from examination of particular cultures. The settlers of the New World, who preceded Columbus by some 25,000 years, were continuously creative in an impressive variety of ways.

Many crops which are important to us were first brought under cultivation by the Indians. These include corn, tapioca, potatoes, tomatoes, beans, peanuts, sunflowers, Jerusalem artichokes, tobacco, and an American variety of cotton. We owe the use of rubber to the American Indians, for, although rubber trees grow in Asia and Africa, no particular use was made of it in pre-Columbian times. The turkey was domesticated by the American Indians, and represents a New World contribution to mankind.

One special kind of American Indian is the Eskimo, and his remarkable technology demonstrates great creativity. The few resources of the bleak Arctic wastes are resourcefully and creatively used by the Eskimo:

> With no wood, the Eskimo builds houses of snow, using the snow to keep out cold and snow in what is an ingenious act of creativity.
>
> With no glass, the Eskimo fashions a window out of ice, from the translucent intestinal membrane of a seal, or from the pericardium of the caribou.
>
> With no crop to spin into thread, he uses sinews from the legs of the caribou, the flippers of the seal, and thin fibers stripped from the surface of bird quills.
>
> With practically no metal, he uses stone for blades, weapon points, lamps, and cooking pots.
>
> With no wood, he makes sleds of bone, ivory, and frozen hides. He makes harpoon shafts from caribou horn.
>
> With no agriculture, he satisfies his nutritional needs by eating the insides of the caribou's stomach, and every part of the fish, caribou, seal, and walrus.
>
> With no coal or wood for fuel, he uses seal and whale oil for heating and lighting.
>
> With no wool or cloth, he tailors excellent clothes from furs and skins.

The Eskimo is surely creative. He survives and thrives in the face of the most difficult environment we know.

Based on the evidence provided by the Eskimo and the evidence of creativity among the other early settlers of the New World, as well as the magnificent list of creative acts represented by the great discoveries of prehistoric man, it would appear that an affirmative answer can be given to the question of whether or not nonliterate man was creative. He was indeed impressively creative.

The contribution of the anthropologist to a consideration

of creativity as presented here suggests that man is, by nature, creative. He possesses powers of imagination, of action, of thinking, of dreaming that are frequently beyond his ability to express. Man is filled with great power. He has an endowment which needs to find expression. It would appear to be a fitting and continuous task for all of us to create and recreate the kind of culture in which there can freely take place the fullest realization of the creativity which is in all of us.

CREATIVENESS IN THE SCIENCES AND THE PROBLEM OF NATIONAL GROWTH

Nicholas E. Golovin

I. *INTRODUCTION*

THE UNDERTAKING of research in any field can be prompted by a variety of reasons. Probably the most frequently voiced are, first, the personal satisfactions, largely of a philosophical sort, which the investigator derives from the research process itself, and, second, the satisfactions resulting from having produced, through research, results that are of general social value. Although there is doubtless a great deal of research concerned with individual creative behavior that is not directly motivated by utilitarian considerations, much, if not most, of such research is justified by the hope that it will ultimately result in stepping up the rate of general scientific and technological progress. This hope is based principally on the belief that increased understanding of the learning and creative processes will provide means for early identification of individuals who are most likely to be creative in science and technology, as well as with insights as to how one can best educate, train, stimulate, and manage the potentially creative persons as individuals or as group members. In my

The views expressed in this essay are those of the author, and are not to be interpreted as representing the official views of his agency or of other members of its staff.

13

opinion the main objectives of the New York University Creative Science Seminar to date have been reaching agreement on the nature of the learning and creative processes and using this increased understanding to find ways to enhance the professional productivity of scientists and engineers.

Since current interest in studies of creative behavior appears to be so generally focused on scientists and engineers, a natural question is why is this the case. The usual answer runs as follows:

1.   Substantially more has been written and said about creative behavior in the sciences than in other fields. One is, to some extent, thereby justified in assuming that more is known about such behavior and that progress from additional research is more certain.

2.   It is natural to assume that, because of the nature of science, scientific creativeness is more likely to be understood through the customary methods of research based on logic and the scientific method.

3.   It is claimed that growth in understanding scientific productiveness will have relatively more spectacular general social benefits than increased understanding of other forms of creative behavior.

These arguments are direct, have an appealing simplicity, and seem to be generally accepted. However, there is a fundamental and general difficulty with utilitarian arguments of this kind, as contrasted, for example, with those based on the desire to increase knowledge for its own sake. The proponents fail to show that the suggested use of resources for such purposes will have more useful consequences in the long run than alternative applications of the same resources. Thus, such justifications based on the intrinsic desirability of increasing knowledge can hardly be questioned in the absence of doubts as to training or competence of the investigators. On the other hand, the justifications based on the anticipation of practical benefits from research programs must survive tests providing comparisons of the relative practical advantages to be gained over the lifetimes of all other research programs which might be conducted equally well with the same resources. In the particular context of interest to us, we can restate this distinction in the form of the following question:

Can the nationally scarce skills of the psychologists, physical scientists, educators, and other highly trained specialists now concerned with research to improve the professional productivity of scientists and engineers be substantially more advantageously employed in other lines of research—for example, in increasing the social effectiveness and usefulness of other occupational groups in our society?

That the question may be important is underlined by the circumstance that our society seems to be entering a period of extraordinarily rapid technological, economic, and social change. Under such conditions the utilitarian consequences of alternative courses of action must be conceptually projected and compounded over extended periods of time if choice of a particular course is to be justified. The main purpose of the following remarks is to carry through a meaningful and hopefully useful discussion of this question.

II.   THE IMPORTANCE OF INCREASING THE
NUMBER OF SCIENTISTS AND ENGINEERS

The principal reason for serious interest in increasing the creativeness of scientists and engineers is the increased rate of technological and scientific progress in recent years. This increased rate, as measured, for example, by the volume of new research published annually, has been substantially in excess of the rate of increase in the number of scientific and technical workers. It seems as if the overall productivity of interacting investigators is an exponential rather than a linear function of their number.

Furthermore, looking at the world situation from an American point of view, a notably disturbing aspect of this general phenomenon has been the disparity in growth rates of the scientific manpower pools of the United States and of other powers. Certain other countries are apparently producing annually more than twice as many scientists and engineers as the United States, and presumably as well trained. Thus, such countries appear to have not only a relatively increasing capability to take advantage of expanding technical knowledge, but also, and perhaps more importantly, the potential for eventually attaining a substantially greater rate of improvement in their capacity to generate new technological and scientific advances. That the benefits to other countries from such trends may not be a matter of the distant future is suggested, for example, by the facts that the Soviet Union's share of the world's technical literature is increasing; its scientific and technical accomplishments in a number of fields have attained levels of sophistication at least comparable with the best available in the West; and its relative industrial productivity, as reflected, for example, by the rate of growth of its gross national product, appears to be increasing more rapidly than our own.

However, there are more comforting views which depreciate the importance of the smaller American output of technical professionals. It is said, first, that the problem is exaggerated, because a technical education is the Soviet society's equivalent of the liberal arts degree in the United States, so that perhaps only a relatively small fraction of Soviet technical graduates practice their professions. In addition, it is usually suggested that competition in total numbers of scientists and engineers is certainly not the answer because it is their quality that really matters. It is then proposed that the simplest way for the United States to ensure maintenance of its superior relative position is to continue raising the individual productiveness of its scientists and engineers by various appropriate devices, with research in creativity presumably providing some of the guidance needed for developing such devices. Finally, the discussion is usually closed on a note of confidence by pointing out that scientists and engineers in the principal competing countries can obviously never be individually as effective as those in the United States. This is claimed to be so because they have to work under authoritarian social philosophies that limit their general intellectual freedom, stunt their initiative, and, therefore, necessarily reduce their capacity to produce new ideas. However, since productivity in science and technology is the primary basis for progress in so many areas of interest to our society, and because correct resolution of the underlying issues between the pessimistic and the comforting points of view is obviously vital to the national welfare, further analysis of these reassuring views is in order.

In the first place, it appears quite clear that the intensity of East-West competition, as well as the stakes involved, have been steadily growing. It would seem, therefore, that programs directed toward improving the United States' capabilities should be focused on reversing dangerous causal trends rather than diverted to preoccupation with relatively superficial phenomena in either the East or West. For example, arguments implying that authoritarianism in politics or economic organization will inhibit personal technical productivity in the physical sciences are almost certainly little more than wishful thinking. There is little, if any, objective evidence to support such a conclusion, and a great deal of logical and factual support for the belief, on the other hand, that intensity of ideological political indoctrination is not likely to interfere with individual creative facility in relatively nonpolitical fields, such as mathematics, engineering, and the physical sciences.[1]

In the second place, it is fairly well established that the principal *necessary* conditions for creative effectiveness in the sciences are:

1. A sufficiently high level of general intelligence to allow construction and retention by the individual of massive accumulations of basic scientific facts and of structural and logical relationships among them.

2. The existence of strong motivations for maintaining *continuity* of the intense intellectual effort needed to acquire mastery of the already available knowledge in the particular field of research interest and to *manipulate* imaginatively the resulting associations and new data until fresh insights on problems under study are obtained.

Now, there is ample general anthropological evidence for believing that portions of the population above any given level of general intelligence are not appreciably different among the principal civilized countries. Insofar as motivations for individuals to undertake intensive technical training are concerned, those in other countries may be greater but, in any case, are certainly no less effective than those our society provides. Furthermore, the availability of educational facilities at all levels for individuals having more than the minimum inherent abilities necessary to benefit from them is certainly not appreciably more limited in the Soviet Union than it is in the United States, while competition to establish the right to use them is, similarly, no less keen in the one country than it is in the other. Thus, it is possible to conclude, with a very high probability of being correct, that if either country is producing scientists and engineers at a rate, say, twice as great as the other, it is at the same time discovering and training outstandingly creative individuals and thereby increasing its potential for the output of new ideas in technology and the sciences more rapidly than its competitor in at least the same ratio.

In the third place, any new developments in techniques for identification of the potentially creative individuals, in their education, and in the organization and management of scientists and engineers in either nation will become almost simultaneously known and available for exploitation by the other. In view of the more centrally directed character of the Soviet management structure and because of its obvious preoccupation with systematized approaches to education and technological growth, it is certainly not less likely that its institutions will take advantage of such new developments, wherever they originate, as promptly as will the appropriate organizations here. It follows that it is highly improbable that the new advances in understanding resulting from research in education or creativity in either country will provide any significant opportunity for the one or the other to gain therefrom any relative advantages in the competition to become scientifically and technically more productive. At most, therefore, initiative in adopting such advances will help us to hold steady the magnitude of our downward drift in relative technological capabilities in relation to our principal competitor, this drift being induced by our continuing relatively lower output of scientists and engineers on whose numbers and utilization such capabilities must ultimately depend.

Finally, in the eyes of the populations of the many new nations now looking forward to rapid industrial development based on modern science and technology, the international posture of the United States is likely to be affected by any growing disparity between the volume of its technically trained manpower and that of its competitors on the international scene. This will be the case because:

1. The competitive appeal to those populations of the world that are relatively backward industrially will be greater for that form of national organization which has acquired both the highest levels of knowledge and techniques, as well as an excess of expertly qualified manpower available for export to communicate them to others.

2. The national group which eventually succeeds in maintaining continuing leadership in science and technology is also likely to acquire in time permanent and growing dominance in per capita industrial productivity.

The first consideration is of basic importance because it is of critical value in developing and holding the balance of world political power. The second is perhaps even more fundamental because growth in per capita industrial productivity is a major national objective of every underdeveloped country, and the nation able to demonstrate the greatest long-run capability to grow and to teach others how to do the same is likely to gain also their following for its forms of social organization and internal management arrangements.

Thus we appear to have concluded that, while the research into learning processes or into scientific creativity may have certain basic philosophical justifications of the same kind as any other research possesses, it is not likely to produce a competitive advantage to our side in science and technology. On the other hand, it seems clear that if we do insist that our international competitive capabilities must be enhanced to produce eventual relative improvement, then we must greatly increase the output of scientists and engineers, particularly of those with the highest educational attainments.[2] Obviously, such efforts will be futile unless we can also ensure that means are provided to make certain that those with the highest creative potential are also motivated to undertake research in science and technology and that the growing number of the highly trained are effectively used by our society.

III.   *THE COMPLEXITY OF THE PROBLEM OF*
       INCREASING NUMBERS

A principal conclusion of the argument in the last section is that it is important for national welfare that our rate of production of scientists and engineers should be rapidly increased and that ways be found for such increasing numbers to be effectively used by our society. We will assume for the sequel that this conclusion is established. Two further questions then naturally arise.

1.   How are these steps to be operationally defined so that they can be effected?

2.   What is the relevance of these steps to our original interests in redirecting emphasis in the research into creative behavior?

Since a program consists of a sequence of planned events

plus the arrangements required to make their occurrence politically, economically, and managerially feasible, we might analyze the problems posed by the first question along the following lines:

1] The current annual production rate of engineers and scientists in the United States is less than one half that of the Soviet Union. We should seek, therefore, to increase our university-level student population in these fields by a substantial factor. Whether this factor needs to be as large, for example, as two and one half is, of course, open to question for various reasons, some of which have already been mentioned. However, it is clearly desirable to make this factor large and increasing, at least because the larger the student population, the greater the number of those highly gifted for productive research that are likely to be discovered, motivated, and trained for professional careers in science and technology.

2] An above-average level of native ability and some secondary school training in mathematics and the sciences are, in general, both highly desirable if an individual is to be motivated to begin and successfully to complete a university-level education in these fields. Thus, it will probably be necessary:

1. To increase substantially the proportion of our general population with the required levels of native ability that completes high school and that chooses, and is financially able, to go on to the university.

2. To improve the general level of education in the sciences and in mathematics in the secondary schools of the United States.

3. To ensure the existence of adequate motivations for individuals to enter into, and complete, the training required and then go on to the practice of these professions.[3]

3] Education through the secondary school level in the United States is a "local" problem, and thus a national effort requiring significant changes from present practices along the above lines will need to be understood, accepted, and, at least in part, financially supported by local governments. Since the demand for engineers and scientists is by no means uniformly distributed geographically, such acceptance and financial support at the local level must frequently be relatively altruistic from the community point of view. These local investments in education will frequently serve merely to increase the supply of trained men who will eventually leave their native communities to make professional contributions elsewhere.

4] A significant proportion of secondary school graduates with high academic attainments do not now go on to college for economic and related reasons. It is not unlikely that there is also a large fraction of capable individuals who never enter into, or complete, high school training for similar grounds or because of special local conditions. A program to alter this situation by providing scholarships or other financial assistance, for example, will almost certainly need to be initiated, coordinated, and probably largely paid for by federal funds. However, there are many parts of the United States, containing a large and growing proportion of its population, where efforts to do so would involve emotionally loaded social and political issues, techniques for the resolution of which have not been appreciably improved after a history of some one hundred years of effort at various levels of government.

5] No marked increase in the extent and quality of training in science and mathematics at the high school level can be attained without a prior increase in the number of qualified teachers. Similarly, no increase by a factor as large as two and one half in the number of science and engineering graduates, at the college and graduate school levels, can be approached without an approximately corresponding increase in physical facilities and faculty populations of universities. Moreover, in recent years, probably because of the large expansion in industrial research-and-development activities, the supply of teachers at all educational levels in mathematics and the physical sciences has tended to shrink relative to needs. Any reversal of this trend would obviously require a prior major upward adjustment in the financial rewards of a teaching career in comparison with similar promise from industrial employment for equivalent levels of individual ability and technical training. However, it is clear that there can be no assurance whatever that any general increase in the salary levels of the teaching profession, even assuming that it could be brought about, would by itself lead to the desired result: industrial rewards for equal skills could, and under present social conditions probably always would, be increased as required to overcome academic competition. Since it is unlikely that any marked increase in the annual output of scientists and engineers could be provided without correlated prior expansion in the teaching force, it would thus seem that some structure of motivations other than those of a purely financial character will be needed to bring about such proposed expansion.

6] The principal demand-supply problem, at the student level, will be that of establishing the system of economic forces which will induce an increase in the number of individuals willing to undertake the rigors of training and later employment in the sciences, as well as the economic basis required for their effective later employment in the national economy. In view of the fact that our economy is able to maintain an average annual growth of perhaps three to four percent in the gross national product, it is obvious that a large increase in the annual increment in such skills simply could not, in the long run, be absorbed by the economy without substantial interference with the free market for them. Some special incentives would need to be provided to maintain entrance and growth salary scales at levels set to "force" increases in the supply required, as well as to absorb into productive effort all the additional adequately trained individuals annually entering the labor market. A firm national decision to accomplish such an objective would then probably require that the federal government enter the market to whatever degree necessary to balance the normal fluctuations in industrial demands for such skills. Since the total number of scientists and engineers currently directly employed by the federal government is measured only in the high tens of thousands, the magnitude of the problem the government would have in maintaining this balance, purely from the budgetary point of view, would be impressive. For example, it currently takes an expenditure of some $40,000 a year to use a scientist or engineer effectively in industrial research-and-development work. If increases in governmental expenditures for the work were required to absorb the additional technologists and scientists provided by such a greatly expanded program, the annual required increase in federal research-and-development appropriations might well reach the high hundreds of millions.

7] The major overall objective for the proposed program in the first place, however, was ensuring continued national technological leadership. But a basic characteristic of such leadership is the increasingly rapid rate of obsolescence of existing industrial installations produced by advances in technology that allow a substantial annual increase in national per capita labor productivity. This means that an effective program along the lines proposed will appreciably raise the industrial automation rate and, therefore, significantly aggravate the overall national problem in coping with present and resulting employment imbalances. Thus, if increased technological capability is to be effectively used for increasing national power, it must necessarily be associated with increased flexibility in handling the results of technologically induced changes in employment and in other related basic economic patterns. On the whole, therefore, it might appear advantageous to moderate the rate at which a relatively forced increase in the supply and utilization of the technically trained is brought about. The longer the number of years taken to overtake the Soviet Union effectively in the annual increase of productive scientists and engineers, the more palatable will be the impact of consequent economic repercussions for which provision must be made separately. On the other hand, the advantages of growing technological capabilities both to military power and to the political effectiveness of our international posture suggest that the shorter this number of years, the more certain will we be of success in these respects.

8] It takes at least four to seven years to convert a high school graduate into an adequately trained engineer or a potentially productive research scientist. In addition, substantial lead times are involved in increasing the supply of basic raw material at the secondary school level and to provide the expanded facilities and teaching staffs before any appreciable increase in the output can be obtained. It would thus seem that a period of ten to twelve years might need to pass before even a vigorously implemented program (assuming prior resolution of the many sorts of difficulties sketched out above) can begin resulting in annual increments of productive scientists and engineers comparable to levels the Soviet Union appears to have reached. During this period, and apparently quite independently of what we might try to do, the Soviet Union will have provided for its own uses, for those of its allies, and for countries it seeks to bring into its orbit a supply of some 500,000 to 1 million more scientists and engineers than the United States will have trained. By 1970 to 1972 it will have acquired a technological capability (at least to the extent that this can be measured by the total inventory of technically trained manpower) substantially exceeding that of the United States. On the basis of the likelihood that technological productivity probably grows more rapidly than proportionately with increases in the number of workers involved, such a relative growth in the Soviet technological manpower pool could result in its having secured by the early 1970's overwhelmingly superior capabilities for scientific, industrial, and military operations, as well as for the further relative enhancement of these capabilities.

These considerations suggest some of the detailed steps and some of the related operational problems and difficulties that must be faced in formulating and implementing a national decision to increase rapidly the numbers of scientists and engineers in the United States and to see that they are effectively used by our society.

Insofar as the relevance of such steps to our original interest in redirecting emphasis in research in creative behavior is concerned, the following would appear to be an obvious conclusion: Our efforts might well be focused less on increasing the productiveness of individual scientists and engineers, more on increasing the productivity and effectiveness of those individuals in our society whose efforts can lead most rapidly both to a greater national output of scientists and engineers with the highest levels of professional training, and to the full utilization of these scientists and engineers in the national economy.

IV.   SOCIAL IMPEDIMENTA TO ADAPTIVE CHANGES

Thus, although in section II we found strong grounds for concluding that it was important for us to expand rapidly our output of scientists and engineers, the discussion in the last section has brought into view a seemingly overwhelming collection of obstacles which must first be overcome. We are forced to conclude at this point that:

1.   There appears to be little that we can do to change trends during roughly the next decade, and that, unless some now undefined new tools are introduced, it seems likely that our competitors will continue making further relative gains during this period.

2.   Any program we begin along the desired lines, even with new tools, will interact strongly with numerous other activities in the national economy and will have its success

seriously constrained and complicated by such interactions.

A natural reaction on the part of the reader might well be to ask, "Why hadn't persons in positions of responsibility long ago become aware of these trends, analyzed their consequences, and properly advised people generally of what lies ahead and what we, as individuals or as members of various organized groups, should be doing about these matters?"

This is an important question. But it could equally well be asked about many other problems which our normal community and governmental processes allow to mature for much too long a time before adequate public exposure takes place. It is useful to note some of the social phenomena associated with this state of affairs. In the following discussion much of what is said is well known, and perhaps for that reason is seldom made explicit in speculations about possible social changes. It seems as if society tends to assign low importance and a connotation of "in poor taste" to concepts if they are well known—and seems to do this most clearly and systematically if some of their implications are critical of the *status quo*.

1] Perhaps partly because of our cultural origins and business history, there is an almost compulsive tendency on the part of our community leadership to moralize optimistically about crucial public issues rather than face them realistically. By "realistically," for our purposes, is meant an interpretation of a problem or situation which is at least not inconsistent with the commonly accepted principles of the physical and social sciences. This tendency is so pervasive that it is almost fatuous to observe that the greatest obstacle to effective (or "creative") thinking and action within our society is lack of realism in recognizing problems and in developing policies and programs for dealing with them.

A simple illustration, in the context familiar to us, is furnished by the once authoritative statement that we must not engage in a "numbers race" with the Soviet Union in the education of scientists and engineers. As previously noted, it can be fairly simply shown by an appeal merely to the "laws of nature" and a few commonly agreed upon facts that the rate of technological progress is significantly dependent on the numbers of specialists adequately trained to push outward the frontiers of science and technology.[1] We can then assert, with a very high probability of being right, first, that we are already in such a race and, next, that we are rapidly falling behind. Clearly, such lack of realism may have gross consequences because, by resolving difficulties through the simple expedient of proclaiming authoritatively that they do not exist, it leads to a false basis for public composure.

2] There appears to be a clear tendency among our community leadership simply to avoid detailed consideration of public issues if it is fairly obvious that feasible approaches will require substantial participation by the federal government. It may be believed, as an aspect of basic philosophical orientation, that such consequences are fraught with greater dangers to the "American way of life" than national failure to solve the problems at issue. As a matter of fact, the circumstance that important economic and political problems at the national level often do not get resolved is attributed by responsible business leaders not to lack of understanding and support of necessary governmental actions by our community leadership, but rather to the fact that such problems would not arise were it not for excessive existing and prior governmental interference with the economy. Such distrust, particularly of the central government, is so ingrained and unquestioned that some three years ago, for example, when the issue of formulating overall national goals for the United States became politically important, it was found most appropriate by the then President to turn the problem over to a group of private citizens rather than entrust it to anyone within the government; also, the work had to be financed by gifts from nongovernmental sources.[4] Such action publicly demonstrated that, in the opinion of the administration in office at that time, the use of governmental appropriations for, or the participation of federal employees in, formulating national goals was either morally wrong or politically unacceptable or both. It is clear that national planning in any sector of the economy traditionally left for handling by the market or by other than private economy means would likely be found to have similar sorts of questionable attributes.

3] The business community has institutionalized the concept of the "market" so that it has come to possess in the popular mind essentially magical properties. Thus, the "market" can be expected to succeed invariably in inducing desirable social and economic adjustments through the mediation of prices, which always reflect the shifting interests of society and the demand for, as well as the supply of, the physical resources available to it. The supply and the demand for practically anything, including scientists and engineers of all varieties and levels of professional education, is therefore established by the essentially free interaction of individual needs and wishes with what other individuals and organizations will accept to supply them now or in the future. Accordingly, it will be argued that, if our society has needs for additional engineers and scientists now or later, demands for an increased supply of them will be forthcoming in a natural and orderly way and as promptly as necessary. If it is protested that recent history suggests that the system does not have sufficient elasticity to produce reactions quickly enough, it will be emphasized fervently that one of the great strengths of our forms of social and economic arrangements lies precisely in the circumstance that adjustments of this character are always taken care of quite automatically and efficiently by the overall system if only it is left alone to operate freely and, in particular, without governmental interference; and that if the system has not responded elastically enough in recent years, then the fault will certainly be found in the excessive amount of governmental tinkering with the market mechanism. This kind of orientation on the part of the business community, and suggested explanations for its origins, are minutely analyzed and discussed in, for example, *The American Business Creed*.[5] It is of special significance to our argument, since little social action, at least that is effective on a short-lead-time basis, can be expected unless ways are developed first to secure the understanding and support of the business community.

4] Mention should be made of the paralyzing inflexibility inhibiting adaptive social changes that is being built into our society by the gradual growth with time in the personal and organizational "payoffs" for conformity. Little can be added to the evidence and analysis in support of this phenomenon within the business community that has not been previously discerned in the studies by Whyte.[6] But these trends apply everywhere in our society. They act largely through two relatively simple types of devices used equally widely in industry, politics, and government:

   1.   The criteria for choice of individuals for strategic positions within the organization are based on group or

political acceptability rather than on intelligence, training, and personal effectiveness.

2.   Continuity of intellectual and/or executive effort in any area vital to the organization is deliberately so limited in time that a major impact on the course of events by any one responsible individual is all but impossible.

Accordingly, joint application of both of these devices is almost certain to ensure long-run organizational *status quo*.

These considerations suggest in part why the large disparity between the United States' and the Soviet Union's emphasis on scientific and technical education, which became fairly clear almost ten years ago, has not become an explicit object of public interest.

Of course there may still be some gnawing concern on the part of the "reader-organization man," that the "real" answer for this lack of interest is not to be found in the explanations given above, but simply in the fact that we are giving the issue much too great weight. Such a reader can always say, "If the issue were really as important as you claim, something would have been done about it." This is, of course, a possible explanation.

But let us conclude this section by mentioning a problem that hardly any reader would class as relatively unimportant and that has been with us for about twenty years—the large and persistent rate of involuntary unemployment. In some countries of the world—France, Germany, and Sweden are examples—the problem has been virtually eliminated largely through the fiscal and planning interference of the respective central governments. What are we doing, and what are the prospects for success? Let me quote the recent comment of Thurman Arnold:

And thus the old folklore of capitalism which I have attempted to describe in this book still frustrates our economic growth. The fact that Western European economies are not so frustrated is a continuing source of bewilderment to us. We are presently sending economists to Western Europe to find out why those countries have no unemployment and are moving ahead at more than double our speed. I suggest that nothing will come of such economic inquiries. Each inquiring economist will look at Western Europe through the spectacles of a preconceived theory. He will then disregard all the facts which do not fit in with the theory. Finally he will come back with the report that the lesson we must learn from the booming economies of Western Europe is to balance our fiscal budget at home. Many reports of this character are already being published in our conservative journals.[7]

v. *THE NEEDED NEW INFORMATION AND THE*
    ESTABLISHED CONSTRAINTS FOR POSSIBLE
    PROGRAMS

Section III developed some of the details of how the problem of increasing the rate of production of scientists and engineers was inseparably linked with a large network of other social problems and needs relating to our society's use of its physical resources. As a consequence, noting the results of section II, it was implied at the beginning of section IV that deterioration of the United States' relative position in science and technology for a prolonged period was a clear possibility. In the last section a brief description was also provided of some of the social processes probably largely responsible for our society's relative inability to adapt effectively even to major influences on its environment, both internal (such as the continued inadequacy in rate of annual overall economic growth) and external (as in competition in rate of growth of scientific and technological skills).

To establish with generally satisfactory validity what our internal difficulties and our external competitive dangers truly are, as well as to define a firm basis for adaptive social reactions, the next logical step in the overall argument might be to make explicit the following:

1.   The kinds of information and means of disseminating it that would be necessary to attain clear public understanding as to consequences to our society of continuing the *status quo,* as well as of the kinds of actions required at the production level of the economy to provide necessary adaptive reactions to the environment.

2.   The boundary conditions established by important current limitations to the flexibility of adjustments in our society.

In the light of an analysis of (1) and (2) one might, hopefully, try to deduce an operationally useful approach to bring about a more desirable course of events.

With respect to matters of information, the basic need appears to be for a factual base which would allow meaningful time-to-time comparisons of our condition as a whole society. In addition to developing a more definite and useful picture of substantive progress and difficulties, it would also help provide a basis for comparisons between the changing physical effectiveness of our society and of our principal competitors' societies. It is doubtful that our society could plan or take effective action to meet major internal problems or external challenges without such data. To put the needs for such information in the perspective of interest to us, we can argue as follows: the United States, as a large and complex physical system, has been challenged to demonstrate continuing superiority not merely in special areas or in the production of particular products, but straight across the board—in education, science, industrial production, space technology, food supply, and so on. We have had no choice but to accept this challenge. But both the challenge and its acceptance are meaningless except in terms of conceptual models of the competing societies as physical systems whose social effectiveness for various purposes can be measured by sets of appropriately defined quantitative indexes. Without such models and indexes we have no way of knowing how we can proceed rationally to the following steps:

1. To define, more or less clearly, where we stand as a whole society in crucial aspects.

2. To discover how we are changing in time with respect to such aspects.

3. To establish how the effectiveness of our industries, and the trends in them, compare with those of other societies.

4. To define operationally effective approaches for improving conditions and trends.

Of course, there are many possible types of indexes relating to the physical operations of the economy, and some of these are currently employed for various business and governmental purposes. Thus, the indexes that might be useful include the gross national product and its rate of growth; involuntary unemployment per capita; industrial labor productivity; relative technological capability, for example, as measured by professionally applied technically trained manpower, and so on. But to be useful for the purposes we are emphasizing, such indexes and sources of quantitative data for them must be developed so that they provide consistent and realistic comparisons not only of the physical effectiveness of our social system with itself at various times to measure growth, but also with equivalent indexes for other social systems at the same and varying times, to measure relative capabilities and changes in them. These are obviously matters in which additional data and fresh ideas, both about our own and about other societies, are greatly needed.

However, to be socially effective it is clearly not enough merely to have such indexes. The following additional step is essential no matter what the details of a program of further social action might be: Such comparative information must be made available to the public in a simple, explicit, and systematic way. This means that considerations of disturbing the so-called public or business "confidence" notwithstanding, the people at large should be made as continuously and acutely aware of the comparative status of our economy as they are currently, perhaps, sated with data about the comparative virtues of competing commercial products.

Furthermore, partly as an introduction to our discussion of the boundary conditions to which operationally useful approaches to improvement of trends must conform, and partly as recognition that the above rather simple statements do not make explicit a number of difficult underlying issues, the following more pointed questions need to be noted:

A. What are the appropriate indexes of overall system performance that are to be used for judging our, and our competitors', general progress, and how can realistic comparisons be actually carried out from time to time?

B. How can agreement be reached, at least among the well informed, so that if such comparisons are found to be unfavorable, the implied necessity for appropriate counteraction will be judged real and not hypothetical?

C. If a need for a social counteraction is recognized by the well informed, what methods will be used to ensure that enough of the population is persuaded of the validity of the findings that a suitable national response becomes a practical possibility?

D. Since a program of general social action to counter undesirable trends in any particular area would have repercussions of varying effect throughout the entire fabric of society, what group or organization can be trusted to examine such repercussions in detail and develop national plans of action in various areas which would be generally equitable, internally self-consistent, and likely to have results the public would be willing to support?

E.   Is it reasonably probable that if we merely establish the mechanics for letting the public know and understand how we, as a nation, measure up to our own goals and to external challenges (in terms of various indexes of basic material and technological progress and their rates of change), that the normal operations of our type of democratic society will lead promptly enough and vigorously enough to individual and organizational actions below the federal government level, the overall effect of which will be the desired one?

The other matter of interest for this section is to use the results available from the discussion up to this point for specifying the boundary conditions limiting freedom in choice of operational procedures for defining potentially useful courses of action. Since the quite preliminary analysis we have been able to attempt above largely does nothing more than scratch the surfaces of the major problem areas, the following specification obviously can be no more than heuristically suggestive:

1] Since realism with respect to both United States and Soviet activities and accomplishments is a prerequisite to a meaningful approach in developing a program of action, the individuals and organizational devices to be utilized for providing facts and generating ideas must be selected in full recognition of the general social, organizational, and individual impediments to objectivity outlined earlier.

2] Since the Soviet Union is evidently pursuing a coordinated, long-range plan of national development focused on overtaking the United States in all significant material measures of national power and has made substantial progress in so doing in a number of them, future efforts of the United States cannot simply follow the relatively laissez-faire approaches of recent years. The advantages and difficulties of more general and longerrange overall planning and coordination of national development in various areas of the economy, accordingly, must be investigated.

3] Since in a popular governmental system like that of the United States all policy and coordinated social action requiring countrywide scales of participation must be understood and accepted by a large fraction of the population, an effective program of ameliorative actions must explicitly define and implement adequate operational approaches for popular communication and the securing of broad public support.

4] Energetic activity by the federal government in seeking to bring about public understanding and acceptance of overall national planning and coordination in a broad spectrum of areas (other than under conditions of war or similarly declared national emergency) would probably be deeply suspect by other levels of American government and no doubt vigorously opposed by business and other community leadership throughout the nation.

It is probable that conditions (1), (3), and (4) would be generally accepted as valid by most of us, while condition (2), in spite of all that has been said above, would probably still be violently rejected by many as an unwarranted and biased extrapolation of available experience. It might be useful to repeat at this point only one additional argument in this connection. We have, in fact, been competing with the Soviet Union in all significant material areas for at least fifteen years, and during this period the traditional laissez-faire approach toward national coordination has been the basis of national policy. We appear to have lost ground in many areas during this period and may be continuing to do so. Such relative trends must be halted or reversed during the next decade or so if the Soviet Union is not to be given an opportunity to reach a position of general technological and industrial domination. Is it prudent policy, then, and is it in the public interest, to assume that these trends will somehow be reversed in the near future by some set of unspecified, automatic safeguards which are reputed to be built into the system?

In closing this section, it may be useful to restate the above four boundary conditions in the form of more direct strictures implied by them on practicable lines of action.

First, in the absence of war or a declared national emergency, it is unlikely that the federal government can successfully take the political initiative for developing and implementing, within the critical time span of the next ten or so years, a long-range plan, of the breadth and rigor probably required, for coordinating economic efforts at the national level. If such initiative were attempted, it is improbable that popular support could be developed and maintained.

Second, continuing broad public support (in time of

peace) for any program involving a substantially increased role for the federal government can be developed and maintained only if influential elements of the business community support rather than oppose such a changed role. This means that any operationally useful approach must be based, for example, on the understanding and support of organizations such as the Advertising Council, the Chamber of Commerce of the United States, the American Manufacturers' Association, and so on. Furthermore, the development of such understanding and support could be initiated and carried through not by the government but probably only on the initiative of organizations financed and directed by individuals fully acceptable to the business community.

Third, on the other hand, because of boundary condition (1) above, and the impedimenta previously discussed, the requirement for realism and objectivity in the general formulation of a plan and program should not be delegated to a representative segment of the business community. Furthermore, no non-profit institution, depending importantly on the continuing financial support of members of the business community, direct or indirect, should be put in the position of assuming such functions or responsibilities.

VI.   *A POSSIBLE APPROACH*

One of the psychological handicaps in dealing with problems of the kind we have been discussing is an acute awareness of the small probability of avoiding inconsistencies, of being naïve about human nature and its role in determining what is socially attainable or impossible, or simply of committing absurdities because of the enormous complexity of modern society in contrast to the poverty of firm principles concerning its activities. Part of society's conditioning of the organization man is to instill in him associated feelings of awe and inadequacy which, in addition to his enormous real difficulties in dealing with social problems, further inhibit his will and ability to understand and question. The appeal of axiomatically simple pronouncements about society in general originating in household economies (such as "bankruptcy inevitably results if a fiscal budget is not kept balanced") can probably be traced in part to inhibitions of this kind, and there is little question that they are among the principal obstacles to participation by nonspecialists or the public in rational consideraton of social adaptation. Accordingly, it is to be understood that it is only with misgivings that we accumulate the bravado to persist in this discussion.

We have now reached the point in the argument where most of the elements necessary for constructing a concrete (but by no means necessarily successful) initial approach to the overall problem of accelerating the rate of general national economic growth have been indicated. More specifically, we seek to bring about a favorable change in the effective output of scientists and engineers. This also is the point at which it is possible to specify areas in which applications of research into creativity can find their most socially useful returns. It is simplest to develop this proposal largely in the form of direct implications from conclusions previously developed by the argument.

1] There is little, if any, basis for believing that enough public support can be generated in the foreseeable future for acceleration of national progress in the directions of interest to us unless effective means are created for doing at least the following:

A. Development and definition of a comprehensive series of material measures, or indexes, of the overall social effectiveness of the economy of the United States and of selected foreign economies, which indexes can then be employed by us as guides for defining appropriate national goals. It is assumed that the measures developed can be validly used for comparisons between different national economies, as well as in the form of comparisons over time for any one economy.

B. Establishing procedures for ensuring realistic comparisons, using these indexes, of the relative progress of ourselves and any of our competitors, as well as for securing agreement at least among those involved in these studies as to the validity of implications to be drawn from such comparisons.

C. Devising the structure of concepts and organizational arrangements, including those with all levels of government, which it would be feasible to employ for communicating the findings to the public and, in particular, to the opinion-forming segments of our society; for resolving problems of interpretation and understanding; and for formulating programs to secure the necessary level of general public understanding.

D.   Conceptually developing national programs of action in all of the relevant areas which are internally self-consistent, based on the attained levels of public understanding and support, and of a character which can be practically implemented by the governmental and industrial arrangements available.

E.   Conceptually developing and preparing recommendations for modifying conventional governmental and market procedures which would be required if national goals specified by the program and accepted by the public are to be effected in the required time phasing.

As can be seen from their content, (A) through (E) define essentially a purely intellectual task, a species of a complex operations and systems analysis type of undertaking. As was implied by prior discussion, the aim would be to undertake this task using available knowledge and accepting the resulting constraints on validity of the results. It can be argued that one of the important obstacles to necessary social change in recent years has been a tendency on the part of our intellectual leadership to rely perhaps too exclusively on academic research, publication in professional journals, and discussions among specialists—in the expectation that the results of such research will somehow be transferred by others in our society into useful plans and action programs—rather than using what is already known for specifying and advocating pragmatic approaches to social phenomena. Accordingly we add:

F.   At any given time use what we know *then* about human behavior and society and take practical advantage of the existing system of personal and organizational relationships, as well as of the available natural resources, for attacking important internal problems or for overcoming external challenges. The emphasis on "use what we know then" arises because time has become perhaps too scarce a resource to throw away by avoiding use of present tools in the hope that new and improved methods might become available around the next research corner. We might here keep in mind the Russian proverb, which is said to be displayed in Soviet laboratories, perhaps particularly

in those concerned with the scientific and technical problems of competing with the United States: "The better is
the enemy of the good."

2] Assuming that the means referred to in (1) have been
created, and are generating the levels of information outlined in
(A) through (F), the question arises as to how this information
should be employed to be effective in producing the required
social adjustments. The analyses of the preceding sections suggests the courses which could be employed, either individually
or jointly, depending on the means available for such purposes.
They are as follows:

A. Disseminate publicly the information generated as a
result of (1), perhaps in much the same media through
which current data concerning American business conditions are made available to the public. The methods of
dissemination would need to be modified, however, so that
the public remains continuously and clearly aware of
trends in the time series not only for the United States, but
also in comparison with the same time series for selected
foreign countries. The basic objective of the disseminated
information would be to make all sectors of the public
conscious of, and concerned about, the status of the production economies of the United States and other countries. In view of the fact that the present practices of public news media tend to focus on selected highlights of
largely favorable news relating to the United States, and
selected, largely unfavorable views concerning some other
countries, this course would not be without its difficulties.
Assuming that it could be pursued, the hope would be
that the resulting public interest and discussion would
eventually, but much sooner than without such action,
lead in a more or less natural way to appropriate action
at the community, business, and governmental levels.

B. Establish and liberally support a special public organization specifically to develop and execute intensive
adult education programs concerning implications of the
data generated by (1). The primary task of this organization would be to ensure that the opinion-forming segments of all sectors of the economy (the leaders in business, labor, government, the professions, and so on) know
and understand the facts, the trends, and the implications

as to the nature of possible national responses at all levels of the national economy. In many respects such as organization would be similar, on the one hand, to nonprofit public associations in the public health field, for example, and, on the other hand, to the organized, special-interest, for-profit lobbies now focusing their attention on one or another public sector. But there must clearly be one major difference between the type of organization required for this broad national purpose and the private interest lobbies—it would have to conduct its work completely in public view and without the use of special pressures or inducements, since to prevent unwarranted public suspicion and to maintain effectiveness it would indeed need to be purely educational in carácter.

c.   Assuming the availability of adequate resources, a combination of the above two approaches would be clearly preferable to either alone. But it is far from clear in what mix they might be combined at the start, in view of the need to ensure that the beginning of the effort is not met with violent rejection by any important opinion-forming segment of the public.

3] In view of their unsuitability from the points of view either of the business community, of some levels of government, or of the public, the sources of financial support for the activities required by (1) and/or (2) could not be any level of government, any organization financially dependent on government, or the profit-making business community. Accordingly, only the large, nonprofit foundations would be suitable, and this means that one or several of these must first be persuaded that, within the structure of the American system, such foundations indeed constitute the principal, if not the only remaining, source of support which might be suitable for direct employment in ensuring the continuing viability of the system through processes of the type being here proposed. No other source of support would be likely to have as much initial business and public confidence in its objectivity or in its fundamental sympathies to the aim of preserving all that can in fact be preserved in the existing institutional and cultural structure. Some factual evidence for this conclusion is perhaps supplied by the support from these sources that was employed for the President's Commission on National Goals during the last administration.

4] The "effective means" to provide the basic data and ideas for the undertaking we are describing must, of course, be itself an organization. The establishment of an organization to provide the intellectual leadership for the entire process is obviously a most crucial element. The principal difficulties will be those in selection of the managerial and professional staffs and in the arrangements made by which these personnel can approach their work with maximum independence of those constraints to uninhibited and original thought such as now limit the effectiveness of individuals facing issues of this kind in government and private life. What we now know about the necessary conditions for effective creative thinking might well find one of its most important applications in the processes of devising the details of this organization, in identifying and acquiring the key staff, and in establishing the optimum conditions for its management and use.

5] Finally, it is necessary to comment on the problem of how a beginning might be made. Probably most of the details are unimportant except for assurance that a relatively small initiating group be formed, that it contain a minimum spectrum of the needed skills and interests, and that its work from the day of formation is completely exposed to public view and discussion. No flavors of special political or economic interests or of proceedings hidden from the public view could be consistent with the objectives of the kind of undertaking we have been talking about. The argument of this essay might form a convenient initial basis for the group's developing its own improved and agreed-upon foundation for further inquiry—or for concluding that the general approach here proposed is itself unrealistic (or unsuitable for other reasons) and should be replaced by some different and hopefully more effective process.

6] A good case could probably be made that a group of the composition of the New York University Creative Science Seminar, perhaps with additions of some skills and interests not now represented, is of the type that should be formed and persuaded to take the first steps. This possibility is reasonable because of the direct relevance of the plan proposed to creativity in science, as should be clear from what has been said above, namely:

1.   The major obstacle to a substantial increase of scientific and technological creativity in the United States lies

in the limitations imposed by our society on the numbers of gifted youths who are motivated and able to acquire the necessary education.

2.   These limitations and others associated with overall planning and coordination in our economy tend to constrain the effectiveness with which we can benefit from changing technology, increase our rate of economic growth, or otherwise improve our capabilities in the national interest in relation to other societies.

3.   There is no task for research in creative behavior which is more complex, intellectually demanding, or socially essential than that of finding ways to use scientific knowledge now available for devising conditions and procedures useful in the mass reeducation of our community leadership so that leadership can think and act objectively and imaginatively to bring about operationally effective cooperation between business and government to the end that the national planning and coordination of the physical processes of our economy, made mandatory by the technology of modern life, become as much desired by the public as they are now proscribed.

VII.   *CONCLUSION*

On a recent occasion Arnold Toynbee is reported to have voiced the opinion that in wartime democracies are more effective than dictatorships because they can secure more readily public enthusiasm and support, whereas dictatorships are more efficient in peacetime because they can ensure superior employment of their overall resources through centralized management.[8] The purpose of this essay has been to suggest how one might try to devise tools to make our democracy more efficient in peacetime without compromising its essential character.

In retrospect, the main purpose of the argument was twofold: first, to describe what makes it unlikely, in the absence of a new approach, that any major change in the national economy, such as a substantial increase in the annual production of scientists and engineers, can be brought about as quickly as it might appear physically possible; and, second, to suggest an approach for attacking pragmatically the general problem of making our society adapt itself more quickly to an environment whose rate of change in recent years has been greatly increased largely by scientific and technological progress.

The approach suggested can be briefly described as an attempt to induce an essentially revolutionary change in the general public's views about management of the national economy, this change to be effected through systematic mass reeducation of various segments of our community leadership, as well as of the public. It is implied by the general argument that, except perhaps in details, some such approach is essential if our forms of social organization are to be viable in the face of evident internal and external difficulties. It is also implied that the so-called intellectual segment of our community leadership must assume the initiative in defining and implementing the necessary steps, largely on the basis of already available knowledge. Such initiative cannot be expected to come from anywhere else, nor is there time to wait indefinitely for breakthroughs from new researches.

REFERENCES

1. Taylor, Calvin W., and Barron, Frank. *Scientific Creativity; Its Recognition and Development.* New York: John Wiley & Sons, Inc., 1963.
2. The President's Science Advisory Committee. *Meeting Manpower Needs in Science and Technology.* Washington, D.C.: U.S. Government Printing Office, 1962.
3. Wiesner, Jerome B. *Education and Productivity in the Sciences.* Address to the New York University Conference on Education and Creativity in the Sciences, New York, June 1963.
4. The President's Commission on National Goals. *Goals for Americans.* New York: Prentice-Hall, Inc., 1960.
5. Sutton, F. X., Harris, S. E., Kaysen, Carl, and Tobin, James. *The American Business Creed.* New York: Schocken Books, 1962.
6. Whyte, William H. *The Organization Man.* Garden City, N.Y.: Doubleday & Co., Inc., 1956.
7. Arnold, Thurman. *The Folklore of Capitalism.* New Haven: Yale University Press, 1962.
8. *The* [Washington, D.C.] *Sunday Star.* August 13, 1961.

CREATIVITY IN AN ACADEMIC ATMOSPHERE

Sidney G. Roth

GENERAL INTRODUCTION

CREATIVITY in the sciences results from the interaction of an individual with other individuals or an environment. The creative individual is generally operating within some social or institutional complex—industry, government, his home, or an academic framework. It is this latter atmosphere which shall be examined here.

Creative science may be defined in a number of ways involving such parameters as process and product, originality, novelty, and utility. However, the process or product results from a long series of intellectual experiences, the great majority of which are traceable to the relationship of the creative scientist with his teachers at all levels, with his experiences as a graduate student, with his scientific peers, and others. Since most basic scientific research is performed within university or university-related laboratories, their structure and atmosphere are significant in almost any analysis of creative science.

Thus, creative science and the educational process are irretrievably interwoven. The intellectual environment of a particular school or university is a parameter of an individual's creativity. If the teaching or research conditions favor concentration

42

upon the problem at hand, the atmosphere should enhance cerebration and its resultant products. An atmosphere with frequent perturbations of a nonscientific nature will assuredly dampen the creative current and stem the scientific output.

This paper will examine the relevant educational issues, with particular stress upon higher education, that must be resolved to enhance scientific research and the search for knowledge. It will analyze some key segments of the environment that academic institutions must provide to continue gathering unto themselves what Paul Klopsteg has called "the best minds and skills for works of such supreme importance." Among these problems are the reforms affecting structure and substance of education at all levels; the relationships of higher education with the federal government; and the competition for the "best minds" to help develop academic institutions as the breeding grounds for future generations.

Examination of this area requires observations on teaching, research, and administrative practices. Inasmuch as education is truly a continuum with almost arbitrary cuts denoting levels of accomplishment, major reforms at the elementary and secondary levels are necessary before significant gains can be achieved in the college and graduate school. Since the nation does not have an unlimited time scale in order to effect desirable change, concurrent experimentation at each level is called for. Finally, an understanding of the forces that act upon the educational system from without is required. For example, the role of government in its financing of education and research has to be clarified and shaped in order that academic institutions, especially universities, do not become servants to insistent demands, thereby relinquishing their role as independent leaders in intellectual activities.

BACKGROUND ISSUES

The academic institution is constantly changing and evolving. While relative emphasis upon subject matter, research, and society's problems may vary from generation to generation, the nation's schools, elementary through the university, represent the cultural institution primarily responsible for the transmission, synthesis, and creation of knowledge. Training, education, and research are the means of performing these tasks.

Thinking and learning are probably the most important activities that can happen in any *educational* institution. These are difficult processes to master, but they are fundamental for the creative intellect. Their significance has apparently been rediscovered by the American Council on Education, which stressed in a report that "learning to think, to relate, to do [result from] native curiosity and the concern to know and understand, stimulating teaching, adequate preparation of the student for the work he confronts, effective tools with which to work, and an ethos conductive to intellectual effort." [1] It seems odd that the American Council has had to issue this type of statement in 1960 to a nation committed to universal education for the past hundred years. Or has education as practiced within the country differed significantly from these precepts?

With one fourth of the nation directly involved in the educational process, the nation is in the dilemma of seeking high quality education but not agreeing upon the substance, purpose, methods, or cost of education. In his essay "The Function of Education," Clarence Faust states:

Our first task is to decide whether we really mean to make intellectual development the prime purpose of our elementary and secondary schools and of our institutions of higher learning. We must ask ourselves whether when we have talked about the education of the "whole child" we really have meant almost everything but intellectual development, or have at best assigned a low position to it. We must ask whether intellectual development is not in effect subordinated to other things when we speak of the schools as "child-centered rather than subject-centered."

If we are confused about these matters, as I think we are, the fault is not with our schools and our schoolmen so much as with the general public which has exhibited great ambivalence about the intellectual aspect of education and indeed about intellectual life in general. In our new concern about the substance of education, the intellectual substance of it, there is a tendency to find a scapegoat in the leaders of elementary and secondary education or in certain twentieth century movements among educators. But the real fault lies with us, the general public, which has set no great store by intellectual achievement and has found it amusing to deprecate eggheads.[8]

Considerable progress has been made toward developing some respect for the "scientific egghead." Yet the country has a long road to travel to eliminate the seemingly innate anti-intellectual attitude which pervades most levels of our culture. Paul Woodring poses the question of educational controversy in more somber terms: "Like the Greeks of Aristotle's day we are engaged in controversy over what is real, what is true, and what is important. But the Greeks never solved their basic educational problems. Greek education declined, and with it the Greek culture." [32]

Dr. James Conant's analysis of the high school and the junior high school leads him to believe that nothing radical need be done to improve their position. He advocates the comprehensive high school and sees no valid educational reason for having a high school with a graduating class of under one hundred. His major criticism of secondary education is that "the academically talented student, as a rule, is not being sufficiently challenged, does not work hard enough, and his program of academic subjects is not of sufficient range." [6]

A continuing problem for almost every community is the financing of its schools. As parents we certainly want good, if not excellent, educational opportunities for our children. But, as taxpayers we are loathe to pay for them.

The total bill for all forms of education in this country approximates 4 percent of the Gross National Product, or $22 billion; higher education takes about $6.5 billion of the total. Since the great majority of schools at all levels are continually seeking improvements in such areas as teacher salaries and facilities, it is clear that either:

A.   We must introduce more economic methods into education, including better utilization of staff and facilities, along with a hard look at the curriculum;

B.   We require considerably greater sums within the system to pay for the necessary reforms such as higher wages and improved facilities; or

C.   We may require both attacks.

Apparently, education is one of the major areas where we qualify as Spartans. For while we groan at the prospect of higher taxes for this purpose, our voluntary expenditure on liquor is $11 billion annually, with at least a $1 billion additional involuntary economic loss due to hangovers (according to the Center of Alcoholic Studies formerly at Yale), and we manage to gamble at a conservative level of $20 billion.

Science is among the more important concerns of formal education. Since the education of scientists and the development of scientific knowledge are essential functions of the schools and universities, it is necessary to understand the role that these institutions play in this total process. While universities should tolerate only that intellectual climate necessary to encourage the scholar along the disciplined path of knowledge, recent phenomena at these centers indicate counterforces at work which seriously threaten the university as focuses of creative science.

For example, the nation's colleges and universities are charged with becoming the places where Merle Tuve observed, "a professor's life nowadays is a rat race of busyness and activities, managing contracts and projects, guiding teams of assistants and bossing crews of technicians, plus the distractions of numerous trips and committees for government agencies necessary to keep the whole frenetic business from collapse." He continued, "Too many of our academic leaders, of course, have chosen this pattern of activity and personal power in preference to the quieter and more difficult life of dealing with ideas and scholarly initiative." [31]

Other anti-intellectual phenomena are those of bigness and group activity, which represent a trend in university life. This trend has already developed an organizational rigidity in certain institutions which can easily negate curiosity and the search for the new, especially along unconventional paths. The convergence of university administrative practices into those associated with corporate management appears to be rapid. In one sense this trend is long overdue, because universities have lacked sound business practices for optimal use of their resources. But the zeal for reform may easily have led to excesses. Perhaps W. H. Whyte, Jr., overstated the case with his comment, "every one of the trends to be found in corporation research can be found in academic research, and with consequences far greater. . . . Like his brother in management, the scientist is becoming an organization man." [30] However, these storm signals have been flying for some time.

A critical issue facing the academic world is the so-called population explosion. The demands upon the colleges have assumed huge proportions, and these will be dwarfed by those about to come. Within the past six years, college enrollments at the undergraduate levels have increased 45 percent, compared to an increase of one tenth that in the 18–21-year age group. Within a decade we shall have some seven million students, double the number in 1961, without any possibility of meeting the staff requirements if we continue to operate under the same ground rules.

This increase is attributed to two elements. First, we are approaching a level of 40 percent of high school graduates entering college, with every indication that this may rise to 50 percent by 1970; whereas only 15 percent entered college in the 1940's. Second, the demand for graduate and postdoctoral training is changing the character of many institutions. In effect, the universities are attempting to combine two trends: accommodation to mass education and the "pursuit of excellence," especially in the scientific curricula and research.

For too many years American education has been prodigal with its treasured human resource. Only some 40 percent of those entering college graduate from their selected curriculum within the allotted time.[4] Attrition within the technical curricula is even heavier. Colleges follow essentially two patterns of admission to their halls of learning: high order of selectivity or permissive entry. The latter procedure, in effect, says, "Let all enter who care enough and who meet minimum standards. We, the College, will observe you during your first year and request those who cannot make the grade to leave!"

Neither procedure is hitting the mark! Colleges, somehow, must discover who is a good bet for admission. With the extraordinary attrition rate, how can current procedures be justified? While the psychologists of learning [12] continue to debate issues of stimulus-response functionalism, neobehaviorism, Skinner's analysis, mathematical models of psychological theory, and the like, application of theory is in order. The gap between research and practice must be closed. College Board scores, high school averages, and a few nonintellectual factors are currently the *sine qua non* for college admissions. Somehow, one has the impression that Model-T methods are being used in a jet age; statistical empiricism is called upon when more sophisticated processes may be available. Psychologists have developed a number of predictive models for intellectual and professional achievement, but their research goes essentially unnoticed.[24] Too many colleges have adopted the attitude that because the prestige institutions adopt certain admissions procedures, such as the College Boards, therefore institutions using these same criteria are identifiable as "good institutions." Can one truly demonstrate that the elaborate paraphernalia of entrance tests—which have developed into a national annual traumatic competition with special arenas for 11th-year and 12th-year students—have yielded significant predictive factors for success in college?

Finally, the national discontent over school curricula, especially in the sciences, has led to a vigorous exercise of soul-searching at elementary, secondary, and college levels. Much of this reexamination stems from concern over Soviet achievements and with disaffection for the excesses of Dewey's misguided disciples. However, an educational revolution is in the making that requires exposition. Perhaps educational change for the mere sake of change can diminish the realization of problem-solving and creative abilities of young students. Excesses of reform replacing excesses of dogma accomplish little.

The issues at each educational level should now be considered in order to arrive at a basis for suggesting certain judgments on "creativity in an academic atmosphere." To keep the theme within manageable proportions, the discussion will be confined to creativity in the sciences. This signifies more than problem solving by logical methods. It means developing intuition, guessing, heuristic reasoning as parts of the process that eventually includes the rational, logical order. However, one must step back and examine a few educational practices in the large before concentrating specifically on creative science and scientists.

THE SCHOOLS

The two horns of the educational dilemma are *quantity* and *quality*. This is clearly elaborated in the many writings on secondary school reform, good illustrations of which are *Images of the Future* [26] and *The Schools*.[17] The first study is directed toward the organization of facilities and instruction to make the secondary school experience more meaningful to all types of students. *The Schools* is an exposition and comparison of primary and secondary school practices.

The most meaningful potential reform, however, is that which results from the realization that instruction in mathematics, the sciences, and language has been woefully inadequate. The experiments represented by the New York University Dual Progress Plan,[25] the School Mathematics Study Group, the Illinois teams headed by Beberman and Page, and the Physical Science Study Committee are illustrative of several attempts to bring about major new learning situations. New mathematics and physical science courses are being introduced into the schools from the early grades through high school. And several studies of their effectiveness are under way.[27]

In particular, large-scale experiments are called for before the schools abandon classical mathematics to a large degree. One may charge some of the reformists who insist on large doses of "modern mathematics" for elementary and secondary school children with being faddists.

By way of illustration, mathematics has long been taught as a discipline concerned with abstract reasoning and an emphasis, in Euclidean geometry, on the deductive method. Rarely have the materials of the elementary or secondary school mathematics courses correlated with the scientific or everyday experiences which young people enjoy. Problems in standard textbooks were essentially sterile or lacking in identification with life situations. No wonder most youngsters could see little value in the study which emphasized manipulative techniques in a mysterious manner. The Gestalt was lacking and the methods employed were foreign to the student. How many teachers or supervisors of science would focus upon heuristic methods, the educated guess, a truly valid application? Not many, for after all mathematics, the "queen of the sciences," has its own distinctive language! It is at this level that strong differences exist between those who advocate mathematics as a study for its own intrinsic beauty, form, and formal logic versus those who regard mathematics as a living, organic part of science with much to offer through problem-solving, conceptualizing techniques.

The least that should be stated, however, is that experiments of the School Mathematics Study Group and the Physical Science Study Committee have caused an awakening to the teaching that these subjects have suffered through the years. Since imaginative and creative youngsters could easily be crushed through their experiences in mathematics and science courses where formulas rather than reason ruled, probably goodly numbers of potential scientists turned to other fields which seemed more promising. These experiments have brought into being new materials and, hopefully, better teaching methods. Most importantly, they have brought together, after many years, an articulation between schoolmen and university scientists. This communication channel is a healthy development and augurs well.

In addition, new methods of teaching through the techniques of the mass media are now very much in evidence. By means of educational television, an exceptional teacher can reach students in schools not blessed with an abundance of such. Here again, before our children are lured permanently to the "idiot box" or to programmed-learning machines, must not large-scale experimentation demonstrate that these newer methods will enable the best teachers to lead more students to higher levels of achievement and understanding than other techniques?

Secondary education has oscillated between two poles: the specialized high school and the comprehensive high school. The latter achieved considerable prominence with the need for better facilities, better teachers, and more diversified curricula. The old academy concept of the high school gave way with the universal appeal of education and the demands of vocational training. However, it is no longer undemocratic to suggest that talented youngsters or even those of retarded development can achieve higher levels when placed in learning situations that are challenging to them. Thus, the specialized school is reappearing and academic high schools are offering advanced courses for seniors to enable them to enter college with advanced standing. Again, do educators really know that these trends will produce more creative scholars, or are these simply political manifestations?

Finally, in the twelve-year span of education leading to college, what can be done to bring student achievement to a higher level than heretofore? And, what can be done to reduce the total period so that qualified youngsters can enter college at age sixteen instead of eighteen? The few pilot programs of early admissions demonstrate that the foreshortened period is feasible for at least better students. A major controlled experiment on a national basis, with large numbers of students of varying abilities, should pay dividends in testing a number of hypotheses, of which the following are representative:

1. A heavier academic load can be absorbed by students of college-entrance caliber.

2. A longer academic year can shorten the total time span from elementary school to college entrance.

3. A significant increase in independent study can bring those in the upper 30 percentile to college at an earlier age and with better preparation than standard methods. Each of these experiments is directed toward the youth who, if sufficiently motivated, will provide the creative talent of next scholarly generations. It should be clearly understood that this type of talent is not confined to the "genius" category. Furthermore, the most creative scientists are not confined as a class to those who achieve highest grades in school or college. Roe, Stein, and others have presented significant evidence on this point.

THE COLLEGE AND UNIVERSITY

The place and role of the university in our society has changed perceptibly during the past century. Woodrow Wilson, fifty years ago, defined a major purpose of the American university to be "serving the nation." [15] In Wilson's terms this meant training the qualified young people to become the educated leaders of the nation or "society of men." Wilson's words would be about the same as those we use today to describe the role of higher education. But, the meanings have altered!

By the 1950's "serving the nation" acquired an additional connotation of "serving the state," a social machine or something beyond the individual. Because the government at both state and federal levels had assumed a major position in the support of higher education through, among other factors, the shift of students to public universities in large numbers and the heavily sponsored research and training programs, the "state" as an entity had acquired major importance. The state's anthropomorphic character had developed important needs to which the individual may be asked to yield. The accent was on *service* rather than *leadership*.

In the recent past, the more demeaning faces of the state's image were emphasized. Not only had the rights of individuals suffered but the intellectual leadership of the university had been shaken by the focus upon immediate, insistent problems put before it. "Service" in the handmaiden sense took root.

Under the celebrated American talent to formalize and organize all types of movements, Universitas has developed disparate meanings for different sectors of the culture. Whitney Griswold and Robert Hutchins [10] exemplify those who would have twentieth-century educational values equated to the absolutes of Aquinas. In effect, the "Greats"—to use the Oxford term—had come to grips with the major problems, and the university's purpose was to illumine their answers. At the other end of the spectrum is the educator who deems it desirable and democratic for American universities to respond to most calls from the government and the economy. This position, generally associated with the publicly supported university, is familiarly known as the "service-station" concept. This latter view may be regarded as resulting from an excess of zeal on the part of American educators who have not developed, as has occurred in Europe, other types of educational facilities for numerous specialized vocations and professions.

Somewhere between these two extremes should be the American university in principle. One educational goal on which most observers will agree is that these centers of learning have the mission to develop basic understandings. Professor A. N. Whitehead stated that a university "preserves the connection between knowledge and the zest for life by uniting the young and the old in the imaginative consideration of learning. The university imparts information, but it imparts it imaginatively." [29]

Universities have attempted to fulfill this function since the founding of Bologna, Paris, and Cambridge. In each country and century such institutions have served their particular purposes: to train and educate the clergy, the barrister, the medical man, the engineer, and now the businessman. The university as the prime intellectual force should develop a wholesome and educated individual and concomitantly develop a more wholesome society. Charles V. Kidd emphasized this role of universities as "the places in our society where the maintenance of free inquiry into the unknown by individual thinkers is a prime goal in itself." [13]

Another educational dilemma results from piling upon the time-honored structure of the liberal arts college that of the university, with its diverse set of functions. One of the seeming contradictions within our universities is the antithetic role of the liberal arts college and that of the graduate school. Since the latter dominates, Earl J. McGrath believes,

It is not surprising that life within the liberal arts colleges has become confused and often aimless . . . and that it lacks the vitality which it once so abundantly had. . . . If the liberal arts colleges are to regain their proper functions they must free themselves from the dominance of the graduate school. They must again affirm, and begin to live by a set of genuine purposes expressed in unmistakably clear language. Unless they do this, they will undergo complete disintegration, as many have already begun to do.[16]

Here is a charge of consummate importance not only for scientific creativity but for education in general. However, the decline of the liberal arts college influence within the university may be attributable to other causes as well. For example, a major concern of the undergraduate college is to combat the ever-increasing specialization of its curriculum and the vocational or professional trend of such schools. Perhaps "training" would be a more suitable word for such activity. To be sure, there have been several notable attempts to develop new syntheses within the scientific and humanities curricula in general education, as at Chicago, Colgate, and Columbia. But has this type of education really resulted in the more educated and, we hope, creative person? Or is higher education producing graduates who become technologically outmoded upon completing the four-year curriculum, since they do not have either the benefit of a general education or the advantage of a higher order of specialization? To paraphrase Montaigne, the object of education should be to make the scholar as well as the man.

More specifically, science as a discipline has had to burst through two disparate boundaries in order to be recognized as culturally and technologically significant and worthy of study in an academic institution. Certain academic intellectuals simply closed their minds and pretended that science didn't exist.* [2,22]

The second barrier was that of nonunderstanding and noncommunication between science and engineering, between scientists and industrialists. Most "pure" scientists "were above" application, technology, and industry; engineers and industrialists, on the other hand, distrusted change and the radical behavior usually associated with scientists. But the impact of science upon education, technology, and the state has become critical only during the past few decades.

With the rapid increase in scientific knowledge, the colleges and professional societies are taking a hard look at the intellectual baggage of the scientific courses and methods of teaching. In mathematics and the physical sciences a number of

---

* Sir Eric Ashby believes, "the scientific revolution had occurred not through but in spite of the English universities." [2]

significant experiments are well under way to determine whether the student may enter the twentieth century intellectually without sifting through many outmoded approaches to these subjects. Modern mathematics, as indicated earlier, has been introduced into secondary schools and elementary undergraduate courses. It is rapidly displacing classical subject matter, and the beginning student is introduced to set theory, linear algebras, matrices, and the like in courses recommended by the Committee on the Undergraduate Program, Mathematics Association of America.[5] However, it will be necessary to know what happens to the mathematical literacy and understandings of young people subjected to this experience before we close the door upon the more traditional form of mathematical education.

The reform movement has probably held sway without too much opposition because of the lack of a unified body of applied mathematicians in this country. With little exception—New York University, MIT, Brown, RPI, Stanford, and Harvard, to name a few institutions—the mathematics departments have been trained in the pure fields. There is undoubtedly a place for both pure and applied mathematics in most universities, and in the national interest such opportunities must be afforded the aspiring student.[9]

Similarly, the chemical bond has been introduced as the theme in the introductory chemistry courses. In physical and biological sciences, other innovations are occurring. These attempts are all designed with the view that major concepts will become meaningful—that the student may cut a swath through a jungle of needless information and technique and emerge into the clearing of scientific understanding and cultural literacy in a considerably shorter period than heretofore.

THE RESEARCH PROBLEM

The discussion thus far has attempted to portray the background and university atmosphere in which basic research has become a primary endeavor. Scientific research, equated here to creative science and technology, is a dominant aspect of the university campus and has been for the past fifteen years. These programs are supported from many sources, university, foundations, industry, but essentially by the federal government. By 1961 this latter sponsorship amounted to approximately $1 billion, probably 20 percent of the total expenditure for higher education in the nation.

The federal research program has wrought and "is stimulating conspicuous changes within higher learning, changes which deserve thoughtful and informed study. . . ." James McCormack and Vincent A. Fulmer develop this theme and maintain that "society would be the loser if government administration failed to use university research resources or proceeded to use them without comprehending the educational forces which dominate the academic community. The university would be the loser if it seriously inhibited the access of its science and engineering faculty and students to the powerful technologies of our time, in which government support is often crucial to meaningful participation." [14]

This growth of program has developed into manpower and organizational phenomena of considerable magnitude during the past two decades. Professional research staffs have grown on many university campuses or on campuses devoted exclusively to research. However, such staff members rarely enjoy the full rights of the faculty, even though in many instances they are fully qualified scientists and scholars. These men have little or no relationship to the teaching program of their institutions.

Thus, an anomaly has arisen: universities generally regard the poundage of a faculty member's research output, rather than the quality of his classroom performance, as the basis for promotion in rank and salary. This procedure forces ambitious faculty members to seek means of reducing their teaching loads to a minimum in order to have more time for research and publication. As a result, the undergraduate and graduate teaching loads of senior faculty especially are considerably less than they were before the war.

On the other hand, large separate or coordinate research staffs have developed in many science and engineering departments. These persons, as indicated previously, include many capable independent investigators who do not seek or are not given faculty status. If they teach, it is ancillary to their major duties. Yet the nation is witnessing a steady worsening of the manpower shortage in the college classrooms. This second-class citizenship for qualified persons is not calculated to develop an environment conducive to maximal creative output.

A variation of the above theme is the separate campus-related research organization or the self-contained, independent research institute. These groups are not inhibited by ranges of faculty rank or salary. Consequently, they can and do attract large numbers of creative scientists who find the atmosphere more congenial than the industrial laboratory and, at the same time, are not "burdened" with the direction of graduate students that is the lot of the university faculty scientist.

This latter type of organization poses another sort of problem. Men who ordinarily would be teaching and training the next generation of scientists have withdrawn from the process at a time when the universities need them more than ever before. Warren Weaver has aptly called the full-time university research scientists "intellectual eunuchs, not at all involved in the propagation of their kind." [28]

FISCAL PROBLEMS

A concomitant effect of the large sponsored research effort is the major impact of these programs upon university purpose and structure and the concern of university administrators with the problem of costs, both direct and indirect. The traditional pull between faculty and administration has undoubtedly heightened. University presidents spend inordinate amounts of time on fiscal problems and have to use "indirect financial levers" to "achieve such educational change" as they can. The faculty has, as a rule, a weakened role because of "the professor's lack of real interest in the university as a total institution." As in the past, there exists a minority who have "thought deeply and analytically about educational programs." [7] Faculty members are first and foremost subject-matter specialists. Relatively few, because of entrenched positions and interests, are educators in a comprehensive sense.

A whole corps of administrators has developed in the period since World War II, both within the academic framework and the government, to "protect" their respective interests. While it is certainly necessary to assure the solvency of the universities —and greater efforts are required along these lines than heretofore—a side effect, to be avoided assiduously, can result in intellectual strangulation.

The present system of contracts and grants is not always a bed of roses; or, perhaps, it would be more accurate to state that the thorns are ever present to prick the unwary. Since major support for scientific research is not readily available from institutional funds, the faculty member must play the game if he wishes to pursue his work on the scale he hopes to become accustomed to. He spends too much of his valuable time on his administrative and financial problems.

According to National Science Foundation estimates, the total sum spent on research and development in the nation during the fiscal year 1960–61 was some 100 times greater than that expended during 1940. Academic basic research is almost 50 times that of 1940, with another factor of 20 for training and fellowship programs. In terms of federal support, in 1940 approximately $15 million came to the campus; whereas it is estimated that $1 billion was spent during 1960–61 for research and allied activities on the campus and associated facilities.*

Any investment of this magnitude brings its peculiar problems and tends to overshadow equally significant programs of lower cost. The extraordinary support of university research programs by federal agencies may be gleaned from the fact that of the $830 million available for research in 1958–59, only $160 million, less than one fifth of the total, came from university resources; $170 million came from foundations, industry, and other private sources; and $500 million was derived from the federal government.[11]

Universities are the major bases for the performance of basic research. For example, of the $5.5 billion in the 1960 budget of the federal government for research and development, the President's Science Advisory Committee estimates that "about 6 percent is earmarked for basic research." Thus, of the estimated $330 million allocated for basic research, universities will have spent approximately $250 million, 50 percent derived from federal funds and the balance from academic budgets, foundations, and industrial grants. Since the vast majority of this support is for science and technology, one would hope that substantial uni-

---

* It is necessary to be aware of the difficulty of comparing and identifying current research expenditures on a meaningful basis with research levels of ten or more years ago. Numerous analysts urge caution on this point. For example, David Novick of the Rand Corporation believes that only $400 million out of the $10 billion research and development sum spent in 1959 is for what he terms "Brave New World" and "Possible Use of New Discovery." He suggests that "adjusting this [$400 million] for price change and Big Wheel and Big Deal administrative practices, a basic question is raised as to how much more we really are doing now than we were ten or twenty years ago."

versity funds would be freed to help nourish the arts, humanities, and the social sciences. However, this may not be the situation at all. The large research and training programs sponsored by these extramural funds may be placing a burden upon the institutions because of the need to develop space and facilities and to acquire staff. Furthermore, the costs of these programs are not fully borne by the sponsor.

Thus, in the quest for bigger and better science programs that will enable universities to bring to bear greater resources upon this vital area, such programs may be in danger of inhibiting the development of other valid educational activities. Dr. Alan T. Waterman, the first Director of the National Science Foundation, stated the problem this way: "As the scope of federal research programs increased, the volume of federal support to many institutions has disturbed the normal balance of research and has caused financial strain through government failure to pay full costs." [31]

A part of this very problem is an untenable situation foisted upon the universities, a situation whereby a scientist may shop around for the best financial terms to undertake a research problem with the support of a federal agency. For example, not only NSF is interested in basic research: so are the scientific arms of the Department of Defense, the Atomic Energy Commission, the National Aeronautics and Space Administration, the National Institutes of Health, and others. Strangely enough, it is possible to submit essentially the same problem to these various agencies but one element may have to change—the budget with which to carry out the study. Many recommendations have been made to make this support element uniform, but to no avail as yet. It has been impossible thus far to educate the several members of Congress responsible for these many fine programs to the realization that the penurious policy enforced upon two major agencies, NSF and NIH, is endangering the universities' ability to continue these activities. No longer is the deficit in funding measured in hundreds or thousands of dollars. Rather it is well into the many millions.

SOME OTHER ASPECTS OF RESEARCH

Most support for scientific research arrives in the form of one- or two-year contracts or grants. But basic research is essentially a long-term affair, as the report *Basic Research in the Navy* indicates. That study reveals "The overall time required for this process [planning, getting the team, performing experiments, analyzing and publishing results], as measured by the current average life of Office of Naval Research projects, is 5.1 years." [20] Universities, under the present system, are expected to make commitments and develop facilities that are neither advantageous for the staff nor for the institution. Any significant cutback in research funds would threaten the solvency of some major institutions if they were to make long-term commitments and damage the cause of education and research on a major scale. The threshold of this situation was dangerously close in the fall of 1957.

Despite many brave words calling for increased understandings of the university-government relationship and the transformation of our universities through these large programs, the nation still lacks the policy and mechanism for significant improvement. Wallace R. Brode, in his 1959 presidential address to the AAAS, addressed the issue as follows:

A national science policy is needed for a wise and rational distribution of scientific activities so that space, defense, education, atomic energy, oceanography, and medical research are not bidding against each other for limited available support. The growing demand for scientists in the face of a limited supply of scientists, materials, funds, and facilities requires major policy decisions as to the distribution of resources. These decisions should of course include the extent to which specialized agencies may recruit by scholarship, fellowship, and research support.[3]

The National Science Foundation has, during the past few years, finally taken the lead in delineating the background from which a national policy can develop. Its recent report *Investing in Scientific Progress* [19] analyzes the scientific and educational requirements of the decade ahead, and should be an important document for carrying out previous recommendations.

The universities have been too willing, in general, to accept research support without well-developed policies concerning the place of large-scale programs within their structure. The President's Science Advisory Committee stresses in a wholesome manner the provincial attitude prevailing on too many campuses and the shortcomings of university centers. It enlarges upon the thesis that basic research and scientific education represent a necessary union in a university locus and the university-federal government partnership is the indispensable basis of first-rate science. This partnership demands high university "standards of freedom and excellence" and minimization of fears that large-scale federal spending will subvert university goals. Of particular importance are the several charges:

. . . our universities have been slow in finding effective ways of encouraging scientific research and training at all the new levels and in all the new ways which the Age of Science makes possible. Graduate education is not as good as it should be. Outmoded rules of study too often impede the student's access to the experience of modern science. Research programs are too often kept in isolation from the mainstream of student life. Special research installations are too often not imaginatively used as a source of learning and teaching. New fields of study are ignored because they inconveniently cross departmental barriers. Strong understanding of the meaning of the Age of Science is too rarely found among university administrators. The universities themselves have much to do.[22]

The separate research institute or installation, steadily growing in influence, represents one type of response to the problems posed by large-scale research. As the President's committee stated, they are "not imaginatively used as a source of learning and teaching." Dr. Waterman, in his paper cited above, goes further and views it as introducing "another quite serious problem in the view of many" because of its isolation from the education process or, because of size, it may tend to monopolize.

An almost classic issue to contend with is the one dubbed by former President Harold Dodds of Princeton as "projectitis." It has two facets. From the university point of view: a faculty member, after an initial research period, may develop a team. Too often, regardless of accomplishment, the size of the staff is maintained or, through the inner mysteries of Parkinson's First Law, even enlarged. This situation results in a continuing search for support, with an incredible amount of time devoted to nonscientific matters and surprisingly little time for science. To correct the imbalance, administrators enter the picture, with the consequence that a larger share of the research funds are devoted to overhead costs.

From the sponsor's viewpoint: it is easier to permit a project to run on beyond its useful life than kill it. One makes fewer enemies, and there is always the possibility that the research will yield significant results. Both of these elements are symbolic of the fact that we are not very creative in our approach to the problem of research administration.

SOME RECENT ACTIONS

Within the past few years, several moves by the learned societies, university groups, the federal government, and the private foundations offer promise that the nation has awakened. The educational crisis is here. Those in strategic positions must be confronted with the need for thoughtful, responsible action. If one may pinpoint a date for the realization that our educational philosophy and scientific programs require overhauling, it would be October 4, 1957, that of the first Sputnik. Many schools and universities took decisive action, the National Science Foundation quickened its pulse, and the National Defense Education Act burst forth in 1958 to promote and develop requisite foreign language, mathematical, and scientific programs. NDEA tackled the need for better trained teachers and better educational programs at the elementary and secondary schools and provided the means for expanding sorely needed graduate programs in many disciplines.

Universities had banded together in a number of instances to tackle scientific programs not amenable to any single school's limited resources: for example, the Associated Universities Incorporated, the Oak Ridge Institute, the University Corporation for Atmospheric Research, and the Graduate Research Center of the Southwest. These consortiums have received governmental, foundation, and industrial support. However, the areas of such cooperation must increase considerably within the near future if the specialized needs of graduate and postdoctoral programs in this burgeoning scientific era are to be met. Faculty, libraries, students, and facilities will increasingly be organized on a compact basis in a number of key areas, in order that institutions have access to, and not replicate needlessly, expensive and highly specialized programs.

The private foundations have used their resources to encourage experimental programs among the more dynamic universities. Despite vaunted claims of two thousand and more institutions of higher learning, the graduate and research programs take place in some two hundred institutions, with only some fifty sharing an important role in this process. Twenty of these are "first-rate academic centers of science," according to the President's Science Advisory Committee. The broadening of this base is a high priority item for America.

An almost incestuous relation exists, whereby the strong institutions often incubate their own undergraduate students for continuing study at the graduate level at these same schools. A brief analysis of the NSF graduate fellowship roster will indicate the really few institutions attracting the best scientific students. To counteract this influence, NSF established the Cooperative Fellowship Program, which enables each university to nominate candidates in proportion to the number of doctorates awarded by the institution in the previous year. Although this program broadens the base of institutions participating in training outstanding students, it does not provide the answer to having good graduate students move to other campuses competent to offer advanced training.

The federal government—insofar as most universities are concerned, this is not an entity, but a federation of grant-giving agencies—has already corrected a number of inequities and "soft spots" which have inhibited the growth of educational and research programs. It has recently shown an imaginative perception in its relationship to these problems, a number of which have been highlighted in this paper. Others are now stated because their solution may well be the key to our future.

The interaction of the mathematical, physical, and biological sciences has led to the need for mutual understandings and simultaneous attacks upon basic problems. Materials science, mathematical models for social behavior, and the physics of physiology are examples wherein large-scale support has begun. The Advanced Research Projects Agency, the National Aeronautics and Space Administration, and the National Institutes of Health are currently investing in programs of this nature.

Basic to all attempts, however, is the necessary support which will ensure the creative scientist that his program can proceed without undue negotiations or administrative interference. Thus, under Public Law 85–934, certain federal agencies are now permitted to offer grants for basic research in addition to contracts. Within the past three years, the several basic research arms of the Department of Defense and NASA have introduced this form of support. Of course, NSF and the NIH have used this instrument for their support programs for many years with increasing success. The grant system provides a more favorable atmosphere in longer term support, up to five years, in reducing administrative procedures and, above all, in moving toward the desirable goal of support for the man and his program rather than for the immediate problem. Its spirit is most commendable in that emphasis is properly placed upon the scientist's requirements and necessary administrative details are minimized. This grants program for basic research is a major step toward implementing the government-university partnership. The institution-grants plan initiated by NSF and NIH is undoubtedly the forebear of new concepts which will radically alter our present system.* We are moving toward a system akin to that of the British. Their University Grants Commission, though working with funds awarded by Parliament, dispenses relatively large sums to each university independent of political influences.

Even though this liberalization tendency has set in, a number of federal agencies believe strongly in having universities utilize their own funds in a given ratio to those supplied by the sponsor. As more than one college president has indicated rather ruefully, this cost-sharing concept may have been valid when the number and size of research contracts were relatively small. But now that they approach or exceed a quarter of many institutions' budgets, amounting to millions of dollars in large universities, the latter must become selective about utilizing their resources. A dollar of matching funds spent for sponsored scientific research may well be one sorely needed for other scholarly programs not the recipients of federal interest. Furthermore, these impoverished programs may be more important to the human race in the long run. If the universities do not support the humanities and arts fields, for example, who will?

Another element is among the most serious for the welfare of individual scholars and our institutions. Because relatively large sums have been available in areas of interest to the major federal agencies, certain phases of science and technology have developed rapidly. Others have received token support at best. Since the Department of Defense and the Atomic Energy Commission, and now the National Aeronautics and Space Administration, provide major support in the physical sciences, university-based research in these fields has developed strong ties to the goals and missions of these supporters. What does this trend

* The Sustaining University Program of NASA, instituted in 1962, is an example.

signify for the development of science? Is it depriving other areas of normal growth through the lure of support dollars and facilities? And by tying the research programs to defense and space needs, is an environment created whereby the government in effect can decide what areas are worthy of study on a priority basis? A charge of this nature was leveled at the major foundations by Congressional committees in the past with regard to the social sciences.

What effect does this situation have upon the researchers —and upon their institutions? It has created a large body of scientists and graduate students in certain fields. Each year for at least the past decade funds for basic sciences have increased in selective fields. Yet firm information concerning the adequacy of support in the basic sciences does not really exist. However, there is evidence that a considerably greater magnitude is called for. In support of this judgment, the National Science Foundation has stated: "The potential of its [United States] scientists exceeds the support available and probably exceeds it by a considerable amount. . . . The Foundation has been able to provide grants to only about one third of the investigators applying for basic research funds for proposed work judged by scientist reviewers to have great merit." [18]

It is known that in certain fields, especially in the medical sciences, a saturation point has been reached whereby a few competent investigators do not receive the support they require. To derive a better basis for judgment in this total area, NSF asked New York University and the University of Michigan to study their own institutions to determine what happens to men and their ideas when their proposed studies are not supported. The conclusions indicate that in several fields—engineering and the social and biological sciences—a significant number of competent scientists are engaged in less research than they would like, or are doing research not of their own first choice. The principal cause of this state is lack of support for programs judged worthy of execution by these two institutions. More data must be developed from a larger sample of institutions before this conclusion can be generalized. However, discussions with research scientists and administrators in different sections of the country tend to confirm the tentative conclusion. Also, recent recognition by the NSF of the importance of engineering and social sciences through the development of separate research divisions for these fields represents additional evidence that greater support is required.

It is clear that more definitive information is called for. More importantly, appropriate action by institutions and government must be taken quickly to provide the funds to support creative science.

As one may quickly gather, the federal government is playing a significant role at all levels of education at this time. Its support has brought important programs, experiments, and reforms into being. At the same time, university administrators and government officials are wondering what type of influence has been released upon the educational system. The Carnegie Corporation, through its own resources, and the Brookings Institution, with NDEA funds, have engaged in studying this very issue of impact of federal funds upon higher education. Their findings substantiate the several judgments expressed herein, pointing to certain excesses. The Brookings report reinforces the belief that federal support has been salutary and should be established on a more permanent and rational basis.

Another dilemma has emerged from current methods of research support. Scientific and technological programs may have different purposes for the sponsor and the researcher. This could be a good arrangement, provided there exists a clear understanding concerning the conditions under which a grant is made. However, if a large part of the basic research program at a university is tied into the "programmatic research" of an agency, then the institution is not building upon a solid foundation. Agency interests can shift through administrative direction or Congressional desire. What may have been a high-priority problem can easily be relegated to the ash heap.

Finally, can one ever measure the number of creative scientists who left a promising field of scholarship because it lacked support, in favor of a "more interesting" field which was particularly "hot" that year and thereby drew a good level of support? In principle one may argue that such people are free to move into whatever fields they wish. Furthermore, they have a real opportunity to become productive scholars where apparently productivity is required. This line of reasoning leads to the conclusion that the nation is no longer experiencing a free, random development of science. Rather, the group with the king-size purse string may be dictating the course of development.

Which fields really bloom under this system? Is it essentially only those selected areas which have their roots in military and industrial application and therefore enjoy relatively large support? High-energy and solid-state physics, materials science, numerical analysis, and computing are examples of areas important for national survival. These disciplines have grown dramatically under the impact of need and have succeeded in attracting their quota of young scientists.

Thus, we come face to face with educational and scientific issues whose import have only recently resulted in major discussions. Among the major queries are the following:

What can the nation do to ensure greater productivity and creativity in the sciences within the universities?

How can institutions preserve and foster "an atmosphere and a social climate in which the productive individual is honored and rewarded"?

What is the basis of a better education for the oncoming generations in the scientific fields?

How does one develop educational programs better suited for this era in order to open opportunities for young people through education and training?

What role does the government play over the next several decades to help the universities solve some of these common problems?

What can the universities accomplish by way of communicating and interpreting the scientific revolution to the nonscientist who must face up to this age of miracles? To bridge the abyss between "the traditional non-scientific culture and an up-and-coming scientific one" described by C. P. Snow?[23]

How does the system assure what Peter Viereck calls the "private elbow room, free from the pressure of centralization and the pressure of adjustment to a mass average" for the "creative imagination of the free scientist and free artist"?

And finally, how can the nation be assured that it will have the best in the advancement of science? Can we really meet the challenge of the President's Science Advisory Committee: "the best is vastly more important than the next best"? Can we afford not to?

These are the issues!

CONCLUSIONS

There is little doubt that the nation's schools and universities are, as a class, considerably superior to those of pre-World War II vintage. Much has happened to them which has forced change for the better upon them. In the spirit of cooperation that has emerged among the schools, foundations, industry, and the government, the joint attack upon these many problems must be sustained.

Mass education should not signify mediocrity. Rather, all persons should have full opportunity to realize their potential. This is particularly critical for research scientists. The schools and universities have much to do, but they require resources and support that are beyond current efforts by orders of magnitude. In short, the scope of the problem is staggering.

For the first time, legislative leaders have realized that large-scale improvement and reform in education take as long to accomplish as scientific advance. This means providing significant sums on a continuing basis—not to be cut to balance national budgets—that can bring requisite brains and facilities to bear on the issues.

At the school level: basic experiments and action programs are called for that will enable the budding scientist to develop his interests and capabilities optimally. The several programs aimed in this direction require careful scrutiny: alternative programs and approaches should be supported. Thus, one aim of a mathematics and science program, even at elementary school levels, should be to develop the capacity for intuitive solutions and understanding of their implications. This goal, for example, may well be in conflict with those currently stressed by the School Mathematics Study Group. One may read in that "scientific journal," *The New York Times,* an exchange of views on this issue with the proponents of SMSG expressing their side with great eloquence. I should like to recommend that the National Science Foundation, which has supported SMSG handsomely, and perhaps the Ford Foundation, with its major concern for science and education, invest comparable sums to develop alternative programs. In general, there is no one best method for accomplishing reforms. A number of leading mathematicians are convinced that

SMSG is actually performing a disservice, with consequent effect upon future development in mathematics and science.

Second, a similar program of alternatives should be supported in the several natural sciences. The Physical Science Study Committee, under Jerrold Zacharias, has revolutionized the teaching of high school physics through a gigantic effort started in 1956. The new course and materials are now being tried in more than 2,000 high schools, with large success. Yet it seems that some physicists are dissatisfied with a number of features of the program. Again, the requisite support for alternatives should be forthcoming to permit physicists and high school science teachers to bring their own ideas into suitable form. With all due respect to PSSC, unless adequate aid is given to the field for this type of experimentation, its significant contribution will degenerate into another prescription handed down by authority. The very process of creating a new curriculum should do much to aid teachers become better guides for potential scientists.

Third, considerable progress must be made to salvage many of the better minds in the educational arena by increasing the number of qualified persons for college entrance. Because college entrance applications are multiplying rapidly one cannot infer that they are from the best students. The high attrition rate among good students has already been cited. Therefore, certain approaches are called for which should yield better answers than the schools currently have. For example, how far may the schools go successfully with programs of independent study? If one purpose of education is to develop critical facilities among individuals, the independent path seems worthy of experimentation on a large scale to determine, on a controlled basis, its feasibility for the college-bound youngster—for developing skills, insights, and knowledge at a pace dictated by the student rather than by such authorities as the school curriculum experts. The major aims of such experimentation are to learn how well young people can organize the learning process, with proper aid from teachers, and to determine whether the time scale for precollege education can be foreshortened.

Fourth, a recent change in attitude of those responsible for elementary education practices has resulted in reading, arithmetic, mathematical, and certain scientific concepts being introduced in the very early years on an experimental basis. Some of the work of Patrick Suppes at Stanford, David Page at Illinois, and others should be scrutinized carefully, replicated, evaluated, and modified. Then, on a continuing experimental basis, reforms in scientific education should be introduced as quickly as possible. Here, I suggest that the gap between education, research, and practice can be narrowed most perceptibly.

Fifth, at the elementary and secondary school levels, continuing experimentation with programmed learning and high-speed computers are necessary. Not only is this a major hope for meeting the shortage of qualified personnel, but better teaching should result from understanding the several methods employed. Evidence is beginning to appear that teachers can learn new approaches to pedagogical problems from the actual process of programming a lesson. In addition, computer methods may vary significantly from pencil-and-paper approaches.

Sixth, there is little hope of preparing science and mathematics teachers of the quality and quantity that would be required to staff classes of twenty-five to thirty through twelve years of schooling. The preliminary evidence of early admissions with the bright sixteen- and seventeen-year-old suggests that the educational period can be shortened. It is recommended that controlled experiments be established in various sections of the country to determine the optimal periods of instruction at each level in order to advance good students along as rapidly as possible.

At the colleges and universities, considerable experimentation is likewise under way. However, a number of major areas require penetrating investigation to reduce the sharp losses of capable students, to ensure the integrity of the research programs which are of primary importance, and to enhance creativity within these institutions.

First, the college entrance criteria seem to concentrate more and more on CEEB scores. Since the validity of the CEEB aptitude scores as a predictive factor of college success is seriously open to question, I recommend that a new educational agency be established, not directly connected with a testing program. This agency should have scholars of several disciplines examining psychological, social, and intellectual factors that represent the differential profiles of professionals in diverse fields. Furthermore, it should evaluate the many types of testing programs for college admissions and help, in general, to develop sounder methods for college admissions.

Second, the programmed learning, language laboratory,

and computer devices should be enormous aids to teachers and students. These will represent a means of providing greater individual study opportunities, of reducing the number of formal class lectures, and of enabling the creative teacher to become involved with larger numbers of students. Once again, theoretic and action programs are required to help determine the disciplines in which these devices can best be used and how best to utilize these newer approaches in order that the higher educational institutions can meet the demands of the near future.

Third, to what extent can computers be utilized to aid scientists not only with methodological problems but as large-scale informational storage, retrieval, and generative devices? University libraries, except for a few major institutions, are finding it difficult to purchase and store the ever-increasing materials. The lack of budgets is almost as painful as lack of space. Through computers and other devices, universities can pool resources and provide almost instantaneous service to research scholars and faculty members. A major experiment involving varieties of collegiate consortiums should be financed to determine the extent to which technology must be improved to make this type of informational resource a reality on an economical basis.

Fourth, the scientific research support of the academic world has been geared to a program of grants and contracts. The shortcomings of this system have been delineated. An immediate remedy is called for in order that the creative aspects of science do not move from university campuses. A number of critics are already predicting that the heyday of the university as a center for creative science has passed. If they are right, the nation is probably in more difficulty than imagined. To stem the tide, the federal government must combine support of research with support of higher education on an institutional grant basis. This can be accomplished by an outright grant to each institution having federally supported programs of a given percentage of such federal dollars; by a matching grant for support of facilities or whatever use the institution wishes to make of such funds; by the equivalent of scholarship or fellowship monies based on the number of students, books in the library, or similar indices. In other words, if the federal government were to supplement the budgets of all accredited colleges and universities on an annual basis by 10 percent of these budgets, the total cost would be approximately $500 million. An expenditure of this kind would probably yield rich dividends almost immediately through increased facilities, more teachers, more research, more libraries, and support of fields not currently eligible under the restricted programs.

Fifth, bright young investigators and promising teachers have to receive encouragement to develop ideas and programs. National fellowships of adequate proportions have to be doubled or tripled to permit these young scholars to commit themselves to their work without distraction.

Sixth, because the scientist of Nobel laureate distinction and comparable stature can probably be the source of inspiration for students and younger faculty members, it is proposed that to each such scientist a major foundation and the federal government provide a ten-year grant to aid him to develop an "institute." This may not be necessary in certain instances, but men of such capability can often generate major ideas in large numbers provided a critical number of competent scientists are working together. An additional responsibility of these major scientists should be to spend at least one year at another campus, preferably in another section of the country, to help stimulate scientific developments elsewhere.

Seventh, a major talent search should concentrate upon the underprivileged groups of the nation to make certain that such persons are provided intellectual opportunities. Similarly, effective means must be discovered to keep the talented female scientist in science during her family-development period and thereafter.

Eighth, how quickly can undergraduates and young graduate students become involved in the research process? The current undergraduate research program of NSF is a modest beginning, to be sure. But, in a sense, a really bright and potentially creative scientist could forego formal class work in his major field if he were to work under supervision of a keen faculty member. Experimentation is desired to ascertain the optimal type of education for this type of person.

Ninth, and most important, the institution of the university as a dynamic force for the development of new knowledge and scholarship must be examined on a continuing basis. Differentiation in aims and objectives among types of colleges and universities should be clarified; interdisciplinary groups developed for the systemic approach to problems that transcend the interests of the traditional department; and students and faculty encouraged to explore the paths of knowledge in novel ways.

Tenth, the university as an organic structure which encourages and promotes research requires study. Its administrative practices and organization vary widely to meet local conditions. However, as a class, universities are essentially conservative and meet new conditions only after seemingly endless discussion. A major investment of talent among educational leaders, scientists, government research chiefs, and comparable persons from industry and the foundations is called for. The problem might be stated in somewhat oversimplified form: What organization models of universities will provide the optimal advance for creative science?

In short, the nation's future is inseparably linked to the future of the university. These institutions must provide the stimulus for free scientific inquiry which will enhance creativity at all levels. They must develop the scholarly atmosphere that will match research methodology with problem,* along with the resources that will make such creative work possible. This is the problem the nation must solve to ensure survival.

REFERENCES

1. American Council on Education. *The Price of Excellence*. Washington, D.C., 1960.

2. Ashby, E. *Technology and the Academics*. New York: St. Martins Press, 1958.

3. Brode, W. R. "Development of a Science Policy," *Science*, 131 (January 1, 1960).

4. College Entrance Examination Board. "Where the Loss of Talent Occurs and Why," *The Search for Talent*. New York, 1960.

5. Committee on the Undergraduate Program. *Collected Reports of the CUP*. Mathematical Association of America, 1955.

6. Conant, J. B. *The American High School*. New York: McGraw-Hill, 1959.

7. Corson, J. J. *Governance of Colleges and Universities*. New York: McGraw-Hill, 1961.

8. Elbers, G. W., and Duncan, P. (eds.) *The Scientific Revolution*. New York: Public Affairs Press, 1959.

9. Greenspan, H. P. "Applied Mathematics as a Science," *American Mathematical Monthly*, 68 (November 1961).

10. Griswold, A. W. *The University*. Unpublished interview, Center for the Study of Democratic Institutions, Santa Barbara, California, 1961.

11. Keezer, D. (ed.) *Financing Higher Education: 1960–1970*. New York: McGraw-Hill, 1959.

12. Kendler, H. H. "Learning," *Annual*

* Allen Newell and Herbert A. Simon have suggested that matching the "good problem" with "good techniques" is an important element in solving really complex problems, such as simulating human thinking through computers.[21]

nual *Review of Psychology,* **10** (1959).

13. Kidd, C. V. *American Universities and Federal Research.* Cambridge: Belknap, 1959.

14. Knight, D. M. (ed.) *The Federal Government and Higher Education.* Englewood Cliffs, N.J.: Prentice-Hall, Inc., 1960.

15. MacLeish, A. "What Is a True University?" *Saturday Review* (January 31, 1959).

16. McGrath, E. J. *The Graduate School and the Decline of Liberal Education.* New York: Columbia University Press, 1959.

17. Mayer, M. *The Schools.* New York: Harper & Bros., 1961.

18. National Science Foundation. *Basic Research, a National Resource.* Washington, D.C., 1957.

19. ———. *Investing in Scientific Progress.* Washington, D.C., 1961.

20. Naval Research Advisory Committee. *Basic Research in the Navy.* Office of Technical Services, United States Department of Commerce, June 1, 1959.

21. Newell, Allen, and Simon, Herbert A. "Computer Simulation of Human Thinking," *Science,* **134:**2011–17 (December 22, 1961).

22. President's Science Advisory Committee. *Scientific Progress, the Universities, and the Federal Government.* Washington, D.C., 1960.

23. Snow, C. P. *The Two Cultures and the Scientific Revolution,* Cambridge, England: Cambridge University Press, 1961.

24. Stern, G. G., Stein, M. I., and Bloom, B. S. *Methods in Personality Assessment.* Glencoe, Ill.: The Free Press, 1956.

25. Stoddard, G. D. *The Dual Progress Plan.* New York: Harper & Bros., 1961.

26. Trump, J. L. *Images of the Future.* Urbana, Ill.: Commission on the Experimental Study of the Utilization of the Staff in the Secondary School, 1959.

27. United States Department of Health, Education and Welfare. *Research Problems in Mathematics Education.* (Cooperative Research Monograph No. 3, 1960.)

28. Weaver, W. *A Great Age for Science.* New York: Alfred P. Sloan Foundation, 1960.

29. Whitehead, A. N. *The Aims of Education.* New York: Mentor Books, 1949.

30. Whyte, W. H., Jr. *The Organization Man.* New York: Simon and Schuster, 1956.

31. Wolfle, D. (ed.) *Symposium on Basic Research.* Washington, D.C.: American Association for the Advancement of Science, 1959.

32. Woodring, P. *A Fourth of a Nation.* New York: McGraw-Hill, 1959.

INDUSTRIAL RESEARCH MANAGEMENT AND CREATIVITY

Harold W. Mohrman

THE POSITION OF MANAGEMENT

ONLY A LITTLE THOUGHT is necessary for one to appreciate the importance of science to our economy and national strength. What is not so readily recognized is that every new invention or bit of technical improvement had its origin in some individual's brain—the product of creativity. This idea was nursed through the working model, the developmental stage, and then offered for sale in the hope of making a profit. Our system of free enterprise has produced the world's highest living standard, and it also has attracted its share of creative scientists. Our problem is to keep this system working, adapt it to changing demands, and to supply research scientists in numbers and quality adequate to meet future requirements. World political problems have made scientific manpower one of our most important resources. Industrial research, the largest employer of such manpower, is vitally concerned with its most effective use.

Industrial research has grown as an integral part of most companies which trace their origin to modern technology. As the results of research produced new products and new markets, industry has plowed back a significant portion of its profits into more research. In the twenty-five-year period from 1936 to 1961,

74

the annual research-and-development investment by American industry has grown from $200 million to over $5 billion. U.S. government expenditures, including such costly projects as space exploration, show an even more spectacular rise, climbing from less than $40 million to $8 billion in the same period. This rate of growth shows no slackening and, indeed, in the long run may only be slowed by lack of scientists to provide the new fundamental knowledge upon which new technology can be based.

During this period of growth, industrial research has earned new status in the eyes of the scientific community. This is shown by the changed attitude of Ph.D. graduates toward employment in industry: now scientists feel as much at home in an industrial research laboratory as in a university, and the frequent shifting of personnel between these groups shows their common understanding. Industrial laboratories, tied as they are to the financial interests of the company, have generally had a much narrower range of objectives than their university counterparts. However, this distinction is also disappearing as industry finds it profitable to dig deeper into fundamentals in the search for new knowledge. Today, industrial research and free inquiry are part of progressive business operations, and industry depends less on outside sources for scientific results. The development of completely synthetic fibers, stemming from the Du Pont support of Carothers' pioneering work, is an example. Many others may be cited: synthetic diamonds by General Electric; polyethylene by Imperial Chemical Industries, as a result of exploring the effect of high pressures upon organic chemicals; and the principle of the transistor, discovered at Bell Telephone Laboratories by the Nobel Prize-winning team of Bardeen, Brattain, and Shockley.

This rapid proliferation of research laboratories, the overriding demands of the defense program for new technology, and increasing competition have brought on an apparent shortage of technical manpower. This, in turn, has led to serious study of our scientific manpower resources along four principal lines: (1) science teaching in the schools; (2) a number of governmental and university studies seeking means of earlier identification of scientific talent; (3) study of the phenomenon of creativity itself by an increasing number of psychologists and educators; and (4) means of better utilization of available scientific manpower. It is the last area with which industrial research management is primarily concerned and which will be discussed here.[1]

Industrial research management has the task of bridging the gap between the corporation's commercial objectives and the work of the research staff. The research director must translate commercial objectives as defined by the company management into research projects and, conversely, must see that commercial possibilities are realized from research results. Since creative research workers usually have an independence of mind (comparable to that of company presidents), it is apparent why research management devotes so much of its time to achieving a degree of harmonious understanding between research workers and corporate management. As the result of a survey of 622 representative industrial scientists and engineers by Opinion Research, Sidney M. Cantor reports, "It may come as a surprise to some management groups that, on general morale, scientists and engineers score considerably less than management and other white-collar groups and, in general, are highly critical of the way in which management handles them." [2] This critical attitude may be a trait of creative workers and may have no relation to their productivity, but it cannot be ignored by management. The success of the research director depends not on the size of the new laboratory he has obtained, but upon his ability to translate the results of "creativity" into marketable products.

Creativity is defined by Stein as "that process which results in a novel work that is accepted as tenable or useful or satisfactory by some group at some point in time." [19] This definition is quite appropriate when applied to industrial research, as long as the "point in time" is not too remote. For industrial research, "productivity" becomes almost synonymous with "creativity" as industry seeks to compress the time required to move from idea to cash register.

Since a research department depends for its life upon the flow of new ideas from its creative thinkers, there is ample justification for studying the creative man and how he can be made more productive, even though in industry this must be done largely on the basis of commonsense observations and experience, rather than controlled scientific experimentation. In addition to being the subject of study from all sides by his management, the research scientist is the subject of research by psychologists, social scientists, and educators, as further efforts are made to develop our resources of creativity. All of his personal history, foibles, and interests are categorized and related to his performance in a characteristic American effort to develop a standardized type and, thereby, breed more. Someday, perhaps, we shall be able to identify and train scientists for creativity in any field to meet some governing body's estimate of our needs. In the meantime, industry has taken the practical approach of making employment in research more attractive. To attract the scientist, industry has located laboratories to offer the most congenial living and working conditions, rather than as an adjunct to a factory in an industrial zone. Buildings are arranged in campus style to appeal to the academically inclined, and employment advertisements sometimes read more like invitations to vacation resorts than to research work. It is heartening to see the research scientist joining the elite in our society, but continued creativity and industrial growth will be necessary to maintain this new position.

Organizations such as the American Management Association and the Industrial Research Institute conduct a variety of conferences and seminars on the subject of research management, bringing together research administrators and university scientists for the purpose of comparing experience. The publications of such organizations are very useful sources. From firsthand experience as well as from the experience of others, there are certain essential factors which can be distilled to serve as guides to research management in the effective use of creative workers. These can be summarized as follows:

1.   Establish objectives by deciding what the company objectives are and what role research is expected to have in their attainment.

2.   Select and assign the best available men whose efforts can be expected to achieve these goals.

3.   Establish organizational structure which, together with services and facilities, is most likely to enhance productivity or, conversely, one that is least likely to interfere with creativity.

4.   Provide adequate and fair compensation or recognition for creative contributions.

Volumes have been and more will be written on these subjects.

Each is a matter of continuing study, so it is presumptuous to do more than elaborate briefly on their qualitative relationship to creativity.

COMPANY OBJECTIVES AND CREATIVITY

First, the matter of objectives for the industrial research function. Without a clear understanding of corporate objectives, the research function faces the risk of finding its efforts of little interest to company management and its continued existence imperiled. In common with many other of life's good things, there is a popular tendency to believe that if a little research is good, more will be still better. This has led to the expenditure of large sums to erect and staff laboratories, with little more in the way of research objectives than to impress stockholders and financial analysts. Unfortunately, without clear understandings of objectives, management is certain to be disappointed in the results of research expenditures. Serendipity has been the source of many new developments, but it is no substitute for sound objectives and good planning. Lack of well-considered company management participation in setting research goals is one of the principal sources of discord and dissatisfaction between research workers and management.[14] The fruits of successful exploratory research can be gathered only if the company can carry the product through the developmental, pilot plant, and market-testing stages to commercial sale. Research is risky at best; there should not be the added disappointment of having to drop a technical success for lack of company interest in its development. Research personnel also miss one of their most rewarding experiences when the results of successfully completed laboratory work are not commercialized. They become frustrated and insecure in an organization which lacks management leadership to capitalize on successful research.

Important as the problem of basic objectives is to the productivity of a research group, it has been frequently overlooked, particularly during the rapid postwar expansion of industrial laboratories. More than buildings, budgets, and people are necessary if management is ultimately to realize a profit. Perhaps some managements have believed that scientists do best when left alone and have carried this to the extreme of not defining problems for research to tackle—hoping in some way that research will build a better mousetrap to attract the world to the factory door. There is a difference between telling a professional research worker what to do and telling him how to do it. "What to do" is part of setting objectives; "how to do it" quickly restricts freedom of thinking and becomes regimentation. A statement of the problem and its importance poses a challenge and provides a target. Directing how the work should be done removes all challenge and the problem becomes the director's; the researcher to whom it is assigned does not personally associate himself with it as long as he is not free to try his own approach.

If research is to contribute to company growth, management by objectives, with realistic goals for the research function, is the first step. If such objectives and goals are not available, the research director's first job is to take the initiative in this definition. Management should outline a policy and program for growth within which research can be assigned a specific place. Research is not an end in itself, and the ultimate payoff depends upon many other functions—finance, marketing, engineering, production. Therefore, closely coordinated team play is required with top management calling the signals. With broad objectives agreed upon, research can select projects with full confidence that management is ready to exploit any successful results, and the creative thinkers are inspired by the importance of their work.

In setting objectives for industrial research, one of the important but difficult problems is the amount to be spent on exploratory or basic research. There is no ready answer, but whatever level of research is chosen should be one that can be supported on a continuing basis. By its nature, fundamental research requires a greater measure of management faith in its research staff, yet too often it is the first area to lose support when budgets are pared. The "yo-yo" system of varying budgets with business cycles is wasteful of money and talent and is particularly frustrating to the scientist who looks upon such economic retrenchment as a lack of confidence in his work.

With the large sums being spent for basic research by government and universities, the results of which become available through publication, it may be argued that a company need do no fundamental research, but rely entirely on published information as it appears. The fallacy of this is simply that a scientist cannot appraise the importance of a new basic development unless he is actively participating in the field. A company must add to the stock of basic knowledge upon which its business depends, and it must have people who can quickly recognize and understand what is happening when important new developments occur. Fundamental research is also the best source of basic patents, a highly desirable commodity. Nevertheless, top management must seriously ask itself whether it is prepared to take the long, hard road and the risks that are involved in supporting truly creative people in fundamental research. It is better for management to take no steps of this sort, intentionally, than to deceive itself by saying it wants creative people and then assign them to applied research or gadgeteering.

PERSONNEL SELECTION AND CREATIVITY

Industrial research runs the gamut from long-range fundamental problems involving almost complete reliance upon the researcher to set his own goals, to short-term, well-defined problems involving practical application, or "troubleshooting." In every case, creative thinking is a requisite, but the individual best suited and most productive in different types of projects will vary widely. At one extreme, we may have men who make a career of studying molecular structure, spending years perfecting a new device or technique for measuring angles between atoms, while the troubleshooter may have thrown at him the problem of an immediate remedy for the unexplained appearance of poor color in a process stream, with each hour's loss of product representing thousands of dollars of loss to the company. The selection and assignment of men to such varying requirements is obviously important if creative talents as well as money are not to be misspent.

Recruiting of personnel is as highly competitive as any other aspect of corporation existence. It is the steady flow of fresh creative talent that provides the new ideas for research upon which industrial growth depends. The selection of research workers becomes an economic evaluation since, in salary alone, the average graduate research worker, during a forty-year career, will cost his employer over half a million dollars. Against this must be balanced the return on this investment which is expected from his work.

In hiring really creative workers, salary costs should not be the determining factor. The very best man for a research job may cost 50 percent more, but he will be many times more productive and, in addition, will attract more competent younger men who desire to be professionally associated with a leader. Such men are needed to build the environment that stimulates less creative individuals to greater productivity.

When hiring new graduates, selection is usually made on the basis of scholastic record and personal interviews. Selecting men for creativity can best be done on the basis of past performance. We have as yet no reliable tests which can be used by a personnel placement office to predict scientific creativity. Mandell and Adams, from a study to validate a battery of tests intended to measure originality in the selection of physical scientists, found that the biographical information produced the most promising correlation possibilities.[8] Later work by Mandell using a group of 600 chemists, physicists, and engineers suggests that certain tests show promising correlation, but results are sufficiently imperfect to make the use of such tests of little value *unless* they are part of a continuing research program within a laboratory or group of laboratories to validate their relevance to creativity as measured by the individual's actual performance in the industrial research environment.[9] Such long-term studies are needed if testing for creativity is to become a reliable tool in personnel selection.

A doctoral thesis and a penetrating interview covering the work involved are presently the best indication of creative potential. Recommendations from professors are valuable if the professor's rating scale is known. Testing of intelligence, aptitudes, attitudes, interests, and other characteristics has been widely used by industrial laboratories as a guide in recruiting, placement, and advancement. When faced with a rapid expansion or a major reorganization, the use of various psychological tests may be very helpful in supplying a mass of information which otherwise might only result from years of close association with a competent supervisor. Further research by psychologists may give more reliable measures of potential creativity, but present tests are inadequate in two important areas—creativity and motivation. If environment and associates are important factors governing these traits, then we cannot expect to have meaningful test results unless the working environment can also be controlled.

The promising research chemist who, because of his wife's insistence on living in her home town, left a position in fundamental research to take a control laboratory position in another city will, no doubt, have his creativity potential determined by environment, regardless of tests of creativity.

Tests are also resented by many budding scientists as prying too far into personal matters which are none of the employer's business.[3] Prospects either take a strongly antagonistic stand or relax into a state of muffled conformity, and some recruits have rejected offers of employment because of psychological cross-examinations by interviewers. In fairness to testing and the research which has gone into test development, most of the problems seem to have arisen from misuse in the hands of untrained personnel department staffs, from overselling by consulting firms, and from management's willingness to let such an outside group carry the responsibility for personnel selection and advancement. Another weakness arises from using test scores as the prop for decisions which are at variance with the man's achievement record. Test results become as fixed as a man's blood type, and poor test scores have cropped up to outweigh a solid record of creative productivity.

It has been said that "industrial organizations are not interested in all-out creativity. They are interested only in creativity that leads to profit-making products."[21] This is perfectly legitimate, but, regardless of the limitations to be applied to the products of creativity, industrial research cannot exist without creative personnel. There are certain easily recognized characteristics which appear common to the more creative individuals, and these same traits are frequently the cause of friction between management and its scientific staff. The traits are primarily centered around an independence of mind, intelligence, a high level of mental energy, dissatisfaction with existing knowledge, and a questioning skepticism of authority.[17] These characteristics do not guarantee that the possessor is creative, but, when added to a scholastic record, a doctoral thesis, and a professor's recommendations, they certainly improve the basis for selectivity. Without the benefit of a research thesis, Bachelor's and Master's graduates, although of equivalent creative potential, are at a disadvantage in seeking to establish themselves, and the recruiter must rely more on the panel interviews and references for evaluation.

RESEARCH ORGANIZATION AND CREATIVITY

The organizational environment into which the individual research worker is placed will have a profound effect upon his productivity.[20] This includes the status or tradition of research in the company, the quality of the research staff, location of the laboratories, as well as all the service facilities associated with research work.

A formal organization is necessary for several reasons: to provide communication channels,[12] for delegation of authority, for planning, for financial control, and to provide a means of developing leadership. The necessary organization should, however, be so structured as to enhance creativity, rather than to look good on paper. Professional management usually tries to set up an ideal organization chart based on a "command" situation and to accommodate superior-subordinate relationships. This is usually not the best climate for creativity, as has been established by attitude studies of laboratory groups. There is no relationship between an orderly organization chart and creativity, but an effective organization can serve to make a research group much more productive.

To obtain the most creativity from an organization, it is necessary to have managers who are, themselves, more than ordinarily creative in conceptual if not in technical matters. Such managers can be the product of an upward influence from subordinates who insist on creative approaches to problems, or creative managers can be the result of planned organizational effort to identify, select, and train the more creative of the managers on hand. The effective manager must identify himself with the best interests of his group. He, obviously, must recognize and support his most creative and productive men if he is, in turn, to be accepted by them and effective in stimulating their thinking.

Organization along lines of special disciplines, such as physics, organic chemistry, and analytical, was formerly favored in industrial research laboratories. More recently the pattern has shifted to an organization designed to spur product growth, with emphasis on moving a product from the idea stage to market as fast as possible. This results in an organization grouped around such functions as pioneering research, pilot plant, product applications, and process development. These correspond to the stages in the development of a product during its life in research. Some highly market-oriented organizations have their principal research groups based on specific major markets, such as surface coatings or detergents. This allows very close contact between research and the customer and eliminates the communication chain which exists between a functionally organized group and customers.

The following figure shows schematically the progress of a typical industrial research project through various phases, from exploratory to commercial operation, and the relative number of men who may be involved. Fundamental research is shown as the foundation under the entire structure, since results may be useful to all stages of a development. This scheme may serve as the basis for structuring a research organization: the fundamental and exploratory activities are grouped together, while the various steps of laboratory and pilot-plant process development and product application are handled by separate groups, with critical review by management as the project is advanced and requires more effort. "Telescoping" of research to gain time is also possible by having the successive phases of a project overlap as the work is carried on by different groups. It is also frequently desirable to form a special team or group to handle a major project, under a leader who coordinates all the specialists who may be concerned in the development. Such a procedure may upset a formal organization chart, but when the project leader is given full charge and can assemble an adequate staff, it is extremely effective in obtaining concentrated interest and fast action. This is where the team approach works best, with clear objectives and specific assignments for each participant. Some data have shown that the length of time a group has worked together is a factor in creativity, with maximum performance in groups having an average association "age" of less than twenty-four months.[18] Also, new members stimulate and, in turn, are stimulated by the group they enter.

This chart also illustrates another interesting feature of industrial research. By far the largest proportion of the manpower and costs are devoted to process development and application research which, in turn, stem from a relatively small amount of

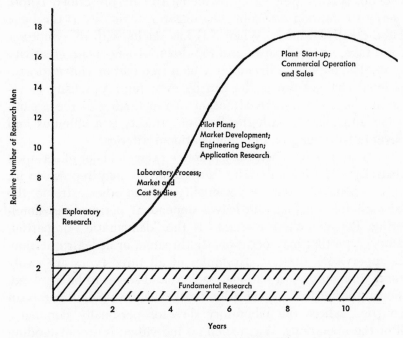

Plant Start-up;
Commercial Operation
and Sales

Pilot Plant;
Market Development;
Engineering Design;
Application Research

Laboratory Process;
Market and
Cost Studies

Exploratory
Research

Fundamental Research

Relative Number of Research Men

Years

TYPICAL RESEARCH PROJECT PROGRESS CHART

exploratory work. This highlights the value of selecting highly creative personnel and giving them freedom, with guidance from company objectives, in order that a wider choice of projects is available from exploratory work. There is a heavy mortality of ideas at the point where exploratory research is shifted to process-and-application-scale study. A creative exploratory program is the least costly part of a research manager's operation, but it provides the seedlings from which developmental projects are selected for transplant and intensive cultivation. With more available, a higher level of potential profitability can be used in selection.

It has actually been recommended by Burton Klein that duplication of exploratory work for military research be fostered, since it is less expensive to make mistakes at this stage, and many good ideas may be lost if all competition is stifled in the interest of eliminating duplication.[6]

The health of a laboratory organization requires periodic

checkup, so that preventive medicine can be prescribed before a serious condition develops. Organizational rigidity is the bane of the creative worker. When this has set in, with its symptoms of red tape, review boards, and top-down management, creativity is lost. The opposite extreme, in which frequent or violent organizational changes are made, can be even more upsetting to research work. Continuous attention to functioning of the organization and change with the flow of projects is a stimulus and prevents hardening of the organizational arteries.

The type of supervisory practice exerts a major effect upon creativity of individuals. The "authoritative" may repress or irk the independent, creative personality. At the other extreme, the "laissez-faire" organization leaves dependent personalities floundering. Between these extremes is the "democratic," or participatory, type that may occasionally threaten, or at least question, the supervisor's position. Examples of all three types are easily found, and cultural or national background seems to be involved. The "authoritarian" organization works well in several European countries, where the laboratory director personally dominates all of the operations. When such an individual is an outstanding creative scientist in his own right, such a system is extremely productive. Such a leader, however, may find it difficult to train a successor in his own image.

A truly laissez-faire organization is not found in industry, except possibly those rare instances where the laboratory is maintained as a showplace or supervised by a very weak leader. Far more common are the democratic, less authoritative arrangements involving more informal authority with more emphasis on human values and a tendency for leadership to gravitate to the man with information and purpose. Here, industrial research organizations can learn from the traditional university approach to research.[15] Organization structures in business have generally followed the military pattern, but this has little appeal to the research scientist trained in the university atmosphere in which colleague authority and individual initiative are emphasized. The more creative men respond best in a democratic or laissez-faire situation, wherein they have greater independence of action.

The leaders of some of the foremost industrial research organizations, in describing the basic principle in which their laboratories operate, have been at pains to point out that for several centuries the best research results have come from the universities. They have concluded that the closer organizations can approach the atmosphere and methods of working in a university, the better will be their results.[10]

Yet, corporate organizations tend to be authoritarian. Such problems as uniform working hours, labor union relations, and other authoritarian aspects of corporate life have encouraged the move to separate locations for research laboratories, in order to lessen the effect of these factors upon creativity. The separate locations, away from manufacturing centers, take on the appearance of a university campus and, in addition to offering suburban living, provide a more relaxed atmosphere. Personnel relations between scientists and management should be greatly improved, as should productivity.

The primary value of organizational structure in research is to provide effective communications. Much has been written on laboratory organization [1,5,7,11,13,16,22] and the problem of planning and control. Less is available on organizational factors as these may affect creativity.[15] Communications must work both to and from the laboratory worker. He must be well informed if he is to appreciate the company objectives, and he must publicize his own work if he is to fulfill the requirements of being creative and achieve professional recognition. Such communication may be restricted for competitive, commercial reasons, and this has been one of the objections raised by some scientists to industrial research. However, this, too, is changing and many industrial laboratories now encourage publication for its obvious morale and advertising value, as well as the prestige it brings to the organization. Such restrictions as exist usually surround process or equipment-design information or premature disclosure which may interfere with granting of patents.

CREATIVITY AND RECOGNITION

The fourth major factor in the effective use of creative personnel is that of reward or recognition. This includes financial as well as nonfinancial compensation. Here, all types of research —governmental, industrial, and academic—meet on a common ground. The need for some sort of recognition is basic to everyone, and it is here that management can do the most to improve motivation. Everyone works for reward and recognition, whether it is the display of material wealth, security for the future, power, or acclaim by fellow scientists for a notable discovery.

Before providing rewards of any type, there must be an appraisal of the research worker's performance and the value of his contribution. This is an area in which objective, quantitative measures are almost totally absent, and where subjective opinions are the basis for performance ratings. For creative workers, attempts to relate their output to corporate profits must provide for the time lag involved in reaching commercial operations as indicated by the preceding figure, and for the fact that the teamwork of many others is required to reach that goal. There appears to be no substitute for the judgment of research management in seeing that rewards are distributed fairly in the eyes of all involved, and that the maximum motivational value is obtained. There is a tendency to believe that creative scientists, like creative artists but unlike other men, live for their work and are not motivated by money as much as by other forms of recognition. If this were ever true in the past, it would never do to try to operate today at less than competitive salaries. Research workers at all levels of creativity are very much interested in salary and, while nonfinancial incentives are important, monetary reward overrides all other factors in a compensation program. This has been put quite concisely by Crawford Greenewalt, board chairman of Du Pont:

Of all the motivations to which the human mechanism responds, none has proved so powerful as that of financial gain. The importance of financial lure is not that the accumulation of wealth itself is significant, but because money is the only form of incentive which is wholly negotiable, appealing to the widest possible range of seekers. As people differ so markedly, it is difficult, if not impossible, to find any other common denominator of inducement fully acceptable to all.[4]

It is not proposed to discuss salary plans, but a sound plan is essential not only to attract new men but also to retain and motivate experienced personnel. Many salary plans are based on "job descriptions," following the pattern used for routine operations. For creative research or engineering personnel, job descriptions quickly become vague and generalized because of the difficulty of describing what is a highly individualized and varying assignment. The best plans for salary administration must be based on individualized decisions by management. These decisions are an important component of the leadership that the scientist expects from research management. Professional employees do not progress at the same rate, and any plan should allow enough flexibility to accommodate the outstanding individuals. In most research groups, probably five percent are the truly creative individuals who are, in turn, responsible for most of the useful new ideas, and the younger among them are the source of future company leaders. If a pay program is not adjustable to the relative worth of these men, they will go elsewhere or lose their motivation.

The special award type of bonus for outstanding contributions to company profits is an effective method for research workers. When properly administered, it relates the value of the contribution directly to the individual's income and is a powerful incentive to creative workers. In Nazi Germany the inventor, by law, retained rights to a portion of the income from licensing inventions assigned to his employer. This law is said to be the only one written during Hitler's regime which is still in force. It is very popular with German industrial research workers, some of whom now receive more in royalty income than in salary.

Nonmonetary rewards are particularly effective when coupled with competitive salary levels. Since salaries are not published, the other forms of reward which can be publicized get more immediate attention from the recipient's fellow workers. Such nonfinancial rewards are as follows:

1. Opportunity for promotion by both the technical and administrative routes. The scientist frequently wants opportunity for advancement without taking on more administrative duties.

2. Support of activity in professional societies by employees, including attendance at meetings, encouragement to seek office, and maintenace of high professional standards of performance.

3. Maximum freedom to publish and maximum patenting—another form of publishing.

4. Identification with management, through equivalent treatment of such status symbols as parking privileges, office decor, secretarial services, and fringe benefits.

5. Individual treatment. Creativity is an individual matter, and creative people respond best to individual treatment; they do not want to be a nameless part of a

big machine. Many large industrial laboratories have lost some of their most creative men to universities or smaller companies where the research worker can feel more personal importance.

6. Security is often overlooked as a factor in reward values. This means a consistently good reputation for not discharging research people with every business downturn. Lack of security is taken as a lack of appreciation for the man's work. For a continued record of creativity, it is better to have a small staff free of worry about job continuity, than a larger staff working under the cloud of a past history of cutbacks.

7. Identification with successful projects. Recognition through seeing his work earning a profit is a most powerful source of satisfaction to a creative worker. This emphasizes the value of having corporate objectives defined, so that the laboratory workers know that the results of their work are essential to the company position. A management which demonstrates confidence in its research staff as individuals provides a real incentive for productive performance, for the individuals are encouraged to grow up to the expectations set for them.

SUMMARY

From experience, the following are some of the major actions which industrial research management can take to enhance creativity; the converse can be expected to stifle it.

Assure complete knowledge and understanding of company's objectives by research group.

Establish research objectives consistent with company objectives.

Make a real effort to attract and select creative people.

Avoid overcontrolling these people, particularly the more creative.

Provide time, facilities, and supporting staff for the development of ideas.

Recognize that there is no single form of organization which is superior, and be prepared to make radical reassignments occasionally to stimulate new thinking.

Put improbable people together and bring in fresh viewpoints.

Survey continually for restrictive constraints on creativity.

Provide adequate communications, up and down as well as laterally, with reporting at a minimum to serve this purpose.

Permit maximum publication of results and encourage professional growth.

Avoid rigid time plans and be quick to drop projects which no longer meet the original objectives.

Recognize and reward creativity.

Recognize that the creative worker, even more than others, cannot be manipulated; any motivating must be done by the worker himself. The manager does best by setting the stage for effective self-motivation.

Provide maximum commercial use of results.

REFERENCES

1. American Management Association. *Optimum Use of Engineering Talent*. Management Report No. 58, 1961.

2. Cantor, Sidney M. "Professional Attitudes," *Chemical & Engineering News* (January 25, 1960), 7–12.

3. Gellerman, Saul W. "A Hard Look at Testing," *Personnel* (May–June 1961), 8–15.

4. Greenewalt, Crawford H. *The Uncommon Man: The Individual in the Organization*. New York: McGraw-Hill, 1959.

5. Hebb, Malcolm H. "Free Inquiry in Industrial Research." Address to the I.R.I. annual spring meeting, May 18–21, 1959.

6. Klein, Burton. "A Radical Proposal for R&D," *Fortune* (May 1958), 112.

7. McGregor, Douglas. "Getting Effective Leadership in the Industrial Organization," *Advanced Management* (October–December 1944), 148–53.

8. Mandell, Milton M., and Adams, Sidney. "Selection of Physical Scientists," *Educational and Psychological Measurement*, 8:575–82 (Winter 1948).

9. Mandell, Milton M. "Measuring Originality in the Physical Sciences," *Educational and Psychological Measurement*, 10:380–85 (Autumn 1950).

10. Mareson, "The Scientist in American Industry," quoting D. W. Willson.

11. Mees, C. E. Kenneth, and Leermakers, John A. *The Organization of Industrial Research*. New York: McGraw-Hill, 1950.

12. National Society of Professional Engineers. "Management and the Engineer Are Not Speaking," *Chemical & Engineering News*, 30:1076–80 (1952).

13. Pierce, John R. "Freedom in Research," *Science*, 130:540–42 (September 4, 1959).

14. Quinn, James Brian. "Long-Range Planning of Industrial Re-

search, *Harvard Business Review* (August 1961), 88–102.

15. Rabe, W. F. "Organizing for R&D–A Lesson from the Past," *Personnel*, 38 (September–October 1961).

16. Research Management. *Selection and Placement of Research Personnel.* New York, 1961.

17. Roe, Anne. "A Psychological Study of Physical Scientists," *Genetic Psychology Monographs*, 43: 129–239 (May 1951).

18. Shepard, Herbert A. "Creativity in R/D Teams," *Research and Engineering* (October 1956), 10–13.

19. Stein, M. I. "A Transactional Approach to Creativity," *The 1955 University of Utah Research Conference on the Identification of Creative Scientific Talent.* Edited by C. W. Taylor. Salt Lake City: University of Utah Press, 1956.

20. Thomas, Harvey M. "Establishing the Proper Climate for Creativity," American Management Association (Management Bulletin No. 4, 1960), 15–21.

21. Wallen, Richard W. "Unlocking Human Creativity," *Machine Design* (March 20, 1958), 132–38.

22. Wilson, E. Bright, Jr. *Introduction to Scientific Research.* New York: McGraw-Hill, 1952.

INDIVIDUAL AND GROUP CREATIVITY IN SCIENCE

Harold K. Hughes

INTRODUCTION

THE GREAT SCIENTIFIC DISCOVERIES of the past were made by men working alone. Pictures of Archimedes, Galileo, Newton, Pasteur, and Einstein, to name a well-known few, inspire science students from the walls of schools all over America. When these future scientists grow to maturity, however, they will have less opportunity to achieve fame than previous generations because of the rapid trend toward group research in large laboratories. Who can name the inventor of a modern digital computer or of the jet airplane?

Group research is bringing into focus new problems of interaction and communication which individual researchers of the past never faced. Newton, for example, did not provide his colleagues with monthly reports, nor did he care about the length of their tea breaks. Indeed, because of personal attacks on him as well as his work, he even regretted announcing some of his discoveries.

Several of the other contributions to this volume are devoted to the creativity of the individual research worker. This paper is an introduction to the role which communication plays in the creativity of groups of individuals working together on a common problem. In it I discuss the trend to group research, define and illustrate the term "creative product," and develop a few theorems about how consultation between individuals and within groups influences their creativity. The broader field of intragroup and intergroup communication I leave for another publication. The final sections of this paper cover the advantages and the disadvantages of group and individual research.

THE TREND TO GROUP RESEARCH

Modern scientific research is increasingly the product of groups, whereas fifty years ago it was almost entirely an individual activity. Of the articles and letters in journals published by the American Institute of Physics during 1958, 53 percent were by two or more authors associated with governmental, academic, and industrial laboratories in that order of frequency.[1,2] Surprisingly, Soviet scientists are, on the average, more individualistic; the corresponding figure is 44 percent for journals translated by the AIP. The same trend to multiple authorship is also evident in U.S. patents, in articles on psychology,[3] and in British publications.

There are several causes for this trend.[4] In small-scale, individual investigations the frequent or continuous use of equipment is not a criterion for deciding upon a project. Much of contemporary research, however, uses large devices such as accelerators and computers. These are so expensive and need such specialized organizations to operate and maintain them that their efficient utilization is an economic necessity. Careful programming of their available time thus leads to group work.

A second reason for group research lies in the increasing complexity of technical knowledge, which encourages narrow specialization. In interdisciplinary subjects where much interesting and useful work is being done, it may take a large team of investigators to contribute all the required techniques and background of training. Speaking of organic semiconductors, Brophy writes, "organic chemists must learn more about semiconductor physics and . . . physicists must relearn organic chemistry. . . . Communication must be reestablished between them before any real degree of success can be realized."[5]

The insecurity of some research leaders, which is possibly

related to the diffusion of authority in industry since the 1930's, is a third cause of the trend to group research. In their search for more authority, such individuals prevent the growth of their subordinates by recourse to what Fox calls "the principle of maximum dilution." [6] According to this principle, a group leader should not permit individual research and should place his own name and as many other names as possible on all publications by his group, thereby diluting the prestige.

Other group-forming factors are the greater ease of obtaining funds for group work than for individual work, the desire to hasten the completion of a project, the development of operations research, the demand for reducing inventions to practice in the shortest possible time, and the trend toward more generous recognition of the role of assistants.

WHAT IS CREATIVITY IN SCIENCE?

Creativity, like happiness, is an illusive concept and difficult to define. At the very least, a creative person is original in some way, such as in devising a new theory, building an ingenious mechanism, or discovering a new cosmic ray particle. But creativity in science must be purposeful or useful, not just capriciously different. To number the equations in a book in reverse order may be original but it is hardly creative.

For the purposes of this paper, it is most meaningful to measure individual and group creativity by the number and importance of their creative products and to define a creative product function as the sum of publications, confidential reports, patents (issued and on file), new products and processes, and the like, each weighted by a value coefficient. This coefficient reflects the importance of the creative product on some yet-to-be-decided value scale. Among other things, the scale recognizes the added importance of work that opens the door to new fields, what I call "open-ended creativity." It also recognizes to what extent the ratio of the number of explained facts to the number of arbitrary assumptions is maximized. Still another consideration in determining the value of a creative product is the remoteness of the elements of the new combination. The more remote the connections, the more creative is the product.

Creative products are of several types,* of which the following are most familiar:

1. *Closure* is making or completing a new Gestalt, such as devising a new scientific theory, achieving new insight in group dynamics, or presenting a unique and simpler proof of a well-known theorem.

2. *Replacement* occurs by providing an alternate solution to a problem, different and original but not necessarily better than the existing solution.

3. *Deliberate invention* is one obtained by semiroutine procedures such as brainstorming or engineering design. The logical consequences of a situation or specification are followed through such a maze that a high level of skill and some creativity is involved. (Getting the Oak Ridge process for the diffusion separation of uranium isotopes to work included many creative acts, although the basic idea was quite old.) A form of deliberate invention, employed by some writers, is "forced association," in which random, factorial, or other forced pairs or triplets are examined for logical connection.[8]

4. *Recognition of errors.* Among research groups there is often the type of person who is good at recognizing errors in existing solutions and in defining problems, but who contributes little toward new solutions. He is, nevertheless, valuable to the group, and it is fair to describe his contribution as creative.

5. *Partial solutioning.* In complex problems, creative individuals may make advances without achieving a complete solution. Examples of this include developing an existence theorem, recognizing the problem as a part of another one, reducing the degree of an equation, and breaking down the problem into parts some of which are soluble alone (orthogonal solutions in three-dimensional partial differential equations, for instance).

6. *Routinizing.* The person who reduces a complex, recurring problem to a routine can sometimes claim creativity. Thus Yates greatly simplified the calculation of effects in factorial experiments by devising a table of signs.[9,10]

7. *Generalizing* is the recognition of whole classes of problems that are soluble by known means. When Tartaglia discovered the general solution to the cubic equation, he was rou-

* Mednick classifies all creative processes into serendipity, recognition of similarities, and mediation of common elements. The discoveries of X rays and of penicillin are examples of serendipity.[7]

tinizing and simplifying the solution of a problem which could be handled by other means.

8. *Transfer* is applying a solution of one problem to another problem in a different field. The creative act lies in recognizing the similarities in the problems and the solutions. Gordon states that there are two steps in what he calls the "synectic process," a development of brainstorming. The first is to make the strange familiar. This is the preparation stage described below. The second step is to make the familiar strange, using four types of analogy which he calls personal, direct, symbolic, and fantasy.[11] These are illustrations of transfer.

9. *Stimulation and release.* Some individuals have the ability to stimulate and release creative products in others, although they may not be creative themselves. Colleagues, teachers, and research directors may fall into this class. "There is room in creativity for the Toscanini as well as for the Heifetz." [12]

10. *Elaboration.* Once a new idea, material, or other product is established, its extension may be developed with great ingenuity and insight by persons other than the originator. Thus, the laser is an outgrowth of Townes's invention of the maser. Also, the solution of control systems problems requires an eclectic approach, choosing transducers, and other circuit elements fully developed as isolated components. Their synthesis into an integrated system often calls for creativity of a high order.

SIX STAGES OF THE CREATIVE PROCESS

Creation in science occurs in a variety of ways, even for the same individual. It follows, therefore, that the process in groups is even more diverse. In his investigations of problem solving, Graham Wallas identified four sequential stages.[13] There are at least two others. Individuals jump back and forth among these stages and do not necessarily follow them in the sequence given below. Groups may function with more than one stage active at the same time.

1. *Interest.* The creative process starts with interest in a problem. This problem may be unsolved or it may consist of finding the question whose answer is known, as when one seeks to determine the function of a particular transistor in a circuit diagram.

2. *Preparation.* To be accepted, a new scientific theory must seem to account for most existing observations in the field and be consistent with other, well-established laws. Preparation is thus an early stage of the creative process. It may precede or follow the interest stage. Such preparation includes learning specific techniques appropriate to the problem, such as how to use a table of integrals or how to administer a Rorschach test. The preparation stage may serve as the warm-up period which often precedes the rush of creative work.

Science is a cumulative discipline, building upon past data and theories. Thus, scientists are more restricted than artists in their subject matter. A painter can create a canvas without referring to van Gogh, but even so, he often does better work if he studies the past. In this connection, Vasari points out:

At that time the magnificent Lorenzo de' Medici had filled his garden on the Piazza of S. Marco with ancient and good sculpture, so that the terraces and alleys were adorned with good antique figures in marble, and with pictures and other things by the best masters in Italy and elsewhere. And not only were they a great ornament to the garden, but they became a school and academy for young painters and sculptors. . . .

And, indeed, these arts cannot be learned except by long study and by copying good works, and he who has not the opportunity, although he may be greatly endowed by nature, will be long in attaining perfection.[14]

Hodnett expresses the same thought when he writes:

You first have to have an excellent working knowledge of the norm in any field before you can control your deviation with the right skill. Failure to accept this hard truth will put you among the half-baked artists, cranks, inventors, political dreamers, and fakers in all fields who find it much easier to be different than to master the fundamentals from which they are deviating.[15]

3. *Incubation.* The third stage of the creative process, sometimes called incubation, is that period which follows a rest from the fatigue of the preparation stage and during which the mind is reorganizing, turning over new sequences and combinations of accumulated facts, trying new paths, and seeking ways around barriers. By constant reference to notes, complicated facts appear to be simple, numbers are memorized, groups of related data coalesce, symbols are invented to conserve thinking,

and reasoning becomes more abstract. Incubation may be a period of complete physical freshness and quiet well-being during which old thought patterns recede, or it may be a period of frantic stewing about in a mood of frustration. Occasional thrusts at the problem fail, following which new data are sought and the problem is reexamined to see whether the right questions are being asked.

Incubation should not be confused with blocks or discouragement barriers. It may be a valuable period in group research. Directors often plan for them, as for example by saying, "Let's think about that for a while."

4. *Illumination* (also called *inspiration* and *insight*). This is the "quick flash of genius" so popular in science reporting whose antecedents, hard work and discouraging trials, are frequently overlooked. Pasteur nicely capsuled inspiration when he described it as "the impact of a fact on a well-prepared mind." The following quotation of Lyman Spitzer, director of Project Matterhorn at Princeton University, illustrates the transition from incubation to illumination. He became interested in fusion power early in 1951, after reading about the alleged Argentine success in the field.

Shortly after the Argentine story broke, I went to Aspen, Colorado, for a ski trip. In the relaxed atmosphere there, and especially while riding the chair lift, I gave some thought to the problem of how a controlled thermonuclear reactor might be built. Many of the essential ideas of the stellarator stemmed from my thinking during that week, and during the weeks in Princeton immediately following. I don't know quite what this story proves but perhaps it is an argument for more frequent vacations.[16]

5. *Verification.* To compose a beautiful song may terminate an act of artistic creativity, but in science there is one more hurdle, verification. No one can argue whether a wood carving is true or false, but a scientific article or book, to be accepted, must usually pass the closest scrutiny by skeptical eyes. Knowing this, it is the obligation of every scientist to examine his own work critically and to enlist the aid of his colleagues in searching for hidden errors.

The verification stage is the time to examine the utility of a solution as well as its correctness. It is the making of an economic appraisal of an invention or new process, it is editing a manuscript, it is asking whether a solution is reasonable. "You really don't have creativity until you reduce something to practice and demonstrate that it is either aesthetically interesting or useful." [17]

In elementary physics laboratories a simple experiment, using Stefan's fourth-power law, measures the temperature of the filament in an incandescent electric light bulb. I remember one student who forgot to take the fourth root of a number, turning in an answer for the temperature of the filament as 16,000,000,-000,000 degrees. He never considered whether this answer was reasonable.

Many poets go through this intensive creative act, during which they revise their first drafts, sometimes over an extended period of time. Golovin describes this reworking process as follows:

Another very strong impression, easily appreciated, of course, after one has thought about it, is the enormous labor of repeated reworking or rewriting that goes into artistic or literary contributions. We are all familiar with similar necessity in scientific work, but it was just amazing for the writer to find that a 30-line poem, which one reads so quickly and effortlessly, may take several hundred hours to develop and polish up! The case is clearly established that beyond the clue or insight which establishes the initial vague and general pattern of a "creation," the universal necessity in all fields is either for relatively enormous efforts in analysis and verification, as in science, or in repeatedly reworking and polishing up, as in painting or literary work.[18]

Verification need not be by the same person who completes the first four stages of a creative process. Indeed, to insist on it may kill his creativity. An advantage of group work is that the labor of evaluating a creation may be and generally is assigned elsewhere in the group.

6. *Exploitation.* The final stage of the creative process in science is exploitation—putting the new product or theory to use. The creation may be elaborated to other materials or fields. Former theories must be shown to be false or misleading and apparent anomalies explained. Data previously unrelated can be grouped and systematized. In industrial research, exploitation may call for filing a patent application, building a pilot plant, or selling the idea or product.

As with verification, exploitation need not be done by the individual or group that contributed the interest, preparation, incubation, and illumination. Indeed, in most industrial organizations the exploitation of research creativity is generally assigned to groups which are emotionally better geared to it than the originators.

Nonetheless, whether exploitation is properly a part of the creative process is a matter of definition. It is an essential ingredient of industrial research and must be a lively function in any well-established company.

STIMULATED INDIVIDUAL CREATIVITY

A creative research group functions in three modes, as follows:

1. Some of its members may work alone (isolates) with or without support from group services such as laboratory assistants, machinists, or librarians.

2. Individuals may work alone but experience stimulated creativity through intellectual contact with their colleagues. Depressed creativity as a consequence of close intellectual contact with colleagues is handled in this development as negative stimulation. There is general agreement on the existence of a stimulation effect, Samuel K. Allison saying in this respect, "It is a well-known fact that theoretical physics often needs a certain minimum-size group talking together every day before it will generate new ideas." [19] This is akin to the critical mass of a nuclear reactor.

3. Groups of individuals may work together so closely that it is difficult to isolate the creativity of any member. Recognition goes to the group as a whole.

A real group seldom functions in any one of these pure modes. Its members distribute their time among individual, stimulated individual, and group research in ways that depend upon numerous and changing influences.

Interactions among individuals affect their scientific creativity. These interactions are of two broad kinds, depending upon whether the research is individual or group. In this section I consider how research discussions with colleagues affect the creativity of an individual. In a later section, I shall consider the tighter couplings in group research and their consequences for group creativity.

Individuals in a group working on their own problems in the second mode defined above influence each other during informal discussions by such means as challenges, suggestions, criticisms, and endorsements. These contacts occur by pairs, three's, four's, or any size up to the total size of the group. In them no member feels a responsibility for any problem but his own. The effect of discussion is to increase (or decrease if the stimulation is negative) the rate of creativity during the period that the individual works alone and to decrease the number of hours devoted to such activity.

Obviously, the time spent in discussion cannot be spent in creative individual research. It is reasonable to expect, therefore, that there is an optimum amount of time for an individual to devote to intellectual exchange about his research. The length of this optimum time as a fraction of the total time devoted to research depends upon how stimulating his colleagues are and upon other factors. The more stimulating a colleague, the more time should be spent with him. The colleague's total creative product may suffer thereby, however. It is unlikely that for stimulated individual research the optimum fraction of time devoted to consultation is ever as large as one half.

Roe summarizes the results of researches on the optimum amount of contact between colleagues, quoting Pelz as follows:

For those scientists [at the National Institutes of Health] who are very similar to their colleagues, having contact only once or twice a week is the point of maximum performance. . . . But if the scientist associates with people who are quite different from him in terms of values, then daily contact is associated with the highest performance. . . . On the other hand, Shepard found in industrial laboratories that in general the more contact the better, even in basic research groups.[20]

Persons vary in both their ability to do creative work of their own and in their ability to stimulate their colleagues. These two abilities are not necessarily correlated. It is well known from empirical observation that some laboratory personnel should be chosen primarily for high stimulation to their colleagues, while others should be chosen for their own high creativity.

THE CREATIVITY OF GROUPS

It is illuminating to view the total creative product of a group as composed of three terms corresponding to the three modes in which its members work. The first of these terms is the sum of the creative products of the members when they operate as lone individuals or as organization-supported individuals with no stimulating or inhibiting influences from other members of the group. The second contribution to the total creative product of a group is the sum of the creative products of those members who consult with colleagues (stimulated individuals).

The third contribution to the total creative product of a group is by those members who devote most of their time working closely together, not as individuals. They work under informal or formal rules which ensure close interactions with their fellows, and thus communication has more influence on their creativity than it does upon creative scientists operating in the first two modes.

Group creativity is a reflection of the synergism and symbiosis among its members (antagonism, parasitism, and similar detractors are treated as negative synergism). Group creativity is useful as a concept principally because of our ignorance of the details of the mechanism of individual creativity in the presence of quick feedback and high input from other members.

Talking of group creativity achieves a simplicity that is similar to that achieved in gas theory by describing the behavior of vast numbers of molecules in terms of their observable group parameters, such as pressure, volume, and temperature, instead of in terms of their individual momenta, directions, and interactions which are not observable. "Similarly, it is impossible to predict the behavior of a complex protein simply from a knowledge of the electrons, protons and neutrons of which it is made. The properties are all there in theory but you have to go into a larger domain to see them." [12]

Group creativity as measured by creative products is the consequence of such close coupling among the members that it may be impossible to decide from whom a particular contribution comes. It is the sum of subgroup creative products rather than a sum of individual creative products. The collaboration between the theoretical physicists Lee and Yang that brought them the Nobel Prize in 1957 is an example of group creativity.

Group creativity merges imperceptibly into individual creativity, and few members of research laboratories operate in a pure mode. They distribute their time among the three modes in ways depending upon their inclinations, the problems, and the environment.

One of the mechanisms of group creativity is explained by Berkner as follows:

We can dissect a photograph into appropriate bits of information and resynthesize this photograph at a distance out of those same bits to reconstruct the photograph with a definable measure of deterioration. But, even more important, we can surpass the human capability for assimilating such information very considerably by scanning a whole series of rather poor photographs of the same thing and reproducing a single photograph out of all of this information which is very considerably and definably better than any of the foggy originals simply by statistically suppressing the random noise in the final reproduction. . . .

New creative ideas take several months to incubate and the process leading to them involves a discipline of study and thinking that is well defined. Moreover, the presence of several differently trained brains, with resultant group access to a wider variety of programs, produces a composite image that more clearly defines a new idea. The high noise of conditioned response of each individual, which is random among a group with diverse training, can be sufficiently suppressed in the composite to provide a greater insight previously obscured in any one of them by his own internal noise level. Therefore, strategic thinking may be more effective in group study because of enforced thinking through group discipline and because of suppression of noise in generation of clear insight.[21]

ADVANTAGES OF GROUP RESEARCH

How are the interests of society and its members best served in the field of science? Should most organized research and development be done by groups or by individuals? These questions have not been settled among industrial, governmental, and institute research managements. The answers depend as much upon the goals of the organization and its members as upon their psychology.

The principal advantage of group research derives from its directed character. It may be efficient in achieving a specified goal, particularly under conditions of stress, and be equally inefficient as a device for unprogrammed research.

In group work, the individual has little or no choice of the problem, the method of solution, his hours of work, the place of publication, or even whether his results will be published at all. As partial compensation he has more companionship, less technical frustration, regular hours, less responsibility (a questionable asset), less worry about money, and better equipment. The better equipment may be a mixed blessing since, if its cost is very high, he may be obliged to stick to problems soluble with it. As Siu says, "the more exorbitant the price, the higher the ransom." [22]

Other advantages include:

1. Creativity is contagious. A few good men in a group may inspire others to perform far above their normal level of achievement. Writing with a background of Eastern wisdom and Western knowledge, Siu, Technical Director of the U.S. Army Quartermaster Corps, has this to say about group research:

Symbiosis is common in nature. Frequently two species of organisms are found producing jointly a result which neither is able to approach alone. Algae and fungi, for example, live symbiotically as lichens. There are thousands of other groupings, the members of which stimulate each other's development. The availability of this advantage is one of the inherent characteristics of organized research with its varied scientific disciplines and skills in the same sociological unit. [22]

2. "Team work provides systematic opportunities for cross-fertilization of ideas." [23] These opportunities are not left to chance encounters.

3. "Groups do not have the fear of criticism that often exists in the loose, individualistic approach." [23]

4. "Another freedom that can be realized only in group effort—a soccer team, a family, a research laboratory—is the wider latitude of error of the individual. There is always the covering of each other's mistakes, the retrieving of each other's losses, and the compensating for each other's weaknesses among the members of the unit." [22]

5. "But the greatest benefit of organized research as a contributor to the growth of scientists . . . is the extension of the range of effectiveness of their thinking and effort to the public domain. . . . In many cases organized research is the only means by which freedom in action can be experienced by a researcher. The force of a technically continuous organization provides the momentum to the initial concept of a scientist through fruition in social good." [22]

6. The "audience effect," a striving for group approval, may stimulate an otherwise unproductive research worker.

7. Low turnover, absenteeism, and personal anxiety are correlated with strong group cohesion.[24] In every organization, including all research and development departments without exception, there are always events and people that tend to destroy individual and group morale and so tend to destroy their creativity. Within limits, good group coherence will ride out surprising doses of morale breakers.

8. As is typical of institutions, groups tend to have a longer life and provide more continuity in program than do individuals. This is a distinct advantage in corporate, governmental, and institutional research, particularly during a period of stress. Few organizations in existence today have not had and will not again have such periods. Stress may be a consequence of competition, political pressures, embezzlement, fire, financial problems, or unionization, for example.

9. It is possible to assign parts of the total creative endeavor to different members of the group according to their interests and abilities. Not only does this relieve the more creative members of some of the drudgery of research, but "many minds, many skills, many disciplines can hasten the development of an idea." [8]

10. "By many minds chipping against each other trying to find a piece of flint and a piece of steel to make the spark in one of the minds you may well get the idea sooner because there is a group." [8]

11. Reporting the findings of Kurt Lewin, Mann and Likert point out that participation in group discussions and group decisions concerning future action sets into motion pressures for action which are more effective than when individuals alone are concerned.[25]

12. Organized groups, usually having greater resources than any single individual, may react faster and more effectively to good ideas.

DISADVANTAGES OF GROUP RESEARCH

Some of the disadvantages of group research were mentioned in the opening paragraphs of the section immediately above. There are certain other disadvantages:

1. Creativity is contagious; its destructive technical effects often spill over into personal relations, creating problems of

morale with which research management may not have learned to cope. The inevitable result of the conflict is a loss of personnel and of the creativity of the remaining members of the group.

2. "A truly new and dramatic breakthrough in knowledge probably comes rarely at best, but almost never as a result of closely managed team activity. In our society, outstanding original thinkers are unlikely to be willing to work under close management." [23]

3. "Group functioning erects certain psychological barriers that impede creativity. The most daring idea out of a group represents the most daring idea of the least daring members." [23] The group may set its standards of acceptable performance too low.

4. "Healthy individuals tend to fear anarchy more than they fear autocracy." [26] But group research partakes of both these qualities through less involvement by individuals in important decisions.

5. Cohesive groups tend to be less tolerant of creative deviants than loosely coupled groups.[24]

6. It is more difficult to pinpoint responsibility.

7. Otherwise creative members of a group may give up their individuality and creativity for what they think are greater values—security, freedom from the need to make decisions, and shorter hours. "Today, the complexities of life in the United States are such that recognition of the individual contribution becomes increasingly difficult. The great problem is the harmonizing of personal achievement with the needs of a society many times larger and more intricate than that of the early days." [27]

8. Group creativity is easily disrupted by poor communications.

9. A group may be so dominated by one man that it expresses only his creative impulses. This is not altogether a disadvantage if the dominating leader is very creative.

10. There is evidence that for many individuals the tight coupling by regulations required for creative group work inhibits their individual creativity. Thus, the total creativity of some individuals may be lowered by organizing them into a group.

11. A group may react too slowly or not at all to a good idea.[28]

12. By its very nature, creativity is destructive of established patterns, yet an implied goal of most organized groups is their own survival. When forced to choose, groups often prefer the latter. While management can avoid this inherent conflict

between creativity and survival, on some occasions it displays neither the wisdom nor the desire to do so, for creativity is disruptive of management as well.[29] Out of this conflict arise many of the advantages and disadvantages of group research.

CONCLUSION

With the rapid growth of industrial laboratories and of governmental participation in scientific development, group scientific work is occupying an increasing fraction of the total creative effort of American scientists. It appears that this trend will continue for many years, even though group creativity often is less productive than individual creativity. This fact is stimulating management to learn how to motivate and satisfy groups at high levels of creativity. In the average group it may be that creativity can never equal the sum of its members' individual creativity and that management will have to accept this as one of the prices of bigness.

The communication problem, which rises factorially with the size of a group, may be one explanation of this loss in total creative product. In this connection Pelz observes:

One may hypothesize that in both settings [National Institutes of Health and in industrial laboratories] some interaction with colleagues is better than none; but the optimum—the amount of contact needed for best performance—may be lower in an individualistic than in a cooperative atmosphere.[20]

It is convenient to describe the problems of motivating and satisfying groups of research scientists in terms of the communications which they have or do not have with their peers and with levels of supervision above and below them. Such communications and their lack carry not only orders and reports but subtle feelings. To recognize the latter and to interpret them correctly is one of the most difficult responsibilities of research management.

This paper is an introduction to the role of communications in the creativity of groups. It is limited to some intragroup interactions. In the future, I plan to continue the study with considerations of intergroup interactions and the effects of the environment, which is generally under management's control.

REFERENCES

1. American Institute of Physics. *Documentation Newsletter.* January 4, 1960.

2. Gilvarry, John, and Ihrig, H. K. "Group Effort in Modern Physics Research," *Science,* 129:1277–78 (May 8, 1959).

3. Smith, Mapheus. "The Trend Toward Multiple Authorship in Psychology," *American Psychologist,* 13: 596–99 (October 1958).

4. Thomson, George P. *The Strategy of Research.* Southampton, England: University of Southampton, 1957, p. 12.

5. Brophy, James J. *Frontier.* Armour Research Foundation (Summer 1961), p. 8.

6. Fox, H. H. Private communication.

7. Mednick, Sarnoff A. "The Associative Basis of the Creative Process," *Psychological Review,* 69:220 (1962).

8. Smith, R. F. W. Private communication.

9. Davies, Owen L. (ed.) *The Design and Analysis of Industrial Experiments.* New York: Hafner, 1960.

10. Yates, F. *The Design and Analysis of Factorial Experiments.* Imperial Bureau of Soil Science (Technical Communication No. 35), England: 1937.

11. Gordon, W. J. J. *Synectics.* New York: Harper & Bros., 1961.

12. Coler, M. A. Private communication.

13. Wallas, Graham. *The Art of Thought.* New York: Harcourt, Brace and Co., 1926.

14. Vasari, Giorgio. *Lives of the Artists.* New York: Noonday Press, 1957, p. 281.

15. Hodnett, Edward. *The Art of Problem Solving.* New York: Harper & Bros., 1955.

16. *Scientific American,* 199(4):22 (October 1958).

17. Mohrman, H. W. Private communication.

18. Golovin, N. E. Private communication.

19. Allison, Samuel K. "Physics in Egypt," *Bulletin of the Atomic Scientists,* 16:317–21 (October 1960).

20. Pelz, D. C. "Relationships Between Measures of Scientific Performance of Other Variables," *The 1955 University of Utah Conference on the Identification of Creative Scientific Talent.* Edited by C. W. Taylor. Salt Lake City: University of Utah Press, 1956.

21. Berkner, L. V. "Can the Social Sciences Be Made Exact?" *Proceedings of the IRE,* 48:1376 (August 1960).

22. Siu, R. G. H. *The Tao of Science.* New York: John Wiley & Sons, 1957, p. 108.

23. Deutsch and Shea, Inc. *Company Climate and Creativity.* New York: Industrial Relations News, 1959.

24. Seashore, Stanley E. *Group Cohesiveness in the Industrial Work Group.* Ann Arbor: University of Michigan, 1954.

25. Mann, Floyd, and Likert, Rensis. *The Need for Research on the Communication of Research Results.* Homewood, Ill.: Dorsey Press, 1960, p. 62.

26. Argyris, Chris. "Employee Apathy and Noninvolvement—The House that Management Built?" *Personnel,* 38:12 (July–August 1961).

27. Greenwalt, Crawford H. *The Uncommon Man: The Individual in the Organization.* New York: McGraw-Hill, 1959, p. 4.

28. Roe, Anne. Private communication.

29. Reich, Irving. "Creativity in Research Organizations," *Research Management,* 3:217 (Winter 1960).

CREATIVITY IN ENGINEERING

Mary-Frances Blade

ABOUT A MILLION MEN and a few women in this country are engineers. Many of them are specifically engaged in being creative in their day-to-day work. While some of them are doing sales or other nontechnical work, most of them are involved in changing the things of the world and even of the space around it.

There has been a quickening of pace in most industrial, governmental, and university research-and-development activities to apply the discoveries of science to advanced types of weapons, space vehicles, and other governmental projects. Engineers have been largely responsible for the design and manufacture of these things, but scientists have also been engaged in the engineering aspects of the work so that the most recent and sophisticated scientific knowledge could be used more quickly.

The pressure for rapid change, invention, and improvement has also affected other areas of the engineer's work such as industrial, civic, and household hardware, machines, utilities, and systems, although in some parts of our industrial plant there is comparative stagnation.

With the increased demands on the engineer to use new scientific principles and discoveries, industry has influenced engineering colleges to change their programs and include more basic science and mathematics. The trend today in most engineering colleges is to seek to strengthen the fundamental scientific and mathematical preparation of students and at the same time to broaden their humanistic studies.

At the same time these changes are under way, there is national pressure for our technology to be at least equal and preferably ahead of the progress of foreign countries. There is thus a growing concern by government and industry that our engineers be creative.

However, educators as a group have not yet been concerned with the problems of creativity. Identification of creative talent and its stimulation in the classroom are not yet recognized as the tasks of engineering educators. This raises an important question: Is it true that the least likely place to foster creativity in engineering is the American college? In exploring this question and its answer, I shall first try to define and differentiate the engineer from the scientist.

ENGINEERS ARE DIFFERENT FROM SCIENTISTS

Engineers and scientists differ in training, values, and methods of thought. Though it is difficult to distinguish between them in some of their day-to-day work, there are differences in their individual creative processes and in their creative products.

Scientists are concerned with discovering and explaining nature; engineers use and exploit nature.

Scientists are searching for theories and principles; engineers seek to develop and make *things*.

Scientists are seeking a result for its own ends; engineers are engaged in solving a problem for practical operating results.

Scientists create new unities of thought; engineers invent things and solve problems. This is a different order of creativity.

One of the problems in the education of engineers today is that the distinctive nature of scientist and engineer as well as the particular contribution which each can make to society is not clearly recognized. Because of sudden demands on the engineer, for example, to apply modern physics, chemistry, and more mathematics to such novel designs as atomic reactors for satellites, some engineering educators are switching engineering college programs into a kind of science training ground and neglecting the art of engineering design. A clarification of the two fields, physical science and engineering, would enable us to define our educational goals more explicitly. We would be able to select and teach these different groups for their separate though overlapping creative endeavors.

Simon Ramo, one of the outstanding creative engineers of today states:

Even aside from the nontechnical factors which should be added to today's common concept of engineering to turn it into the "greater engineering," engineering is still not synonymous with science. Even the "science" needed by the "engineer" is different from the "science" needed by the "scientist." In certain respects the engineering profession does not have to include as much study of conceptual science as is required for the education of a basic scientist who will pursue research on the laws of nature as his life's work. The engineer does not need the same skills in the handling of certain tools for doing research to discover new scientific fundamentals. On the other hand, the engineer has to be trained to do certain things with scientific knowledge that need not be part of the bag of tricks given to the basic researcher. The engineer must learn to synthesize scientific fact into formulations useful for design. . . . The heart of the engineering problem in the technical sense is design, of course, not merely the analysis of the relationships amongst the parameters. . . .[10]

Various psychologists have studied engineers to determine their differences from scientists. One of the most interesting is MacKinnon, Director of the Institute of Personality Assessment and Research at the University of California. His results suggest that the engineer is more narrow in his interests and information, is less inclined to follow interests and independently explore problems of his own setting, has relatively low aesthetic interest and appreciation, and is more interested in what is useful and productive.[7]

It easily can be demonstrated that there is little notion of the creative engineer in the mind of the public, although the image of the creative scientist is widespread. A test of this can be made by anyone. Informally I have been polling my friends and colleagues in this fashion for many years. "Name five outstanding creative scientists who have done their major work in this country." This question is always quickly answered. The list is never the same but there is no hesitation in their response. Next I ask, "Name five outstanding creative engineers who have done their major work in this country." Now the answers are slow in coming. The names of Edison or Steinman may be recalled, then, after a long pause, the names of a few men known personally may be added.

Though engineers are anonymous, mistakenly thought of as scientists, the products of their creative efforts are all around us. These products may be complex, dramatic, and novel things such as rockets, atomic reactors, and space vehicles; or commonplace things such as the television set in the living room; or the simple and inexpensive device which maintains a constant temperature for a shower bath. These products are the results of an engineering design and construction which can be characterized as an innovative conception and problem solution.

In a sense every engineering achievement may be considered creative if we rule out repeat problems with repeat solutions. This is true to the extent that we consider any outcome creative if it is new and original (although some investigators such as Bronowski, in considering the highest type of creative endeavor as "perception in disorder of a deep new unity," would not consider the inventions, clever rearrangement, and problem solving of the engineer as highly creative). However, this is the nature of most of the creativity of the engineer. He designs and constructs something new and original, and creativity in engineering is the mental process of conceptualizing and evolving such a design.

The practice of engineering, as well as any other pursuit, is hedged with limitations. In solving engineering problems these limits are generally very restrictive and involve public or governmental policies; the limits of cost, specific materials, time, known scientific principles which can be utilized, size, shape, manpower, appearance, auxiliary services available; and restrictive codes, methods and procedures, union labor rules, and other limits. As a result, the most important feature of engineering problem solving and design is *compromise*. He has even been labeled an artful deriver rather than the artful contriver. This is a necessary, ineluctable characteristic. Even within the many limits usually imposed on the engineer as he seeks to solve a problem, there are usually many feasible solutions and, contrary to public notions, it is rare that the final solution is the "best" one. Because of the myriad factors which must be adjusted in even a simple engineering problem, there is no time, let alone enough money, to evaluate all possible solutions. (For example, consider the simple problem of a hot- and cold-water-mixing valve for the even-temperature shower bath.) Generally the engineer seeks *a* solution which solves the problem within the given limits. Sometimes he may be able to make adjustments of some of the limits. Many times the engineer does not find a solution and abandons the problem, the company or the sponsoring agency decides not to spend more money, or another design direction is taken. Further, the engineer may solve the problem but it may not be adopted or it may be delayed in adoption.

However, even though most engineering problems are hedged by restrictions imposed by others and require compromise, some solutions are considered by engineers or the public as more ingenious, innovative, and creatively imaginative than others. Also, sometimes one group of engineers is able to solve a problem which another group cannot. For example, Russian engineers have been able to solve certain problems of space vehicles which our engineers have not, despite relaxation in this country of many of the usually limiting conditions on problem solving.

In much of this discussion I have considered the engineer as an individual. But, increasingly, engineering design results from team effort, groups of engineers, or interdisciplinary groups. For example, any design resulting in a practical operating machine to carry a moon explorer will be the product of many creative engineers, as well as psychologists, astronomers, and others solving new and hitherto impossible problems.

So far I have discussed engineering creativity in relation to situations in which the solving of problems are *assigned* the engineer. In general this is the way problems come to him—by assignment. It is much less often that engineers discover and create a solution to a problem which *they* initiate. The engineer is a problem solver to satisfy the wants of others, who also impose many of the limits. This is in distinction to the creative scientist, who often creates for himself in searching for his ideas of truth and reality and for understanding. Two different situations illustrate the point. One engineer's problem, for example, might be to design an economical washing machine for use in countries with limited water supply, the proposed machine to have as many components as possible which the engineer's firm is presently manufacturing for domestic use. One scientist's problem might be that *he* wonders why tomatoes remain red despite radical changes in temperature and radiation.

The engineer generally has little direct contact with the public or with the customer who desires the problems solved. Especially today, when large numbers of engineers may work on a project, the individual engineer may be far removed from the agency or individual responsible for assignment of the specific problems.

Creativity has frequently been described as requiring freedom of action, but the engineer's freedom to create is restricted in a predefined manner to a much greater extent than is the freedom of the scientist. However, within these boundary conditions and limits imposed by the assignments there may be many freedoms of action that give the engineer an opportunity to create. Some of these freedoms are new uses of old and new materials, new fundamental scientific concepts, reordering of elements, and more powerful technical and mathematical tools and methods. He may be able to get his problem solution into circulation very fast. He may have vast physical wherewithal to accomplish assignments, and he may know what to do with an idea when he gets it. The rapid progress of the Manhattan Project illustrated the advantages of such freedom to solve problems, and the current space program is providing further illustrations.

These outcomes of engineering creativity are all results of societal values in which the engineer solves his assigned problems. Today we tend to phrase everything in a problem framework, and the engineer is valued for his ability to find solutions. We might well ask: What does or could a program in engineering education contribute toward a better solution of engineering problems?

ENGINEERING EDUCATION AND CREATIVITY

Engineering is being challenged today to prepare students to solve future unknown problems. How? Scientists are unfolding an increasing wealth of observations, ideas, and principles which prepares the way for the engineers' inventions and artful contrivances. But the engineer, in his groping for something which will work, also prepares the way for the scientist to plow the field, for knowledge can be useful long before it can be understood. The educational program of the engineering student must therefore contain two important elements, information and exploration. The engineer must be educated today so that he can use the knowledge of modern science. At the same time, he must retain a childlike curiosity and experimental interest in making things work in a new way, thereby solving problems in such a manner as to surpass any of today's technology.

Can a college foster creativity? Many critics declare that the last place to develop creativity in engineering students is in an engineering college. This may seem an extreme view, but it comes from men who have had years of experience and know about the talents of young people and their training. Kettering said, "The educational process is the process by which we eliminate creativity." Neither Kettering nor I really believe this, but what does it mean? What are some of the educational practices which hinder rather than kindle creative processes?

Unfortunately, our youngest engineering students, the freshmen, are generally subject to the most restraining and restricting educational practices, which I would label as "stifling creativity." These youngsters are more susceptible to infectious creativity than any of the upperclassmen, and there are very many of them.

According to Bridgeman,[4] of the estimated 570,000 male college freshmen in the fall of 1962, about 67,000 of them entered as engineering students. In some state colleges as many as 2,000 engineering freshmen are enrolled. These students are assigned to sections, and there may be as many as forty sections, each teaching the same subject. In general the students progress through their subjects according to a standard syllabus, conforming to an educational lockstep. Typically the teacher uses a textbook which contains several hundred short, single-answer problems which the student is assigned in small, regulated doses, and the reader or instructor corrects or reviews the problems solved, usually using an answer book which the textbook author must supply. If the student demonstrates that he can solve correctly a sufficient number of these or similar homework and examination problems, he passes the course.

What is wrong with this? Many things. Only about half of these students survive the process to become sophomores in engineering. Who has survived? We don't really know, since we have not studied those who have faltered, dropped out of school, or switched to another field of study. Have we lost the creative and independent-minded students? Have we lost or not stimulated the student who would be challenged by open-ended problems rather than by closed-ended, single-answer problems, who would be stimulated by laboratory research rather than merely confirming an oft-repeated experiment, or who would become deeply involved in a design problem which could be solved through innovation? I would propose that our educational methods in engineering colleges are stifling creativity and seriously crippling our future national endeavor.

ENGINEERING EDUCATORS FACE A VERY DIFFICULT
DILEMMA, OR "HOW CAN WE POUR A
QUART INTO A PINT POT?"

It has always been assumed that a great deal of fundamental learning of even a rote nature must be accomplished in mathematics, chemistry, physics, or what are called preengineering or fundamental subjects. The question is raised, "How can a student learn the necessary principles and techniques and subject matter which are fundamental to his profession and on which his later engineering courses are based and still have time for creative innovation?" The average freshmen may already be spending seventy hours a week on his educational program! There is increasing pressure to spend more time on these fundamentals, not less. For example, more studies in advanced mathematical analysis are being called for as well as more in chemistry and physics. There is also a continuing pressure for more time to be allotted to study sociohumanistic subjects. These pressures have already squeezed out all the traditional practical shopwork and surveying field instruction and have reduced the time in engineering graphics. It can be seen then that the first year of engineering studies seems much too crowded for creative effort.

We believe it is necessary for students to accumulate information. Yet the psychologists are unanimous in saying that if we wish to foster creativity we must nurture the young in providing opportunities and rewarding innovation; facilitating, not restricting, independent, original solutions; and allowing some freedom for nonconformance.

It would appear that if we are to foster the creative talents of our younger engineering students we must provide favorable circumstances in the classroom and we must change at least the early part of the present program. At least some of their learning should be in engineering design problems. The problems should be open-ended, not necessarily having a single answer, and allow for imagination, innovation, and discovery, with experimental work a part of the discovery as well as the testing phase of the solution. The problems should require the student to work with complex and disorderly elements so he can discover simplifying assumptions and integrating concepts.

This suggested program is not new, for some engineering colleges have been teaching such courses many years to upperclassmen. But very little has been changed at the freshman level. At the upperclass levels of undergraduate engineering education there may be some opportunities for student exercise of imagination and innovation which will encourage him to use his creative talents. But there are still too many classes even in the later years of study in which the single-answer, rote problem is used; and any opportunity for creative endeavor is postponed to graduate study—or must wait the day when the student is employed and assigned a problem in engineering!

In this discussion there has been an assumption that creative stimulation for engineering students can come only through engineering design. Of course, this is not true. Opportunities for imagination, innovation, and independent exploration can be provided in any of the courses required of freshmen as well as upperclassmen. This could well be one of the goals of all college teaching. However, the essential nature of engineering is that a design is conceptualized and something results which can work. Some early practice should be given in that aspect of the training that the student has selected in preparation for his life occupation. Engineering schools should introduce real engineering problems in each year of the student's education and develop courses in interdisciplinary problems and designs. These problems and courses should require not only that the student cut across the customary boundaries between the engineering specialties (such as mechanical, electrical, chemical, and civil), but also the collaborative efforts of teams from other professional groups which characterize so much of present-day technology. Such problems would require a broadening of interests and information which is lacking in engineering students today but which is necessary for solutions of creative problems.

There are new methods of teaching which are perhaps a solution to part of the problem of our crowded curriculum. The programmed learning, or "teaching machines," which B. F. Skinner of Harvard has pioneered [8] may enable students to master much of the rote material of the engineering curriculum through independent study guided by experienced teachers. This may quicken educational achievement. At the very least, these methods may enable students to review, to bone up, or to remedy poor teaching or poor learning habits. At best they may give time for more creative learning.

A serious limitation on any change in teaching methods is the faculty. Any significant trial of the suggested changes would put the colleges in a different situation. Instructors would be required who would be able to carry on engineering design projects at every level of the school curriculum. Some relief would be necessary from the student's general program. If he is engaged in a lockstep, solving hundreds of small single-answer problems in math, physics, chemistry, and other scientific and engineering subjects, in developing a keen analytical sense and a stockpile of information, it is seemingly unrealistic to expect him to exercise his creative talents. It would appear that something must change if we wish our future engineers to be more creative and expect them to be stimulated in the early years of their college experience. In discussing the creative process, Anne Roe says that creative products "emerge from a background of absorption in a topic and begin in a state of imaginative muddled suspense." But these qualities are antagonistic to the concentrated effort required in "memory-oriented" instruction and analytic rather than synthetic approaches to learning and creative problem solving.

It should be possible for an engineering college to study and then utilize its means for individualizing instruction and fostering creativity through key courses in the curriculum. A college can also change its admission procedure to admit students who may have creative talent.

CREATIVITY AND THE INDIVIDUAL STUDENT OF ENGINEERING

Many schools of engineering select their entering freshmen on the basis of tests, while others use the students' records of high school achievement in mathematics, science, and English courses. Some state schools admit any high school graduate. There is a trend today for the colleges to admit freshmen on the basis of a predictive score made up of both tests and high school achievement, with weights given to the various factors, depending on the experience of the engineering college. Present test and predictive scores are used to select students who will be successful in their first year of engineering study. That is, in physics, chemistry, and English studies.

Practically no testing is done to predict graduation. This may be because the greatest attrition in the student body comes during the first year, so that survival of the first year of engineering study is in itself a prediction of graduation. Survival rates of engineering freshmen range from ten to sixty percent, depending on the college. If the freshman can "take it" the first year, the chances are that he will survive the next three or four years with the same kind of instruction. Colleges do not select potentially creative engineers as freshmen nor are such students identified. Grade-point averages mainly reflect the students' achievement in the memory-oriented courses.

There is much to be explored in the area of mental abilities which might predict success in engineering. At one time intelligence was thought to be a single characteristic. Even today people give undue weight to some single measure of intelligence, such as IQ, and mistakenly believe this correlates with the ability to do well in specific vocational and professional areas or even with creative talent. However, the complex nature of intelligence has led us to the theory that there may be many factors, traits, characteristics, faculties, or components of intelligence. Psychologists who have developed measures of human ability have sought to discover independent, or so-called primary, factors. We have today many thousands of psychological tests and identified hundreds of differential abilities of intelligence.[1,5,6]

There may be factors of intelligence which are much more important in identifying creative students than any we are using today. One measure of ability—the figural, or spatial, area of mental ability—has been less explored than others more commonly used, such as verbal, reasoning, abstract mathematical, and quantitative abilities. In this relatively unexplored area may lie such measures as visual perception or an individual's ability for sensing the world through such abilities as vision and touch, and mentally organizing and storing the sensation for later actions.[2,3]

I believe that figural or spatial ability is related to the creative performance of engineering students. Myers postulates that spatial ability is important in the types of problem solving characterized by engineering demands.[9] Blade and Watson found that spatial ability is related to success (eventual graduation) in an engineering school.[3] It appears that, in those students who have in a sense been deprived of certain manipulative and visual experiences as children, spatial ability can be developed by instruction.

It is the future study and knowledge of all modes of thought, including spatial, which will answer some of our questions concerning the individual's creative process.

CONCLUSIONS

While the practice of engineering requires competence in analysis, there is a large synthetic component. We are selecting today's students for their ability to reason, to analyze, to compute, and to learn facts.

But more important for creative engineers may be their ability to perceive order from disorder, to find new solutions, to discover through methods of "cut and try," to fancy, imagine, and be ingenious.

Engineering colleges should value students with creative potential, give opportunities for stimulating creative effort, reward innovation and independent works which are carried out successfully and tested in laboratory evaluations.

Research should be continued in identification of talented, creative students, in methods of developing creative modes of thought in all students, and in the methods of teaching young students.

There is a noticeable decline in the interest of young people in studying engineering. A vitalizing of instruction in early college years which would stimulate creative talents would certainly attract a greater number of able students to the engineering field.

REFERENCES

1. Anderson, Harold H., *et al. Creativity and Its Cultivation*, New York: Harper & Bros., 1959.

2. Blade, M. F. *Some Notes on Spatial Ability and Creativity*, unpublished report, Creative Science Seminar, Division of General Education, New York University, 1959.

3. Blade, M. F., and Watson, W. S. "Increase in Spatial Visualization Test Scores During Engineering Study," *Psychological Monographs* (No. 397, 1955).

4. Bridgeman, Donald S. "Another Look at Engineering Enrollment, Retention and Degrees," *Education*, 52(8):492–95 (1962).

5. French, J. W. *The Factorial Compositions of Aptitude and Achievement Tests*. Princeton: Education Testing Service, 1949.

6. Guilford, J. P. "Basic Traits in Intellectual Performances," *The Sec-* *ond (1957) University of Utah Research Conference on the Identification of Creative Talent*. Edited by C. W. Taylor. Salt Lake City: University of Utah Press, 1958.

7. MacKinnon, D. W. "Fostering Creativity in Students of Engineering," *Journal of Engineering Education*, 52(3):129–42 (1961).

8. Mills, Annice L. (ed.) *Programmed Learning and the Educational Process*. New York: Thomas Alva Edison Foundation, 1961.

9. Myers, C. T. "Some Observations of Problem Solving in Spatial Relations Tests," Education Testing Service Research Bulletin 58–16 (November 1958).

10. Ramo, Simon. "The New Pervasiveness of Engineering," *Journal of Engineering Education*, 53(2): 65–73 (1962).

A CRITIQUE ON CREATIVITY IN SCIENCE

H. Herbert Fox

PREFACE

There was a time when men of ideas engaged in acrimonious debates and impassioned literary duels and freely dripped verbal vitriol over each other's works and, occasionally, on each other's personal characteristics. The literary world has long since gentled, and now it is possible to say almost anything in print without eliciting more than a mild, semiapologetic disagreement. It is probable that the critical faculty was much overworked in the early days, but I believe the pendulum has swung too far to the other extreme and has resulted in a great deal of verbiage which would have been better left unprinted. This is especially true of the literature which has grown up around the subject of creativity and the creative process. To illustrate just what I mean, I quote the following from a work on creativity written within the last ten years by one of the most prominent writers in the field.

In a poem about the creative process, "Long-Legged Fly," Yeats makes a refrain of the words, *"His mind moves upon silence."* Silence, so important to the mystic, implies the absence of pattern, configuration, the explicit matter of expression. But this is not all. The silence of the creative mind, like that of the mystical mind, is sustaining, not an emptiness. It is a substantial profundity of being. Though it comprises the play of energies that tend toward resolution in insight, they yield an impression less of developing meaning than of developing life. Profusely subjective and without representation in the independent form of any configuration, these determinants of meaning still inchoate seem for the time being merely aspects or movements of the deeper personal life. That may be why the creative individual is so much implicated, not in a selfish way, but in a personal way, with what he is doing. In some degree he lives these things, as he lives for them.

The important point in all this is that the field has been all but inundated by a flood of words with little meaning. As a former chemistry professor of mine was fond of saying, "The constipation of ideas is frequently followed by a diarrhea of words."

There are other persons who are aware of this problem, but some of them feel that the problem will go away if ignored. I do not subscribe to this view. The printed word is not readily recallable and, for good or ill, its effects are frequently manifest over long periods of time. Anthropomorphically speaking, errors have a way of perpetuating themselves. They pass from book to book, from article to article, and by this very process acquire a spurious authority unless they are vigorously checked somewhere along the line.

It is my intent therefore to consider some of the ideas which have long been current in the field of creativity and about which much too much has been written, and to reevaluate them with the same rigor I would apply to any problem in my own field of chemistry.

Nothing is more indicative of the loose thinking and the chaotic state of the subject than the fact that one may read millions of words on any of the manifold aspects of creativity without ever once seeing it defined. Authors have used the term with complete abandon on the apparently tacit assumption that readers know what they mean and the word has the same meaning to all readers. This is certainly not so. In the present inchoate state of the subject, there is no surety that others think of creativity as we do, and in fact, we can only hope that our notions and ideas on the subject are in reasonable accord. If they are, we can work and think constructively together. If they are not, we find ourselves at cross purposes and in endless and meaningless conflict.

Illustrative of the many meanings associated with the term is a partial listing culled from the files of a public library under the heading "Creative."

Creative adult
Creative ceramics
Creative chemistry
Creative cooking
Creative crafts for campers
Creative crafts in wood
Creative dramatics
Creative expression
Creative gardens
Creative hands
Creative intelligence
Creative learning and teaching
Creative music for children
Creative old age
Creative personality
Creative power
Creative power of mind
Creative sports of the 19th century
Creative understanding
Creative unity
Creative youth
Creative writing
Creative writing of verse

Even more pertinent are the variations in the definitions assigned to creativity by contributors to a recent symposium on the subject.[1] I might add that, whether good, bad, or indifferent, these were the first definitions I encountered in much reading in the field. For this reason alone, the authors deserve credit. H. A. Anderson, the editor, in his preface says, "Creativity, the emergence of originals and of individuality is found in every living cell. In psychology, we still talk about individual differences in a rather static cross-sectional way. We are just beginning to think of individual differences in a moving, changing, progressing interacting way, a way we are beginning to call *dynamic*. This *flow* and interweaving of individual differences is, by definition as well as by discovery, the process of emerging originals, creativity." Erich Fromm, another contributor, says, "In talking about creativity, let us first consider its two possible meanings: creativity in the sense of creating something new . . . or creativity as an attitude. . . ." About creativity as an attitude, he says,

"The best general answer I can give is that creativity is the ability *to see* (or *to be aware*) and *to respond.*" In the same symposium Rollo May says, "Actual creativity I define as the process of *bringing something new into birth.*" Later he says, "Creativity is the encounter of the intensively conscious human being with his world." Carl R. Rogers defines the creative process as "the emergence in action of a novel relational product, growing out of the uniqueness of the individual on the one hand and the materials, events, people, or circumstances of his life on the other." To P. A. Murray, creation is "the occurrence of a composition which is both new and valuable." and to H. D. Lasswell, "Creativity is the disposition to make and to recognize valuable innovations."

THE CREATIVE PROCESS

The divergencies in views which cropped up in this one symposium suggest that the establishment of a common understanding of the term "creativity" would be very desirable and that the establishment of such a common understanding might be somewhat less than easy. One logical mode of attack would be to examine the literature in the field to determine those qualities, ideas, and concepts which are most closely associated with, and are most frequently implied in, the use of the term. If one looks at the literature with this idea in mind, one finds a surprising uniformity in the presentation of the creative process as a sequence of events which culminates in a generative idea, an ideational spark, a creative flash. Graham Wallas divides research into the following four parts:

1. *Preparation,* involving thorough investigation of the problem by reading and experiment.

2. *Incubation,* involving a conscious and unconscious mental digestion and assimilation of all pertinent information acquired.

3. *Illumination,* involving the appearance of the creative idea, the creative flash.

4. *Verification,* involving experimental testing of the creative idea.[2]

Others have used similar constructions to represent the pattern and chronology of the creative process.

Tinged with magic and flamboyant though it may sound,

the concept of the creative flash is not a figment but is firmly rooted in experience. Too many great men have attested to such flashing insights and too many of us have experienced them ourselves in less notable connections to leave any doubt as to their reality. The chemists Platt and Baker, in a study of the relationship of the scientific "hunch" to research sent a questionnaire principally to directors of research laboratories and chemists, and to a sprinkling of physicists, mathematicians, biologists, and psychologists. Of the 232 replies, 33 percent reported they were frequently assisted by intuition, 50 percent were occasionally so assisted, and 17 percent were never assisted by intuition. Many striking examples have been cited in the literature, and it shall suffice us here to cite but one—the notable description given by Poincaré of one of his greatest discoveries, the theory of Fuchsian groups and Fuchsian functions. After two weeks of a vain effort to prove that there could not be any such functions, Poincaré said,

One evening, contrary to my custom, I drank black coffee and could not sleep. Ideas rose in crowds; I felt them collide until pairs interlocked, so to speak, making a stable combination. In the morning, I had established the existence of a class of functions. There remained merely to set down the results and that was done in a few hours.

Subsequently, I wanted to represent these functions by the quotient of two series; this idea was perfectly conscious and deliberate; the analogy with elliptic functions guided me. I asked myself what properties these series must have if they existed and succeeded without difficulty in forming the series called theta Fuchsian.

Just at this time, I left Caen, where I was living, to go on a geologic excursion under the auspices of the School of Mines. The incidents of the travel made me forget my mathematical work. Having reached Constances, we entered an omnibus to go some place or other. At the moment when I put my foot on the step, the idea came to me, without anything of my former thoughts seeming to have paved the way for it, that the transformations I had used to define the Fuchsian functions were identical with those of non-Euclidean geometry. I did not verify the idea; I should not have had time, as upon taking my seat in the omnibus, I went on with a conversation already commenced, but I felt a perfect certainty. On my return to Caen, for conscience sake, I verified the result at my leisure.

"Then I turned my attention to the study of some arithmetical questions apparently without much success and without a suspicion of any connection with my preceding researches. Disgusted with my failure, I went to spend a few days at the sea side and thought of something else. One morning, walking on the bluff, the idea came to me, with just the same characteristics of brevity, suddenness and immediate certainty, that the arithmetic transformations of indefinite ternary quadratic forms were identical with those of non-Euclidean geometry. . . . Most striking at first is this appearance of sudden illumination, a manifest sign of long unconscious prior work. The role of this unconscious work in mathematical invention appears to me uncontestable." [4]

This is a remarkable description because it encompasses within itself all the elements commonly associated with the creative process.

The four creative acts or episodes related therein are all preceded by a concentrated, conscious effort toward a solution of the problem. Characteristically, two of the "revelations," the last two, came at a time when the problem had been set aside and was entirely out of the conscious and, probably, preconscious mind. In fact, both revelations occurred during periods of diversionary activity. The really exceptional instance is the first one, wherein with conscious mind Poincaré observed the evolution of a creative idea from subconscious sources. It was a peculiar experience of disembodiment, as though he were peering into his own mind from the outside, but the mechanism described corresponds to the widely held notion that the creative flash, or the creative idea, is a synthesis resulting from the interaction of two or more ideas not previously related.

To me, one of the oddest aspects of the Poincaré account is the fact that of the several authors I have read who discuss the matter, none pays heed to the second and admittedly least spectacular creative episode. The one in which Poincaré sets out consciously and deliberately to invent the series called theta Fuchsian. Here, the creative act is achieved undramatically through logical, sequential development. But more of this later.

Another point worthy of note in the account is that background knowledge, such as Poincaré obviously possessed, is an absolute imperative for creativity. No one creates in a vacuum. The triumph Poincaré achieved could only have come to a mathematician with a similar background of knowledge. The combined efforts of all the creative men in all the other disciplines could not have done what he did and, conversely, he and his fellow mathematicians in combined effort could not have done the work of Pasteur or Emil Fischer.

Most authors imply that intense application to the problem is a prime requisite to the generation of a creative flash. It is as though by intense effort the mind generates an enormous voltage or potential which is then triggered by such trivial stimuli that the mind can rarely if ever recall them. The flash that results thus appears to be quite spontaneous, without connection to any preceding thought. In presenting this electrical analogy I do not mean to imply that this is what actually happens. At the same time, I do not wish to disclaim the possibility that the analogy is a rough approximation of the reality. Too little is currently known of the physicochemical mechanism of nerve function to enable us to understand even the simplest impulse transmission, much less the tremendous complexities of a thought process.

The fact is that intense application, though it undoubtedly sometimes precedes the creative flash, is by no means a prime requisite to creativity except at a high level of creative endeavor. This simple idea is not readily garnered from the literature. Much creative effort is directed to the solution or partial solution of less consequential problems, which require modest or very little application. In my own experience, I have on many occasions walked up to a problem, so to speak, and almost immediately and without effort seen a novel solution to it. For example, some years ago the chemist E. B. Hershberg invented a laboratory stirrer made of metal wire hung on a glass shaft and designed to whip through heavy suspensions, sludges, and viscous-reaction mixtures.[5] When it was first called to my attention by a colleague, I recognized its advantages over the widely used glass blade stirrer, but it appeared too clumsy and inflexible, especially inasmuch as the wire stirrer was permanently fixed to the glass shaft, necessitating a multiplicity of wire-stirrer and glass-shaft combinations for the many purposes of the organic chemistry laboratory. Within minutes of seeing the Hershberg stirrer, I conceived the idea of combining the flexibility and keyhole mode of attachment of the glass blade to the principle of the wire stirrer, thus enabling any size stirrer shaft to be fitted interchangeably with any size glass blade or wire stirrer. This minor invention has been in constant use in my laboratory since that day. Similar episodes have doubtless occurred to countless others, which suggest that prior intensive effort is not essential to creativity.

What about the creative flash? Many writers on creativity have drawn their illustrations and hence their conclusions not only from the select few but from the most dramatic statements of those select few—and there is no doubt that the unexpected flash of insight which leads to a successful conclusion is most dramatic. The relevant question is, how much of creativity depends upon this flash as compared to methodical progression and logical development. No figures exist to answer this question, but Platt and Baker, in their study, did elicit the fact that the illuminating flash, or "hunch," is not always correct. Only 7 percent of those who answered the questionnaire said that their hunches were always correct. The remainder varied between 19 percent and 90 percent of correct hunches.[3] Even this result may be skewed in favor of the correct hunch because of the human tendency to remember success and forget failure. Since those questioned were creative men, it would seem that the hunch, or creative flash, plays a significant but minor role in overall creativity.

The literature is quite misleading in this regard. Its preoccupation with the pattern of the creative process as exemplified by the unexpected revelation, while praiseworthy in intent, has served to highlight a minor, if dramatic, aspect of the phenomenon. It would appear that a creative act gets short shrift in the literature if it does not conform to one of the established sequences used to represent the pattern and chronology of the creative process. As was mentioned earlier, Poincaré's description contains four distinct creative episodes. Three of these are always pointed up because they are dramatic and conform to the established pattern. His invention of the theta Fuschian series, on the other hand, is virtually ignored because it resulted from sound, logical thinking without the intervention of the creative flash. It is apparent, therefore, that the patterns devised by Wallas and others to represent the creative process are based on preconceptions of what the creative process should be and as such bear little relationship to reality.

Most creative work is solidly based on the plodding and unspectacular, but nonetheless effective, solutions of problems by methodical accumulation of data and sound, logical thinking. This is the bread and butter of creativity which has built most of modern day civilization. The creative flash is the added fillip, the extra dividend of creative activity. It is fortunate for most of us engaged in creative work that creativity does *not* depend on the creative flash.

Though many of those who have delved into the subject have written as though the creative flash were indissolubly linked to creativity and the creative process, some of them have been aware of creative people who are, so to speak, flashproof: people who get original and creative ideas but principally as the result of ordered and logical thinking. Both Hadamard [6] and Poincaré [4] have divided mathematicians into two classifications, the intuitive and the logical, according to whether they work largely by intuition or by logical development. Similarly, Bancroft classifies scientists as "guessers" and "accumulators" according to whether they accumulate data until the problem is solved by the weight of evidence or make shrewd guesses at the solution long before the supporting data have been gathered.[7] Beveridge, for the same general types, uses the terms "speculative" and "systematic" and suggests that most mathematicians and outstanding biologists have been the speculative type. He quotes the following:

> Newton: "No great discovery is ever made without a bold guess."
>
> Gauss: "I have the result, but I do not know how to get it."
>
> Huxley: "It is a popular delusion that the scientific enquirer is under an obligation not to go beyond generalization of observed facts . . . but anyone who is practically acquainted with scientific work is aware that those who refuse to go beyond the facts rarely get as far."
>
> Pasteur: "If someone tells me that in making these conclusions I have gone beyond the facts, I reply: 'it is true that I have freely put myself among ideas which cannot be vigorously proved. That is my way of looking at things.'" [8]

On the other hand, Bancroft quotes Lord Kelvin as saying, "Accurate and minute measurement seems to the non-scientific imagination a less lofty and dignified work than looking for something new, yet nearly all the grandest discoveries are made this way." He also points out that Faraday, who used hypotheses to gain experimental ends, cautioned others "to distinguish the knowledge which consists of assumption, by which I mean theory and hypothesis, from that which is the knowledge of facts and laws." Similarly, Wertheimer never once suggested that Einstein evolved his revolutionary theory of relativity with the aid of creative flashes, though the two spent many hours together in 1916 recreating the steps in the process by which the theory was developed. On the contrary, the account shows that the theory was the end result of logical, clear thinking, of a methodical development of ideas.[9]

Hadamard, who has probed more deeply than some into the mechanisms underlying creativity, has suggested that the creative process consists of two steps, the construction in the unconscious of a multitude of combinations of ideas, followed by the culling and examination of a few useful combinations by the conscious mind. He says "invention or discovery, be it in mathematics or anywhere else, takes place by combining ideas. . . . Invention is discernment, choice." [6] This overlooks the importance of making the right combinations. The answer, once given, is often obvious to many, suggesting that the discernment of the many may be as good as that of the inventor, whose unique contribution lies in making the right combinations. How this may be done still remains a mystery.

From the foregoing, it would seem quite apparent that there is no *one* creative process, and that there may well be as many creative processes as there are creative people. As Guilford has so aptly said, "Psychologists have all too often fallen victims of the fallacy of assuming that one name means one process." [10] What can we say of the process itself? According to Anne Roe, "There have been millions of words written about the creative process, few of them very illuminating. The reason is not hard to find. The crucial stage of the process takes place in the preconscious or unconscious and is pretty inaccessible to study." [11]

This is only part of the reason. To me, the creative process, so called, is the thinking process directed generally toward a specific goal, the solution of a problem, and culminating in a synthesis of ideas which solve or advance the solution of the problem. For as long as the mechanism and elements of thinking escape our analysis and understanding, so long shall we remain in ignorance of the creative process. Aside from the elements of direction and ideational synthesis, there is no way to distinguish between the thinking process and creative process. Putting it another way, the creative process is neither more nor less than productive thinking. Therein lies the principal difference between the thinking and creative processes. The latter is a special or limiting case of the former. Thinking need not be productive, the creative process must be. In this sense, the process and product are irrevocably linked. In science, at least, the concept of a creative process has meaning only insofar as it produces a creative work of whatever dimension. A process that does not create is not creative in exactly the same sense that a process which does not procreate is not procreative. The male screwworms released by the U.S. Department of Agriculture after sterilization with Cobalt 60 radiation go through all the normal physical mating procedures with the native females, who then produce eggs that do not hatch. This coupling is not a procreative process, as witness the fact that the screwworm menace in Florida, South Carolina, Georgia, and Alabama has been totally eliminated, and no screwworms have been found in these states in recent years.

If the creative process takes place entirely within the mind and is essentially an ideational synthesis, what can be said of the patterned sequences which are so frequently called creative processes in the literature? I think it is quite clear, as I have said before, that these are not creative processes at all. They merely describe what happens before and after the moment of creation. Consider the sequence of steps suggested by Wallas.[2] Steps (1) and (2), *preparation* and *incubation*, are obviously preliminary procedures which intrinsically have nothing to do with creativity. The gathering, digestion, and assimilation of all sorts of information occurs every day in the routine work of countless thousands of people without ever producing a creative idea. Step (4), *verification*, must of necessity come after the fact of creation, and it too has nothing to do with creativity. Any grammar school child who has had to prove an answer in arithmetic is thoroughly conversant with the process of verification. In effect, therefore, of the four steps enumerated by Wallas, three are related to the creative process but not really a part of it at all. This leaves step (3), *illumination*. Here, indeed, is the creative process. It is at this point in time that the new idea is synthesized and creativity takes place. But how this synthesis is effected still remains a mystery, and embedding it in a familiar matrix does not make it any the less a mystery. On the contrary, perusal of the literature would seem to indicate that at least some authors have been misled by their familiarity with the processes of data gathering, data assimilation, and conclusion verification into thinking they had the creative process well in hand. At this point, therefore, it might be well to reaffirm that we do not know what the creative process is and that it is therefore an area wide open to investigative effort.

THE CREATIVE PRODUCT

It would seem, then, that there is no unique entity identifiable as the creative process. All we can identify is the product. And it is from the product that we infer the existence of a process. Since so much seems to depend on the creative product, it would be well to examine it in some detail and determine what qualities and attributes are commonly associated with it. Clearly, the product of a creative act need not be tangible. It can be as abstract or intangible as an idea, a mathematical equation, or a hypothesis. Poincaré's Fuchsian functions and Einstein's theory of relativity are as much creative products as are the earth satellites and the atom bomb. What is perhaps not as clear, but nonetheless true, is the fact that the product of the creative act need not be of monumental or even of very significant proportions. Most creativity is manifested by minor and sometimes almost inconsequential contributions. There are all degrees of creativity, and the products may vary from a laboratory stirrer to nuclear energy. Unfortunately, this view tends to be obscured by the understandable emphasis the literature places on the great discoveries.

COMMUNICATION

I stated above that all we can identify of the creative process is the product. Implicit in this statement is an idea that has received little if any recognition, namely, the necessity for communicating knowledge of the product to others. It should be noted that the communication referred to here differs from that discussed by Hughes [12] in being after, rather than before, the fact of creation. If we are to recognize the creative product, we must perforce know of it. And to know of it, it must be communicated to us. This seems obvious, but it has some less obvious implications. In the present state of our knowledge, we can only identify creative men by their works. Leonardo da Vinci, Galileo, Newton, Einstein—all men of great creativity, yet all would have died in obscurity but for the fact that they communicated their ideas to the world. What if, having had the same burgeoning ideas, they had failed to reveal them to anyone else? Would they then have been creative? If you say yes, how would you have recognized them? What products could you show to prove your point? What standards could you set up for creativity? Without objective criteria, it is quite impossible to place the study of creativity on a scientific foundation, and so far, the creative product is the sole objective index of creativity. I submit, then, that for the sake of an operational concept and for objectivity, we are compelled to the position that a man is no more creative than his works and that it is by our knowledge of his works that we can judge him.

ORIGINALITY

One point of common agreement relative to the creative product is that it must be new and novel or original. This is the essence, the hallmark of the creative act. Without the quality of newness or originality, creativity does not exist. A mental process may involve tremendously intricate reasoning, but it is not a creative process if at least one of the ideas is not original. Of the two terms "new" and "original," the latter is far and away the more important because an idea may be creative without being new if it has the element of originality. The history of science is replete with examples of inventions and discoveries conceived almost simultaneously but quite independently by two or more investigators. Regardless of chronology, each inventor has been creative. Besides, one can be relatively certain of the originality of an idea but never of its newness.

The importance of originality or of new and novel methods of solving problems to the concept of creativity is most effectively illustrated by Max Wertheimer, who vividly retells the story of young Gauss. When Gauss, the famous mathematician, was about six years old, he attended a grammar school in a small town. One day the teacher asked the class to find the sum of all the numbers from 1 to 10. While the others were busily engaged in solving the problem in the conventional way by adding $1 + 2 + 3 + 4$, and so on, young Gauss, who finished far ahead of the class, had used an original and therefore highly creative approach. With phenomenal insight for such tender years, Gauss had seen that in the series

if one paired the numbers as illustrated, the sums of the pairs all equal 11 and the sum of all five pairs was therefore 55.[9] The point to be made here is that the same problem was solved in two different ways, only one of which was a manifestation of creativity —not because it was a superior method, but because it had not been taught to Gauss and was original with him. The rest of the students had solved the problem by rote, according to a procedure which had been taught to them. If the reverse had been true and the method taught to the class had been the one Gauss had devised, then the use of the untaught simple addition would have been a creative act. In discussing the creative process, it was pointed out that it involves a synthesis of ideas. Whether as the result of a logical progression or of a creative flash, an original idea is born which solves the problem or advances its solution. The key words here are "synthesis" and "original," because they imply an original mental construction. Gauss, in effect, saw relationships which had not been taught to him and from them synthesized the idea which resulted in a rapid solution of the problem.

UTILITY

Implicit but largely ignored in the concept of creativity is utility. A creative act must be a useful act and must result in a product which is useful, even though at the moment of creation all of its potential utility cannot be foreseen. To invent a costly, complicated machine to do the work of a ten-cent tack hammer —à la Rube Goldberg—is not a creative act. The well-known Rube Goldberg contraptions often show ingenious methods of transmitting energy through long and amusing sequences, but they remain merely amusing because they lack utility.

I would like to emphasize that in discussing the utility of a creative product, the term "utility" is being used in its broadest sense, since it covers, as it must, all creative products from tools and machines on the one hand, to ideas and abstractions on the other. An idea or theory that contributes even slightly to our understanding of the universe around us may be a useful creation, whereas an airplane with flapping wings that will not fly, for all its novelty and complexity, may not be. Many of the latter have been built and found wanting. The ideas underlying them have not been creative because they have not been sound and hence have lacked utility. Illustrative of the former is the work of Hoyle, the British mathematician-astronomer who elaborated a theory of the creation of the universe which depends upon the existence of a steady state with stars being created and destroyed in a dynamic equilibrium. This notion may or may not prove to have validity, but it does have some merit because in the current state of our knowledge it does not grossly violate any of the established facts and it does give us another way of looking at space, time, and matter. Fifty years from now, Hoyle's theory may be considered amusing and of only historical interest should new facts come to light which make it untenable. The same theory promulgated then would not be creative because it would have lost its usefulness. It is apparent, then, that the creative product must be useful in that it must contribute to the solution of a problem or to the advance of knowledge or of understanding, even if time proves it wrong. Whatever its ultimate fate, it must be useful for the time and circumstance.

A case in point is the phlogiston theory developed by George Ernst Stahl around 1697. Though ultimately shown to be false, it was a creative work because, as the first general principle put forth in chemistry, it served to explain a large number of previously unrelated facts. Its value to the scientists of the time is attested to by the fact that many of them, including such famous ones as Priestley, Black, Cavendish, and Scheele believed in and used the theory. Today it is without creative merit because it has lost its utility. It is this time-utility relationship which causes a product to be creative in one time and culture and not in others. There are many illustrations of this because all outmoded scientific theories belong in this category.

When I first presented to others the idea that the creative product must be useful, it was vigorously attacked by some on the grounds that (1) utility involved a value judgment and was subjective, and that (2) situations were conceivable in which the usefulness of an idea or material creation could not be judged except in retrospect. I can only say that much of science is based on value judgments. R. B. Lindsay writes that "value judgments are by no means foreign to science. We must remember that there are fashions in theories as in other human creations; the attitudes of scientists toward the data of experience are conditioned by many factors including, for example, and in very decided measure, the total cultural environment and background of the scientists." [13]

Our truths are relative, and those of yesterday have given way to those of today, which in turn will change with tomorrow. Not all scientists are in agreement on all areas within the scope of their competence, and their differences are often differences in value judgments. For example, not long ago I prepared a compound and assigned to it a structure which was a reasonable extrapolation from the reactants and the conditions of the reaction and was also in accord with the analytic findings. This is common practice in synthetic organic chemistry, and judgments of this type are valid. The new structure was now a fact securely ensconced in the chemical literature. Very recently, on what I thought was rather inconclusive evidence, a new structure was assigned to this compound by other workers. To settle the matter beyond a reasonable doubt, I performed some critical experiments and found that the other workers were right and my original structure was wrong. All of us had leaned heavily on value judgments in drawing our conclusions.

Regarding the other objection, I would suggest that the time-utility relationship applies in both directions. Indeed, it must if it has any validity. If a hypothesis which was creative and useful a hundred years ago can become useless and without creative merit today, then it is conceivable that one which would have been useless and therefore without creative merit a hundred years ago could be useful and creative today. An excellent illustration of this is provided by a recent article in which the author shows by calculation that the theoretical effect on an insect population of sexual sterilization of 90 percent of the males is much greater than that of killing off 90 percent of the insects.[14] Here is a calculation which could have been made quite readily a hundred years ago. But at that time it would have been regarded as an idle speculation of no merit whatsoever because no means existed for sterilizing insects en masse. Today the concept is of utmost importance, as was pointed out earlier in discussing the control of the screwworm menace in the South.

Another argument against the second objection lies in the fact that science deals with probabilities and the vast majority of creative work is immediately recognizable as such at the time it is produced. The fact that the hydrogen-filled balloon rises does not negate the fact that almost everything you release from your hand falls.

In pursuing the ideas on utility formulated here, it occurred to me that the creative merit of most products diminishes with time—over the long haul. This could be ascribed to invalidation. For example, let us assume that a hypothesis has been formulated which satisfactorily explains the facts known at the time. As knowledge expands, the original hypothesis is strengthened, modified, or discarded to the degree that it accommodates the new facts. If it readily explains them, it is validated and strengthened. If it does not explain them too well, it is partially invalidated and must be modified accordingly. If, finally, it is in marked conflict with the new facts, it may be completely invalidated and discarded. Invalidation seems plausible at this point.

But what of material creations, machines? They are not invalidated. The principles upon which the bow and arrow, Watt's steam engine, and Wright's airplane are based are as true today as they were when they were first invented, though the creative merit of the machines themselves have diminished by today's standards. Machines, too, become outmoded as improvements are made. Why? The answer is *utility*. The creative merit of machines and ideas diminish as utility diminishes. The spear, the spinning wheel, the oil lamp, the Aristotelian concept of the universe, and the phlogiston theory, for all their creative importance at one time, have little or no utility and therefore little or no creative merit in our civilization. On the other hand, the wheel, the lever, Euclid's geometry, and Newton's theory of gravitation have all retained their creative merit because they have retained their usefulness—the last two despite the influences of the relativity theory and our current concepts of the universe.

Much of what I have said here is more succinctly and perhaps better expressed by Teicher, who states, in his article in this book, ". . . the reciprocal relationship between culture and creativity is such that a creative product is not really an invention unless it is socially accepted. The creative product has to operate within the culture; it has to work. If it does not work, then it is a failure as an invention. It may exist individually or mechanically, but it only becomes an actuality when it is socially accepted."

In recapitulation, we can say of the creative product, whether it be an idea or a machine, that:
1. It must be made known.
2. It must be original in conception.
3. It must be useful in the broadest sense of the word.

CREATIVITY: A DEFINITION

I have already pointed out that as with the creative process, creativity has no meaning except in relation to the creative product. In other words, like other talents or abilities, creativity must be exercised to be identifiable. A man may dream great dreams—all of which may be practical and readily convertible to realities. If he never makes or influences the conversion to reality, if he never implements his ideas or transmits them for implementation by others, if, in short, they die with him, then he has not been creative by any standards that can be scientifically imposed. He may have had the potential for creativity but he was not creative.

The exercise of this talent can be widely observed at all levels of human endeavor, and I had assumed that its universality in mankind was generally acknowledged. This may be an unwarranted assumption on my part. Anderson says, in the preface to his book on creativity, "Creativity is in each of us. That is to say, creativity *was* in each one of us as a small child. In children creativity is a universal. Among adults it is almost non-existent." Interestingly enough, the above statement follows closely on another, "Creativity, the emergence of originals and individuality, is found in every living cell." Still further along, in another article in the same book, he says, "There is creativity in everyone." [1]

My avowed purpose in this critique is to attempt to eliminate such ambiguities and to achieve some precise and generally acceptable ideas on creativity. Before proceeding to the formulation of a definition based on the ideas I have advanced, it is pertinent to consider what it is that we want a definition to do for us. By their very nature and purpose, definitions are restrictive. This is as it should be. But by the same token, to be useful to our purposes any definition of creativity must be general enough to be applicable to any and all of the scientific disciplines. (I will attempt to define creativity in art just as soon as someone defines

art for me.) The definition should also be operational—at least
to the extent of providing us with qualitative criteria for judging
what is or what is not creative work. Einstein has pointed out that
for a concept to have real meaning, it must provide a measure for
itself. This is in line with Bridgman's idea that all scientific
definitions should be operational. Indeed, Bridgman contends
that the revolutionary character of the theory of relativity was
occasioned by the failure of early physicists to use operational
definitions for some of the basic concepts in physics. Had they
done so, the transition would have been evolutionary.[15] As a final
condition, the definition should be as simple as is consonant with
the above criteria.

Having established the criteria for a definition and having
discussed at some length those factors which I regard as essential
to the concept of creativity, I offer the following with the expressed understanding that it is not the only nor even necessarily
the best definition possible:

*Creativity in science is the exercise of the ability to solve
problems by original and useful methods.*

The definition can be further simplified if one departs from
the usual vague concepts associated with the words "talent" and
"ability" and assigns to them more precise meanings. Most people,
including those who should know better, confuse ability and
talent with inherent capacity. Admittedly, the difference is subtle,
but it exists nonetheless. Inherent capacities are the natural en-
dowments with which people are born. They are latent and may
or may not become manifest. For example, it is readily conceivable that somewhere amongst the most primitive people of the
darkest corner of Africa is a child who in the proper environment
could become a renowned scientist or mathematician. As it is, he
will probably live a life of primitive savagery. We can say of him
that he has an inherent capacity to become a prominent scientist
or mathematician, but we can never say he has a talent for science
or mathematics until he has demonstrated such a talent. In other
words, capacities may be latent, abilities must be demonstrated.
The measure of a person's talents or abilities lies in his performance. In this view then, *creativity is the ability to solve problems
by original and useful methods.*

Whatever this definition may lack in poetry of expression,
it makes up for in practicality of meaning. It avoids, deliberately,
involvement in the speculative area of mechanism, and is de-

signed solely to provide a common understanding that is precise enough to avoid ambiguity and descriptive enough to serve as a measure of what is and what is not a creative act.

In point of fact it is not far removed from the definition proffered by Taylor and a rather reluctant contribution of Stein. Taylor has defined creativity as ". . . that thinking which results in the production of ideas (or other products) that are both novel and worthwhile." In his view, "creative thinking is also best defined not in terms of process but in terms of product." [16] This is quite in agreement with the thesis developed here. On the other hand, Stein prefers to define creativity in terms of process. "It is," he says, "a process of hypothesis formation, hypothesis testing and communication of results. Creativity may be manifest in any one or all of the aspects of this process." Nonetheless, he feels compelled to add later, "For purposes of empirical research our definition of creativity is as follows: Creativity is that process which results in a novel work that is accepted as tenable or useful or satisfying at some point in time." [17] Substitute the phrase "in a novel product" for "in a novel work" and Stein's definition is not far removed from Taylor's or mine.

CREATIVITY—ITS ROLE IN SCIENCE

A little earlier, in discussing a definition of creativity in science, I indicated somewhat facetiously that I was willing to attempt a definition of creativity in art as soon as an acceptable definition of art had been devised. Upon reading this statement, a colleague forthwith challenged me to define science in a meaningful way, implying thereby that science was no more definable than art and that my definition of creativity in science was no more valid than a definition of creativity in art. It is pertinent then, before discussing the role of creativity in science, to assay a definition of science.

At the outset, it is obvious that many definitions of science are possible, and, indeed, many have already been formulated and published. As is usual, some are more intelligible, more meaningful, and more useful than others. Rather than select one of the better ones, I have decided to devise one of my own. The definition I offer here, therefore, while not necessarily the last word in definitions, is an operational one and thus meaningful in an important way.

Science is the organization of facts obtained by observation and experiment and the development of concepts, laws, theories, and hypotheses from these facts by productive thinking (which is defined elsewhere in this paper) for the purpose of achieving a better understanding of, and a greater control over, the universe in which we live. By the same token, a science is an organized body of facts obtained by observation and experimentation, along with the complex of concepts, laws, theories, and hypotheses derived therefrom by productive thinking for the purpose of achieving a better understanding of and a greater control over the universe in which we live. I have used the term "productive thinking" to preserve the unitary character of this paper, but I might, perhaps to better advantage, have used Polya's term "plausible reasoning" in its stead. As Polya has said, "Anything new that we learn about the world involves plausible reasoning. . . ." [18]

Patently, a telephone book, an almanac, or an encyclopedia, for all that they are full of facts organized according to some system, do not constitute sciences. The distinguishing characteristic of a science is the web of ideas which relates the facts of the science and weaves them into a comprehensible whole. The construction of this web, idea by idea, theory by theory, concept by concept, is the most productive area for creative endeavor in science. Creativity, then, is the *sine qua non* of science.

Not all scientific endeavor is creative, however. There is much in science that is routine and a great deal more that, in the hierarchy of creative work, is of low order. For example, some of the natural scientists of bygone years did a useful job but were not very creative men. Their works, gracefully and entertainingly written though they might be, were weak in originality and ideation and were simply lists of facts and observations palatably presented. Even Charles Darwin was quite in tradition in recording his almost five years of travel and observations as a naturalist on the *Beagle*. The difference with Darwin lay in the fact that his observations provoked within him a mental ferment which culminated in his monumental *Origin of Species*. By his own admission, Darwin was not a man who could merely observe and record. In his *Life and Letters* he says, "I have steadily endeavored to keep my mind free so as to give up any hypothesis, however much beloved (and I cannot resist forming one on every subject), as soon as facts are shown to be opposed to it." [19] To me, the most significant portion of this statement lies in the parentheses. The inborn compulsion to hypothesize is one of the hallmarks of the creative man and provides most of the motivation for the ideational synthesis we call creativity.

On the other hand, Jean Henri Fabre, Darwin's contemporary, spent all of his life observing and recording the life histories, habits, and instincts of insects, from all of which he derived two principal ideas: that insects showed an intelligence irreconcilable with the theory of fixed habits, and that the theory of evolution was wrong.

Or compare Fabre with von Frisch. About all that can be said in resemblance is that they both studied insects. But how differently! Fabre was the passive observer—an almost disembodied pair of eyes to see and hands to record. Von Frisch, in his recent work on the communication of bees,[20] practically projects himself into the life pattern of his subjects. He is all eager, probing, experimental mind—with eyes and hands appended. Fabre was a receiver of impressions. Von Frisch also receives impressions, but in addition he decodes, interprets, synthesizes ideas and transmits them in the form of critical experiments and cogent hypotheses. In a word, von Frisch is an experimentalist—and experimentation is probably the earliest form of creative effort. Underlying every experiment is a hypothesis; and every experiment which is original in concept and results in a useful product is a creative act. In chemistry, for example, the synthesis of a new compound by a well-established general method and of a known compound by a new method are both creative acts, though the latter generally takes precedence in the creative hierarchy. It may seem strange to the layman that the use of a well-established method to synthesize a new compound should be regarded as creative, inasmuch as the element of originality would appear to be lacking. The fact is that in the synthesis of any new compound, variables are introduced which may, and not infrequently do, cause the method to fail.

Despite the foregoing, it should be emphasized that the routine and the mildly creative make massive contributions to science and are not to be despised. They are the concrete and steel for the conceptual bridges that span the unknown. Without the myriad of facts and observations to support our structured view of the universe in which we live, it would collapse like a house of cards.

Most of this seems quite elementary, perhaps too elementary to require discussion but for the fact that much has been written in this area which has served to befog the reader and becloud the subject. A case in point is an item on creativity in science by a professor of physics. It begins with the following paragraph:

It is easy to suspect that the observational sciences cannot be truly creative. The natural scientist discovers things by looking keenly at the world. He does not—or at least should not—invent his data. He may construct ingenious experiments, but he designs them in order to bring into the laboratory whatever small part of the world he wishes to observe more precisely. He may appreciate the grand and free sweep of pure mathematics, but he uses it as an abstract tool to supplement his microscopes and vacuum pumps. And what can be said for the mathematician himself? Are his imaginary structures independent of the natural world, or does he simply discover an objective body of knowledge flowing naturally from laws of human thought? Surely Euclid's discovery that the number of primes is infinite might be reproduced by any talented schoolboy ignorant of the original work. Thus, if we define an act as creative only if it brings something new into existence, scientific activity can be regarded as uncreative. In this sense it is easily distinguished from the literary, graphic, and musical arts.

It turns out that the author does not really seem to believe all this, because he goes on to develop the other side of the question—to deal with the theoretical aspect of science, what I have called the "web of ideas"—and concludes, "From this viewpoint we can regard science as a framework within which creative work of the highest calibre is possible." As a scientist, the author has obviously decided that his chosen field of work allows for great creativity, but only after committing mayhem on some pretty basic notions of creativity. Consider some of the implications of his paragraph:

    1.   Observational sciences are not truly creative because:

        The observational scientist merely looks keenly at the world and gathers all sorts of data, presumably without ever entertaining a thought of the interrelationship or general meaning of the facts he has uncovered.

        Even if the scientist constructs ingenious experiments, they are only designed to help him study segments of the real world with more precision and in the comfort of his laboratory.

        He studies only things which are already in existence and therefore cannot be newly created.

    2.   The mathematician is not creative because:

His imaginary constructs are related to the natural world.

Mathematics really exists in nature as an objective body of knowledge which flows naturally from laws of human thought (whatever that might be!).

Any talented schoolboy, ignorant of the original work, could duplicate the discoveries of Euclid or those of any other early mathematician.

It is true, as I have already pointed out, that some of the earlier natural scientists were merely observers and recorders. I know of no latter-day scientists who, like Fabre, gather data as the big-game hunter gathers trophies. Data, facts, observations, and experiments are no longer ends in themselves. They are only the means to the solution of the particular problem that has captured the scientist's interest, fired his imagination, and sparked his energies.

The spectroscopic study of the elements within the confines of the laboratory enabled man's mind to reach to the stars across countless millions of miles. The rare gas helium was discovered in the sun almost thirty years before it was found on earth. In more recent times man has brought a bit of the stars into the laboratory with him in the form of atomic energy. To consider these merely ingenious experiments is to lift creativity out of mortal range. "There is nothing new under the sun" is a tired cliché which makes poor argument against scientific creativity. Using such a criterion, the creation of a living amoeba in a test tube would fail as a creative act because amoebas already exist! Similarly, the notion that mathematicians are not creative because they simply discover a body of knowledge which already exists in the conjunction of their minds and the real world can be applied to all concepts concerning the universe around us. To be creative then is not merely difficult—it is impossible!

And what if any talented schoolboy of today could rediscover some or all of the Euclidian concepts? Does that negate Euclid's creativity? Not at all. Creativity does not carry with it the implication of absolute uniqueness for all time—as is evident by the many examples of simultaneous invention and discovery.

We have seen, so far, that though creativity is essential to science in our modern concept, not all of science is creative and some of it is creative on a lower order. We have, in effect, within the orbit of scientific endeavor an entire spectrum of creativity which parallels the scope and importance of the problems under attack. When a scientist undertakes a problem of major importance, he is simultaneously undertaking many problems of lesser scope, each of which may have to be solved before a solution to the central problem is obtained. Often the central problem is attended by peripheral problems which may be as important or even more important in a fundamental sense, and whose solutions, while not requisite to the solution of the central problem, may contribute to it in an important way. Inasmuch as the level of creativity is a function of the magnitude of the problem and the originality or novelty of its solution, any problem of major scope provides a wide range for creative activity.

As a chemist, I can illustrate these ideas best by drawing on my own experience in chemical research, but the basic principles are equally applicable to the other sciences.

One problem of recent interest to me involved lycopene, the red coloring matter of the tomato. Lycopene is a carotenoid closely related to β–carotene, the precursor to vitamin A. It has forty carbon atoms arranged in isoprene units and linked to form a highly unsaturated chain. A natural food color of considerable intensity, it has great potential usefulness in the food and cosmetic industries. As a prerequisite to commercial application, some colleagues of mine, in an elegant piece of research, succeeded in synthesizing the compound, thus giving our organization an inexhaustible source for lycopene but, unfortunately, no market for it—it proved to be too unstable for use.

The central problem, then, was to stabilize lycopene without changing its molecular structure. In the original synthesis of lycopene, the synthetic product proved to be chemically identical to the natural lycopene, yet the notion had persisted among those working with it that the synthetic product was not as stable as the natural product. One of the peripheral problems, therefore, was to determine whether or not such a difference did, in fact, exist, and if it did, what factors were causing the difference. It is also known that lycopene in the tomato resists hours of boiling and shows every indication of being remarkably stable. Why this is so has never been determined, though it has often been suggested that the lycopene in the tomato may be bound to a protein in a lycopene-protein complex—a circumstance which could account for its stability. Thus, we have as additional peripheral problems (1) the nature of the lycopene-stabilizing factor in the tomato; (2) the existence or nonexistence of a lycopene-protein complex in the tomato; (3) the character of the protein which may be complexed with lycopene, and (4) the nature of the bond between the protein and the lycopene. All of these are of considerable scientific interest and, though peripheral, could provide valuable information for the solution of the central problem and possibly of other problems.

Subordinate to the central problem are those questions pertaining to the most promising lines of approach in attempting the stabilization of lycopene. Inasmuch as it is known that the instability of lycopene is due to a light-catalyzed oxidation, a direct assault on the problem would suggest the use of an antioxidant, an enveloping matrix, an ultraviolet light absorber, or a combination of all three to protect the lycopene from destruction. There are still lower echelon questions. Which antioxidants? Which matrices? Which ultraviolet light absorbers? And then, How should they be combined with lycopene? And once combined, what method of assay can be devised to determine the rate of lycopene destruction in the combinations? And what stability tests can be set up which would give rapid and meaningful results? These and many other problems subserve the central one, and all require a degree of originality because there are no ready-made answers nor are there known techniques which can guarantee the answers.

The solution of the central problem, necessitating as it does the solution of all the subordinate (but not peripheral) problems, occupies the highest position in the hierarchy of creativity. This is valid, however, only for this specific purpose, since a shift in objectives generally results in a shift in creative values. Thus, to the research scientist in academic circles, some of the peripheral problems mentioned here would appear much more important than the central one. Sometimes, too, the solution of a subordinate problem can assume much more importance than that of the central one, as witness isoniazid, the most effective tuberculostat known to date. Isoniazid was synthesized as a means of arriving at another chemical structure which it was believed might have tuberculostatic activity. The desired structure did have a tuberculostatic activity which in other circumstances would have been quite impressive, but which, in the face of the extraordinary potency of isoniazid and its unique combination of qualities, proved to be of minor consequence.

This discussion of the hierarchy of creativities and of problems brings us to another area of creativity in science which has stirred up some minor controversy. If the creative process involves a synthesis of ideas, it seems fairly obvious that this synthesis must occur within the realm of one mind. Other minds may accomplish the same synthesis, but each mind must do it for itself to validate the claim for originality. On this basis, creativity is an individual, personal, and singularly unique phenomenon. Individuals create; groups collaborate.

Yet the term "group creativity" is widely used, and there are some who contend that a group can be more productive than the sum productivity of its individual members. How can these two apparently opposing points of view be reconciled? In my opinion, they are not in opposition at all. Both are true, but on different levels in the creative hierarchy. It is undeniably true that the creative idea must occur to the individual mind. But consider the case of a group attack on a complex problem whose solution depends upon the solution of subordinate problems. Each member of the group may be assigned to a subordinate problem and may solve it, creatively. In such instance, the sum of the solutions will resolve the central problem, and the term "group creativity" will have real meaning. The atomic reactor is an example of a creative product of enormous significance that was developed by the creative endeavors of many groups.

There is another way in which a group may be creative. It is tacitly admitted that no one creates in a vacuum. Creative endeavor leans heavily on background knowledge garnered from personal and vicarious observation and experience. In a closely collaborating group of diverse backgrounds, one member may say or suggest something which will provide just the idea needed by another for a creative synthesis. Visualizing the creative process as a mental connection drawn between two ideas not obviously related, it is apparent that one of the ideas may come directly from an outside source. Such cross-fertilization may make a group more creative than the sum of the creative potentials of its individual members.

From this point of view, all creative work in science, because of its dependence upon exogenous ideas, may be regarded as a form of group creativity. The creative scientist finds his "collaborators" in the scientific literature and culls their ideas to help him initiate and solve problems. In drawing this parallel, I have no intention of depreciating the uniqueness, the singularity of the creative man. I merely wish to suggest that the question is complicated and the answer is not unequivocal. The individual working alone is generally separated from these collaborators by time and distance. They are passive, and he has only their written word to consult in a one-way communication. The group worker is part of a plexus of oral communication, and the ideas generated in such a system have a pertinence and an immediacy which may be (and, I think, are) especially potent in creativity. The difference between the two situations, I believe, is sufficient to keep resort to the scientific literature from being regarded as group collaboration except as a semantic exercise.

It was more than a year after I devised the definition of science presented here that I was suddenly struck with the notion that the definition had more implications and was more pertinent to the topic of creativity than I had been aware of. If, as I have postulated, productive thinking is the creative process, then the definition not only approaches science in an operational way, but also points up those areas of science which are most promising. What I have called the "web of ideas," that great complex of concepts, laws, theories, and hypotheses which is the most distinguishing characteristic of a true science, is derived from the observational and experimental facts by the creative process. The creative process, or, alternatively, productive thinking or plausible reasoning, is the mechanism whereby isolated facts are related to each other and are woven into the comprehensible whole we call a science.

SUMMARY

Many of the ideas which have been developed and rooted in the earlier literature on creativity are poorly conceived, frequently unsupported, and largely untenable. More rigorous treatment of the subject suggests that there is no one creative process and that, indeed, the creative process is any thinking process which solves a problem in an original and useful way. Since the creative process and creativity itself are recognizable only through the creative product, the creative product must be original and useful and, if the creative product is an idea, it must be communicated or implemented.

Creativity is the *sine qua non* of science, but not all scientific activity is creative. There is, in fact, a whole spectrum of creative activity within science which parallels the scope and importance of the scientific problems under study. The creative value of a solution is a function of its originality and the magnitude of the problem and is subject to change with changing objectives. Because there are hierarchies of creativity and of problems within science, group creativity is a real phenomenon even though, on another level, it is undeniable that the creative act must take place in an individual mind.

REFERENCES

1. Anderson, H. H. (ed.) *Creativity and Its Cultivation*. New York: Harper & Bros., 1959.

2. Wallas, Graham. *The Art of Thought*. New York: Harcourt, Brace & Co., 1926.

3. Platt, Washington, and Baker, R. H. "Relation of the Scientific Hunch to Research," *Journal of Chemical Education*, 8:1969–2002 (October 1931).

4. Poincaré, Henri. *Science and Method*. Translated by Francis Maitland. London: Thos. Nelson & Sons, 1914.

5. Hershberg, Emanuel B. "A New Type of Laboratory Stirrer," *Industrial and Engineering Chemistry, Analytical Edition*, 8:313 (1936).

6. Hadamard, J. *An Essay on the Psychology of Invention in the Mathematical Field*. Princeton: Princeton University Press, 1945.

7. Bancroft, Wilbur D. *The Methods of Research*. Rice Institute Pamphlet XV.

8. Beveridge, William I. B. *The Art of Scientific Investigation*. New York: W. W. Norton & Company, Inc., 1950.

9. Wertheimer, Max. *Productive Thinking*. New York: Harper & Bros., 1945.

10. Guilford, J. P. "Basic Conceptual Problems in the Psychology of Thinking," *Annals of the New York Academy of Science*, 91:6 (December 1960).

11. Roe, Anne. *Creativity and the Scientist*. Address to the Illinois Psychological Association, October 9, 1959, Chicago.

12. Hughes, Harold. "The Role of Communication in Group Creativity," unpublished report, Creative Science Seminar, Division of General Education, New York University, 1959.

13. Lindsay, R. B. "Entropy Consumption and Values in Physical Science," *American Scientist*, 47:377–85 (September 1959).

14. Knipling, Edward F. "Sterile-Male Method of Population Control," *Science*, 130:902–4 (October 9, 1959).

15. Bridgman, Percy W. *The Logic of Modern Physics*. New York: The Macmillan Co., 1960.

16. Taylor, D. W. "Thinking and Creativity," *Annals of the New York Academy of Science*, 91:108 (December 1960).

17. Stein, M. I. "A Transactional Approach to Creativity," *The 1955 University of Utah Research Conference on the Identification of Creative*

Scientific Talent. Edited by C. W. Taylor. Salt Lake City: University of Utah Press, 1956.

18. Pólya, György. *Mathematics and Plausible Reasoning.* 2 vols. Princeton: Princeton University Press, 1959.

19. Darwin, Charles R. *The Life and Letters of Charles Darwin.* New York: Basic Books, 1959.

20. Frisch, Karl von. *Bees: Their Vision, Chemical Senses, and Language.* Ithaca: Cornell University Press, 1950.

PSYCHOLOGICAL APPROACHES TO
CREATIVITY IN SCIENCE

Anne Roe

MANY DISCUSSIONS of creativity and the creative process would have been clarified if a careful distinction had been made between the process itself and the product or result of the process. The process itself, that is, *what goes on within the individual,* is not directly related to any value which may—then, at some future time, or never—be placed upon the product. It is not related to the absolute uniqueness of the product or even to its adequacy. There are artistic productions and scientific theories which were rejected when they were first offered, only to be acclaimed by later generations; there are others which were acclaimed and have since been rejected; but the process within the individual was as creative in one instance as in the other. Similarly, the discoveries a child makes may be true creations even though many other persons have made them before him.

Such specifications as that of Stein, who defines a creative product as "a novel work that is accepted as tenable or useful or satisfying by a group at some point in time," [60] focus upon the social acceptability of the product rather than upon the process. They do, in fact, refer to a particular subclass of results of a more general process, although admittedly to the subclass in which our chief interest resides. This seems to be the most general use of the term "creative" and will be followed here, except that the phrase "creative *process*" will carry no implication regarding the social usefulness or absolute novelty of the results.

The total gamut of scientific thinking includes both the creative process, that is, discovery or invention, and the verification, elaboration, and systematization of the new product. These stages are not always neatly distinguishable; in developing a hypothesis, for example, invention and some verification may alternate rapidly until it finally takes shape and is ready for formal test. We are here concerned primarily with the process itself, with discovery and invention, rather than with its final elaboration.

We are attempting to study a very intricate series of events: the creative process taking place within an individual and resulting in an acceptable product. The process is inseparable from the individual;* the evaluation of the product is inseparable from the social group. We can make no predictions regarding the probability of occurrence of this series of events until we have isolated the relevant variables at each step in the series.

The first problem, then, is to reach some consensus on how to determine that this series of events has occurred: this is the criterion problem. Since only the product is directly observable, this becomes the first point of attack. Having identified creative products, we may go on to identify the individuals who have produced them and the environments and societies which have fostered them. And finally we may approach the process itself.

THE CRITERION PROBLEM

The most thorough discussions of this problem, together with a number of proposals for its solution, are to be found in the Criterion Committee Reports for each of the Utah conferences. The third committee noted that the problem of defining creative products includes the necessity for discriminating between personal and social novelty; between creations and discoveries (which may or may not involve a truly creative act) and breadth of applicability as a measure † of *degree* of creativity. They point

---

* This is true even in the case of a team working together upon a particular problem: although the members may all contribute to a solution, fitting together the pieces (or some of them) takes place within a single mind, although of course it may occur simultaneously in several.

† Measure, as used in such contexts, is not limited to objective and physical scales. It may include ratings, rankings, and so forth.

out that a truly creative product or contribution generates additional creative activity.

For example, an important new scientific theory provides new solutions to problems hitherto unsolved, new perceptions of problems hitherto unperceived, and new discoveries. This characteristic provides a basis for measurement of levels or degrees of creativity. At the bottom of the scale, the creative product simply solves the immediate problem to which it was directed. At the top of the scale, the creative product provides the solution not only to the immediate problem, but also to a wide range of related problems, affects broad areas of thought and activity, and may even open up new fields of research or technology or other action and progress. A corollary, important for the use of products as criteria of creativity, is that the truly fundamental or highly creative contribution is usually rare, difficult to achieve, and requires a high level of creative effort and ability—hence it identifies the highly creative individual.[Sprecher 66]

Creative products of science include such things as patents, oral or written reports, publications, processes, new instruments or methods, ideas, and new products or compounds. These different kinds of products occur with different frequencies in different fields and different situations, hence an across-the-board count as a means of comparing different individuals or groups is not meaningful. For men in industry McPherson considers that a count of patents alone is also not significant,[64] and he suggests application of the concept of "inventive-level." [61]

With regard to publications, however, Dennis has shown the purely quantitative approach to be not without merit, since there is a definite relationship between productivity in terms of number of papers and eminence. He says that

the correlation between fame and fecundity may be understood in part in terms of the proposition that the greater the number of pieces of scientific work done by a given man, the greater the likelihood that one or more of them will prove to be important. No one can foresee perfectly whether a given scientific product will be a fruitful one. While scientists undoubtedly differ in their ability to select areas that will lead to "pay dirt," whether they find it or not depends in part upon chance. Other things being equal, the greater the number of researches, the greater the likelihood of making an important discovery that will make the finder famous.[16]

Another suggestion dealing with the relative importance of published work is to count, not the number of papers by a given man, but the number of times his work is cited in an appropriate selection of journals and books. This is a simple technique but a very time-consuming one. Westbrook has demonstrated its usefulness for identifying laboratories doing the most significant work in a given field. It requires a large sample, and may be distorted by scientific fashions or restrictions on publications, but he considers that neither of these problems need be serious ones.[80] This kind of count is approached qualitatively when raters are asked to make judgments of the influence of the subject's writing and other products in bringing about basic reorientation in the field.

At some place in any evaluative method reliance must be placed on individual judgment. Some form of classification—of ratings or of rankings—is required, based upon the opinions of men about other men. A single variable such as global judgment of creativity or productivity or performance may be used. If a number of variables are employed, they may be combined later into an overall estimate of creativity or may be studied individually. The criterion should eventually be stated in quantitative scale terms for comparative purposes, and, of course, it should have a reasonable degree of reliability and validity. A simple dichotomy of creative or noncreative is not very helpful, although in the earliest stages of work one of "most creative" and "least creative" can be used.

The form of evaluation, who is to do the evaluating, and how personal bias is to be minimized are crucial questions. It is usual to have supervisors do the rating in an industrial or governmental setting; ratings by subordinates would be of interest but have not been reported, except as regards supervisors' leadership skills.

In studies of individuals, peer ratings are most usual. Attribution of eminence, for example, is almost always based upon the judgment of supposedly qualified peers, and refers to their estimate of the value of the potential subject's contributions. There are a number of ways of carrying out peer ratings. Several methods are described by Clark, along with a careful statistical analysis of relationships between various criteria.[11]

Analysis of the basis on which judges make their ratings or of their own possible biases is seldom carried out. It is usually supposed that if the number of judges is large enough, individual bias in them will not significantly affect the final results. This, of course, assumes there is no constant biasing factor, such as the possession by one subject of a particularly unlikable personality. Harmon has reported an interesting study of the determinants of judges' overall ratings of creativity, using a ten-point scale, on the basis of questionnaire data on scientists who had been fellowship applicants six years previously. These ratings were correlated with eight specific questionnaire variables: year of B.A., year of Ph.D., academic level, academic progress, publications, adjusted income, supervisory level, and number of persons supervised. Number of publications received the highest correlations with the ratings in both physical $(+.61)$ and biological $(+.76)$ sciences groups. The multiple R for predicting the criterion from publications, income, and supervisory level was $+.65$ and $+.78$ for the two groups.[65]

That judges with different backgrounds may differ in their estimates of the relative importance of different behaviors was shown by Sprecher. Five psychologists and four engineers made judgments of the relative importance of twelve aspects of creative persons, such as "independent," "energetic," and "communicates." Agreement among the engineers was considerably greater than among the psychologists, perhaps because the engineers had worked closely together for years and were thinking about the meaning of creativity in a specific practical situation. Agreement between the two groups was not close, but both would say that the creative person has a lot of ideas and a lot of unusual ones. Engineers emphasize technical competence and analyzing; psychologists do not.[66]

The most comprehensive study of criteria of scientists' productivity and creativity was done by Taylor, Smith, and Ghiselin at an Air Force research center. After preliminary studies of almost 150 measures, they settled on fifty-six criterion scores, including eleven supervisory ratings and rankings, four monitor ratings, six peer ratings and rankings, nine scores extracted from official records, thirteen scores on reports and publications, one score on membership in professional societies, four ratings from the project researchers, four control variables, and four self-ratings. They report,

The correlations between scores from supervisors vs. peers vs. monitors were usually low, though often significant. The correlations between scores subjectively obtained and scores obtained from objective records were generally negligible. Scores either from supervisors or from peers generally correlated zero with scores on research reports and publications . . . although there were a few exceptions. The control variables, such as age, education, and experience were generally quite independent from the criterion scores. . . . One general conclusion to be drawn from this table is that the data on contributions of scientists tend to be relatively independent when obtained from different sources. The second overall observation is that although the typical correlation is low, the range of correlations often varies widely between different pairs of scores from any two sources of information.[66]

A factor analysis produced twenty-seven factors, sixteen of which are relatively separate in meaning. Most of them appear to be clearly either science oriented or organization oriented, although a few are ambiguous. They are described briefly below, and those seven that might be considered creativity factors in at least some degree, because of the nature of their loadings, are starred.

*1. Productivity in written scientific work.
2. (This factor is rather unclear: perhaps the degree to which a scientist has recently produced a quantity of house research reports.)
3. Judgment of research quality, except for originality.
*4. Originality of work and thought.
*5. Self-perception of creativeness.
6. Number and importance of scientific and professional societies.
*7. Judgment of work output by closest associates.
*8. Judgment of the upper echelons.
*9. Supervisor's overall evaluation.
10. Social likableness, or grapevine reputation.
11. Visibility in the organization.
*12. Organizational recognition.
13. Degree of status seeking.
14. Current organizational status.
15. Contract monitoring load.
16. Total years of experience.

These and other studies demonstrate the complexities and difficulties involved in achieving reliable measures of creativity or productivity. They emphasize the need for very careful specification of the criteria which are actually employed and of the qualifications of those who apply subjective ones. They point out, too, that criteria relevant to one situation may not be appropriate to another. If a study involves several different organizations, fields, cultures, or times, further problems are encountered.

SOURCES OF VARIATION

Once individuals or groups who have made creative contributions have been identified, the next obvious step is to look for factors which may be associated with creative productions. Since eminence in science may come from effective elaboration as well as from contributing important ideas—or both—and since these behaviors are not highly correlated, this distinction needs to be kept in mind in selecting a sample.

Which of the seemingly endless variety of ways in which persons and situations differ are relevant to creativity? For convenience, sources of variation will be discussed under these headings: (1) cultural variables; (2) demographic and socioeconomic variables; (3) developmental experiences; (4) present intellectual and personality characteristics; and (5) environmental variables.

CULTURAL VARIABLES

The nature and number of creative productions shows great variation between cultures and within the same culture at different times. Kroeber has shown that science, like other creative activities of human cultures, is produced in irregular pulses, cycles, or intensive bursts of growth. Although science is accumulative, the production of it is discontinuous. This is also true of the arts and philosophy and of national growth, all of which may wax and wane almost independently, so that only approximations to relations among them all can be stated.

Science and philosophy are likely to have relations in their historic occurrence but need not have them . . . [that] a philosophy which is also a religion or is capable of developing one, can become and remain the fundamental idea-pattern of civilization, in which case scientific growths are likely to lag or be left to foreign introduction; whereas a nonreligious philosophy is likely to be accompanied by a growth of science; but also to be unable to withstand the vigorous activities of a growing organized religion, or to be delimited by an established organized one. . . . On the whole it would seem that the periods of science tend either to coincide with, or somewhat to follow, the periods of culmination in national success or the arts.[33]

In dissenting from West's proposal that scientific advance comes in recurring cycles of 164 years in length,[79] Kroeber adds:

Thus technology obviously is one of the components of civilization that tends to be strongly accumulative. Given sufficient time, it even accumulates in disregard of spatial limitation, in contrast to the arts and religions. As a creative endeavor, the history of pure science behaves much like the history of the arts, in rising intermittently and dying away. But creative science is also closely related to technology, whose higher levels are applied science. So we are apparently compelled to infer that the creative bursts of science—be they rhythmic and cyclic or not—occur on the surface of a cumulatively growing body of permanently retained scientific-technological knowledge.

Even within a national or broader culture, there are situations in which there is more creative production than in others or in which one field or another is given preeminence. Knapp noted in his surveys of the production of scientists in various American colleges that there were changes over time associated with a general cultural shift from a sectarian to a secular outlook.* He considers that science accords well with the early stages of such a shift, but that in the present later stage, "it may well be that one of our difficulties in the recruitment of scientists at the present time lies in the propensity of our culture to place a premium upon expression and competency in human relations rather than on impulse control and concern with the structure of physical things." [64]

Stein has stated,

A culture also fosters creativity to the extent that its parent-child relationships and child-rearing techniques do or do not result in the setting up of rigid boundaries in the inner personal regions. Techniques that result in excessive repression or guilt restrict internal freedom and interfere with the process of hypothesis formation. Attention must also be directed toward the broader aspects of education. For example, does the culture tolerate deviation from the traditional, the status quo, or does it insist upon conformity, whether in politics, science, or at school? Does the culture permit the individual to seek new experiences on his own, or do the bearers of culture "spoonfeed" the young so that they constantly find ready-made solutions available

---

* The issue concerns values, not church membership, which appears to be currently on the rise.

to them as they come upon a situation that is lacking in closure? Furthermore, to what extent do the adults accept or reward and thus reinforce the creative experience that the individual has had? [60]

In any one nation there are also subcultures, within which there is more creative production than in others. There have been no thorough studies of such subcultures in order to determine what are the significant concomitants of this variance. There are, however, a few studies, to be discussed in the next section, which give some leads to possible factors. A study carefully organized for the specific purpose of illuminating this aspect of the total problem would be extremely worthwhile—and extremely complex.

DEMOGRAPHIC AND SOCIOECONOMIC VARIABLES

Geographic In the United States there has been differential recruitment into science associated with geographical area. This has applied to the location of colleges sending on high percentages of graduates to advanced work in sciences, as well as to per capita representation by states in the membership of the American Association for the Advancement of Science. In all of these the Middle West and Far West lead in the production of scientists, and the South is conspicuously low. Other studies have reported conflicting results in relative percentages coming from urban and rural backgrounds, although some of the conflict may be due to changing rural patterns. It has also been noted that such variables as per capita income and expenditure per pupil are important.

In summary, regions poor in economic and cultural resources do not stimulate their inhabitants to enter a scientific career. It is obvious that in a limited educational and cultural environment even the possibility of a scientific career does not become known. Naturally, also, these regions do not contribute to the ranks of eminent scientists.[19,30,31,71,77]

Socioeconomic Background All studies of the parental family background of scientists, of eminent scientists, or of science students agree in reporting that the majority of them come from the middle or upper-middle class, with a high incidence of professional occupations among the fathers and higher than average education of the parents.[9,13,52,69] Few scientists come from wealthy homes, and very few from lower class homes. While there is evidence that differences in intellectual ability are associated with socioeconomic position, the overlapping of intelligence between levels is very great, and all of our tests are affected, to at least some degree, by background. The important thing about socioeconomic differences in this connection is not ability levels but differences in value systems and in interest patterns. There is a very close relationship between the occupation of the father and the likelihood that a high school graduate will enter college, or graduate if he does.[78] Whether or not the home has intellectual interests is a factor of importance, not only in the college attendance of the children but also of the particular college selected for the child and the occupation which he considers for himself.

Race   There have been a few studies on race and its relation to entrance into or eminence in science, and they have been in essential agreement—that in this country proportionally fewer among minority groups achieve eminence. Visher found that Puritan, other English, German, Scottish, and Scotch-Irish stock predominated among the starred scientists in *American Men of Science*.[76] American Indians have about a tenth as many chances for eminence as the population in general, but even so they have almost three times as many chances as do Negroes.[58] Barriers to accomplishment by members of racial minority groups are primarily cultural, not biological. Such groups have great disadvantages in schooling, in job opportunities, and even in obtaining equal recognition for equal achievement.

Religion   There is also good evidence for the differential production of scientists among different religious groups. All of the studies have agreed on the very low proportional contribution to scientists by Catholics and the disproportionately high contribution of Protestants.[31,38] This situation seems not to have changed since de Candolle remarked upon it in the seventeenth century. A study of those whose names were starred in the 1927 edition of *American Men of Science* and who were also included in *Who's Who in America* (an 86 percent correlation) gave the following list of denominations, in decreasing order of their contribution in proportion to church membership in the United States: Unitarians (eighty-one times their quota); Congregationalists (nine times their quota); Friends, Universalists, Episcopalians, Presbyterians, Jews, Methodists, Disciples, Baptists, Lutherans, and Roman Catholics (three of the 1,189 scientists included).[38] Davis pointed out that the ratios of eminent persons from various church groups varied directly with the socioeconomic level of the religious denominations.[15] Knapp recently failed to find religious differences among science and nonscience students,[64] but there are no further studies of this. It is not clear how much of this variation in numbers of scientists is due to the doctrinal position of the church, which is suggested by the greater freedom of inquiry granted by the churches most highly represented, and how much is due to socioeconomic concomitants.

Sex That greatly fewer numbers of women enter scientific careers—and even fewer become eminent—is well known. All studies of interests and activity preferences have shown many fewer girls with scientific interests, at all ages, with the differences between boys and girls in general interest patterns apparent as early as the first grade.[18,37,62,70,75] Girls also tend to average lower than boys in tests of mechanical aptitude and numerical and spatial abilities, although higher in verbal tests; but the differences are not great and distributions for all of these overlap almost completely and may well be chiefly culturally determined.

Even if we assume some genetic variation in aptitudes with sex, there is nevertheless much in the end result that is primarily due to the sometimes subtle differences in the ways in which boys and girls are treated by their parents and by society in our culture. They are *expected* to behave differently and the same behavior may be rewarded with approval for one and punished with disapproval for the other. Drews notes that male scientists easily find a place in the community of scholars, but that "able girls with leanings toward science do not easily find models and typically view the practising woman scientists as queer, unattractive and socially unacceptable." [17]

In the Soviet Union, women appear to be proportionally more highly represented in scientific fields. To what extent this reflects actual differences in interests and how much personal choice is involved are quite unclear. Clinical medicine, in which women are said to predominate, is, in a sense, only peripherally a scientific field.

DEVELOPMENTAL EXPERIENCES

The Home Some relevant factors in the general family background have already been discussed, but there are some special situations in the family that seem to be associated with choice of science as a career or with great success in science.

Two studies have reported a tendency for the fathers of

scientists (and other persons with high achievements) to be above the average age of paternity when the son was born. Raskin reported the fathers of scientists to average thirty-eight at the birth of the son;[48] Visher reported that a quarter of the fathers of scientists were between twenty-five and twenty-nine, and a third between thirty and thirty-five at the birth; the mothers most often between twenty-four and thirty-three.[76]

This is a little surprising in view of the repeated finding that there is a very high proportion of firstborns or eldest sons among scientists.[9,22,41,53,76] Apperley found the same thing to be true of Rhodes scholars.[2] Schachter has recently presented evidence from students which is not in accord with the above, but there is some doubt of its significance here. He also points out that, among college students in general, incidence of firstborns is disproportionately high.[56] College is a hurdle which scientists must pass at the present time, but this was not the case when Galton made his studies, nor to the same extent when Cattell and Brimhall were writing. A number of studies have reported more or less consistent personality differences associated with birth order.[39,43] Until some of the complicating issues are better understood, speculation on this point seems rather futile.

Other aspects of the general family climate may be of great importance. It appeared in my studies that the natural scientists regarded their fathers with respect but seemed not to feel great closeness to them, and a number of them had somewhat derogatory attitudes toward their mothers. Among the social scientists, on the other hand, there was a considerable residuum of parent-child conflicts, and they tended to come from homes in which the mother or a paternal grandmother was a dominant and often a driving figure.

Friend and Haggard in a study of clients of a vocational counseling service, mostly men without jobs, reported that family integration and attitude toward father are important in adjustment but make little difference in achievement. Antagonism for the mother, however, is positively associated with both.[21]

It seems quite evident that family flexibility in permitting or rigidity in forbidding any kind of exploratory activity of the young child, intellectual as well as manual, may have a considerable effect in promoting or inhibiting creativity in him. Terman noted the beneficent effect of breadth of interests in the parents of his gifted children.[69]

McClelland and his associates, in a study of achievement motivation, have reported data which indicate a positive relationship between achievement motivation and emphasis on independent individual development in the family.[40]

Two studies, Roe on biologists and Bell on mathematicians, have noted a high incidence of loss of a parent at an early age. This may have had the effect of decreasing dependence upon others, if not of directly increasing independence.[5,49]

It must be said that relationships in this whole general area have been very little studied and that most of the suggestions come from studies not designed for this specific purpose. They do have, however, considerable psychological consistency, and it would seem that studies specifically investigating these variables could be extremely fruitful. A number of studies have noted that biographical items are among the most effective predictors, but replications have seldom been as successful. Nevertheless, this is one of the most promising approaches to prediction, as noted by Taylor, Smith, and Ghiselin.[66,67]

There are, of course, many individual exceptions, but in general those who become scientists tend to excel at school from their early years.[7,14] It has also been noted that those who achieve eminence were frequently top students in college.[68] Other special achievements of youthful scientists have been pointed out by Cox,[14] Edgerton and Britt,[19] MacCurdy,[41] and Terman.[69] On the other hand, not all who become great scientists give any indication of it in childhood or adolescence, even though many, if not most, do.

Life histories of individual natural scientists indicate that the typical scientist was somewhat late in developing in some respects. He was not much interested in club or group activities, except in the few instances in which there were active science clubs. He tended to spend a great deal of time following up his own interests in a rather systematic way, usually by himself but sometimes with one or two other boys of like mind. He was likely to be very shy and withdrawn socially, not to date until well into college, and was likely to be an avid reader. This general, non-person-oriented attitude appears very early and undergoes very little change.[52,69] Social scientists follow a very different course, being from early days much involved with other persons in a variety of ways, but also being avid readers.

Some differences in developing interests are associated

with the field of science. In general few were gadgeteers except those who went into physical science fields; few were interested in natural history except those who went into biology; but an early interest in chemistry was found in both physical and biological scientists.[53]

INTELLECTUAL AND PERSONALITY CHARACTERISTICS

Intelligence Numerous studies of undergraduate and graduate students in science have indicated that high general intelligence is characteristic of them.[12,Bloom 64,81] A few studies of scientists themselves have also shown this to be the case.[10,59,69]

Studies utilizing traditional factors of intelligence—verbal, quantitative, and spatial—have brought out differences between fields, although a high level of all of these factors is characteristic of most.[8,25,51,55] In general, social scientists and the more theoretically oriented of the physical and biological scientists are relatively higher on verbal tests than experimental physicists or engineers. On the other hand, these latter groups are relatively higher on quantitative tests, along with the theoretical physicists. Tests of spatial and mechanical factors have given rather conflicting results.

The relationship of general intelligence (or any of these factors) to creativity is another matter, however. It seems now to be the consensus that while a relatively high—perhaps about IQ 120—minimum level of intelligence is needed for scientific contributions, either inventive or elaborative, beyond that level other factors are of more importance, and possession of that or higher intelligence is by no means evidence of high creative potential.

Guilford and others have conducted investigations of the relation of aptitude to nonaptitude factors with particular reference to creativity, finding very low correlations between them.[23]

Getzels and Jackson identified a group of high school students in the top 20 percent of their like-sexed age peers on creativity measures but not in the top 20 percent on IQ measures and another group in the top 20 percent on IQ but not on creativity measures. They found that the scholastic achievement of the high creatives was as superior to the generality as was that of the high intelligents.[66] Torrance, in eight partial replications of this study with elementary school, high school, and graduate students, found the same results in six groups. In the other two, the high intelligents had better scholastic records, but in these two schools there was both a somewhat more normal distribution of talent and a greater emphasis in the teaching on traditional, memory-oriented procedures.[73] The implications of these findings for our selection procedures for scholarships and so forth are important and obvious.

Getzels and Jackson interpret their results in the light of Guilford's findings on the difference between divergent and convergent modes of thinking. (Divergent thinking is defined as "generation of information from given information, where the emphasis is upon variety of output from the same source." Convergent thinking is defined as "generation of information from given information, where the emphasis is upon achieving unique or conventionally accepted or best outcomes.") The work by Guilford and Merrifield on the structure of intellect has resulted in a conception of intelligence as factorially much more complex than previous studies had indicated, and they now propose a cubic model, the dimensions referring to *Operations*, with five classes, such as *cognition* and *memory; Products*, with six classes, such as *relations* and *transformations;* and *Contents* with four classes, such as *semantic* and *symbolic*. That is, five kinds of operations may be performed on four classes of contents to result in six kinds of products. Fifty-three of the 120 factors indicated by the model have been identified and corresponding tests constructed. It is Guilford's belief that not all of these factors are involved in creative thinking, but that some are of particular importance. These are the abilities in the general category of divergent thinking—fluency, adaptive and spontaneous flexibility, originality, and elaboration—and those in the transformation layer, involving changes in existing or known information or in its use. He points out, however, that "the weight to be given to any factors in connection with particular instances or classes of invention is a matter of empirical investigation." [24]

There are no replications of Guilford's work and no other studies of the structure of intellect which are remotely comparable to his in extent, complexity, and sophistication. The sheer number of factors involved is rather staggering in its implications for genetic intepretation, for any kind of selection, and like possibilities. Since Guilford has now succeeded in pulling the whole together into a well-conceptualized structure, it may well receive considerably more general acceptance. Guilford's tests were developed to coincide with hypotheses regarding the nature of the creative process, but as yet there have been no studies which could demonstrate whether or not creative persons are in fact consistently high in the tests believed to be related to creativity. Allen, Guilford, and Merrifield have reported a study of the opinions of thirty-five research scientists and engineers and of fifty nonscientists regarding the relative importance for scientific work of twenty-eight of these factors. The subjects were given nontechnical definitions of each factor, with an example of the mental activity believed involved, and asked to rank them for their importance to the creative scientist. Rank correlation was .87. The scientists themselves rated factors in the product category of transformations highest, particularly the redefinition factors, which are also in the convergent-production category. Divergent-production factors were not ranked as high as the authors had expected.[1]

Imagery   Studies of imagery are out of style at the present time among psychologists, but there is evidence in one study of rather sharp differences in preferred types of imagery. Biologists and experimental physicists seem to rely quite heavily upon visual imagery, which may be of a very elaborate sort. Theoretical physicists and social scientists tend to use auditory-verbal imagery predominantly. All groups studied reported a considerable amount of imageless thinking, particularly at crucial points.[50]

Some recent studies on the electroencephalograph and imagery have shown a relationship between the amount of alpha rhythm present and the extent to which visual imagery is used during thought. It is suggested that these differences are related to differences in verbal, as opposed to practical, intelligence.[45]

Gray-Walters, in a personal communication, suggests that there may be a relationship between variability of brain rhythms and the amount of creativity manifested by the individual, but this has not been tested experimentally. It is a most intriguing suggestion, and if it can be demonstrated, would open many possibilities.

Bartlett, in a discussion of the relationship between visual imagery and thought, suggests that visualists probably use more images than are really necessary. Perhaps some may be irrelevant to the immediate purpose and yet spark new discoveries. This could be thought of as a special variety of preconscious thought.[4]

Interests, Values, and Types Interest tests, such as those of Strong and Kuder, show rather clear differences between scientists and nonscientists and among scientists of different specialties. Most of the studies with interest inventories on tests have been made with students. These are reviewed in Super and Bachrach and summarized as follows:

The literature on scientific interest shows that this type of interest develops relatively early in life, that extremes of socio-economic status tend to inhibit or prevent the development of interests which are appropriate to scientific aptitudes, that scientific interest is characterized initially by interest in concrete things or activities and is relatively stable, that successful science students show interest profiles similar to those of successful workers in science fields, that the various fields of science have distinctive but related interests, and that the interests, while not predictive of success in these fields, are predictive of occupational choice and stability.[63]

Highly creative men tend to get high scores on femininity scales, and highly creative women on masculinity scales. Such men are more sensitive than most and have higher aesthetic interests; such women are more interested in things and ideas than other women. Highly creative groups tend to get relatively high scores on both theoretic and aesthetic values.

MacKinnon has reported that the Myer-Briggs Type Indicator * differentiates sharply between creative and noncreative groups with respect to sensation vs. intuitive attitudes. On this test, 75 percent of the general population show a preference for sensation, but 100 percent of architects, 100 percent of mathematicians, 93 percent of research scientists, and 90 percent of writers in their creative groups showed a preference for intuition.[42]

Personality A number of fairly recent studies using different techniques, different samplings, and having somewhat different purposes have attacked the problem of the personality characteristics of creative scientists, in contrast to those of the generality or to such groups as scholars or administrators.[3,10,42,52,McClelland 64] It is quite striking, then, that there is almost no conflict in the results. While most of the studies are not

---

* This is a test designed to assess individuals with respect to the personality types described by Jung: judging vs. perceptive attitudes; extroverted vs. introverted orientation; sensation vs. intuition; thinking vs. feeling.

directly comparable to any of the others, the psychological interpretations are in close accord or dovetail very satisfactorily. These are summarized under general groups of characteristics below.

Creative persons are unusually open to experience. They are particularly observant and often see things in unusual ways. They are extremely curious. Their willingness to see what is there applies to perceptions of self as well as to the outside world, making it possible for them to admit unconventional thoughts, accept and reconcile apparent opposites, and be tolerant of ambiguities.* Disorder does not too greatly dismay them, but they like to be able to resolve it. They prefer complexity and manage to come to an aesthetic ordering of experience.

They are highly independent in judgment, thought, and action, and they need and assume autonomy. They are willing to take a calculated risk, provided that more than chance is involved and that people are not involved. They are self-reliant and not subject to group standards and control. This may lead to unconventional behavior as well as to originality and unconventionality of thought. They do not accept authority on its own terms. This originality and unconventionality do not make for the stereotype of "adjustment," for organization men, or for all-American boys. One of the most disturbing aspects of the Getzels and Jackson study [66] and of other studies of Torrance [73] are the findings that the highly creative are definitely not preferred by their teachers or their peers and that sanctions are frequently invoked against them, though admittedly they often provoke them. Jex and Merrill found that the ability to get high scores on ingenuity tests was antagonistic to whatever is involved in high ratings of teachers by supervisors or principals.[28]

They are high, but perhaps not extremely high, in ego strength, and their superegos are not compulsive. They are capa-

---

* A quotation from Thurber, commenting on the admonition to "Be a guardian not an usher at the portal of your thought," is particularly descriptive: "What I am like at the portal of my thought is one of those six-foot-six ushers who used to stand around the lobby of the Hippodrome during performances of 'Jumbo.' . . . I am *all* usher as far as the portal of my thought goes, terribly usher. But I am unlike the 'Jumbo' ushers or any other ushers in that I show any and all thoughts to their seats whether they have tickets or not. They can be under-age and without their parents, or they can be completely cockeyed or they can show up without a stitch on; I let them in and show them to the best seats in my mind (the ones in the royal arena and the gold boxes). . . . Thoughts like that can spot the usher type of mind a mile away and they seek it out as tramps seek out the back doors of generous farm wives." [72]

ble of considerable discipline and of great perseverance. They tend to be rather dominant.

They are markedly preoccupied with things and ideas and not with people. (This applies to some social scientists, though not to most.) They dislike emotionally toned preoccupations outside of their own field.

They are not gregarious nor talkative. (This also does not apply to social scientists.) They are especially sensitive to interpersonal aggression and have marked distaste for interpersonal controversy in any form. They prefer to deal with disturbing instinctual drives by repressing them or avoiding situations which arouse them.

Their notable persistence indicates the presence of strong motivation, but analysis of the sources has not progressed very far. This is one of the most important factors contributing to the production of a scientist, and it must vary from one scientist to another. There has been considerable discussion of the probability of "neurotic" sources. I am sure that the motivation has a neurotic basis in many instances; I am equally sure that it need not always have, but this negative is much harder to document. Kubie has stated,

[Not only does] a scientist's ability to endure the prolonged frustration and uncertainties of scientific research depend on neurotic components in his personality (both masked and overt), but also there are significant relationships between masked neurotic components in the personality of an apparently normal scientist, and such things as (a) the field of work which he chooses; (b) the problems within that field which he chooses to investigate; (c) the clarity with which he habitually uses his native capacity for logical thinking; (d) the ways in which he attacks scientific problems; (e) the scientific causes which he espouses; (f) the controversies in which he becomes entangled and how he fights; and (g) the joy or sorrow which he derived from the work itself and also from his ultimate success or failure. Thus over the intervening years I have seen men of imagination and erudition whose scientific lives were nonetheless baffled and unproductive, and also men with lesser gifts who seemed to function freely, creatively, and productively; scientists who were happy in spite of failure, and others who became depressed in spite of acknowledged and recognized success.[34,35]

Many have successfully extrapolated a personal problem into a problem to be studied scientifically. I see no cause for dismay in this—in fact, it seems to me to be one of the major inventions of the species.

There has been some discussion of the possible deleterious effects for creativity if psychotherapy modifies a neurotic structure that may be involved in an individual instance. It seems to be the general opinion that creativity is more likely to be enhanced by successful therapy than not.[6,20,27,32,36]

ENVIRONMENTAL FACTORS

The phrase "environmental factors" refers to conditions which are facilitating or inhibiting of creativity. These may be specific for the individual, in whatever setting he is working, or specific for the setting, and applying, more or less equally, to all scientists in that setting. In the latter case, particularly, it should be possible to find some generalizations which would apply to most, if not all, settings of the same type.

Individuals differ in such matters as the way in which they react to low, moderate, or high degrees of pressure; to different kinds of pressure; in the ease with which they can be distracted; in the extent to which interaction with others is helpful or not; and in numerous other ways relevant to their productivity. Situations differ in such things as facilities, pressures, and degree of autonomy and rewards. They also differ in the role demands and expectations which the scientist meets. These concern not only his research work as such, but also his role as a professional, his role as an employee, and his general social role.[Stein 64]

Studies in Organizations Pelz[64] and others at the National Institutes of Health found two uncorrelated orientations in a group of research scientists. One, "science orientation," consisted of importance attached to the opportunity to contribute to basic scientific knowledge, to freedom for originality, and to use of present skills and abilities. The other, "institutional orientation," stressed such things as having an important job, associating with high-level people, and belonging to an organization having prestige in the lay community. Science orientation correlated well with a measure of performance based chiefly on peer and supervisory judgments; institutional orientation did not. Since Shepard did not find such a relationship in industrial laboratories (by analogy—he used different techniques),[57] Pelz suggests that in industry it may be necessary to have both scientific and institutional motivation to be successful in the eyes of the company. This would accord well with Stein's analyses of the roles of the industrial chemist.[64]

Their NIH investigations of possible relations between performance and supervision indicated that these would be different with younger and older groups. They found, in the younger group, that the highest performance occurred when there was lots of interaction with the supervisor but where the younger man had some freedom to make decisions. In the NIH group there did not seem to be any simple tendency for high-producing scientists to have a stronger identification with their immediate group, as Pelz had found in some industrial studies.

The relationship depended upon who was head of the group. If the scientists had a strong sense of belonging to the immediate group and the chief of that group was a relatively competent person, then the subordinates' performance was high. But if the scientists had high identification with the immediate group and the chief was a relatively mediocre man, their performance was low.[64]

It would seem likely that high identification with a problem rather than with a group should relate to performance, but this has not been investigated.

Pelz then looked for relationships between performance and relations with colleagues, using two measures of the latter: amount of contact with five most significant nonsupervisory colleagues and similarity in terms of value orientation. Neither measure alone was related to performance, but jointly they were.

For those scientists who are very similar to their colleagues, having contact only once or twice a week is the point of maximum performance; more frequent contact than that is associated with a decline in performance. But if the scientist associates with people who are quite different from him in terms of values, then daily contact is associated with the highest performance. . . . One interpretation is that if a scientist is thrown in with a group of dissimilar people, he needs a lot of contact in order to bridge the communications gap. Whereas, if he is thrown in with like-minded colleagues, he doesn't need so much contact; too much group activity, in fact, may be a distraction in this individualistic setting. On the other hand, Shepard found in industrial laboratories that in general the more contact the better. Even in basic research groups within an industrial setting, he found more contact associated with higher performance. There is an apparent contradiction between the two sets of results; but I think it may be resolved by more knowledge of the nature of the task and the goals of the organization. One may hypothesize that in both settings some interaction with colleagues is better than none; but the optimum—the amount of contact needed for best performance—may be lower in individualistic than in a cooperative atmosphere.[64]

Sprecher, investigating the meaning of creativity and working with engineering personnel in a large industrial organization, suggests that many factors not ordinarily thought important affect ratings of creativity. He found that measurements of work-habit characteristics were important variables and that work-sample criteria may be the most useful and predictable measures of creativity at present.[66]

Taylor has reported studies in the Navy Electronics Laboratory at San Diego and at the Naval Ordnance Test Station at China Lake. He used checklist rating scales for scoring the subjects (103 engineers and scientists at NEL and 66 physicists at NOTS) on creativity in research-and-development work and seven-step rating scales for six variables on productivity and a number of standard tests. Correlations between creativity as rated by the immediate supervisor (which proved more satisfactory than combining them with ratings by a secondary supervisor) were from .03 for the Strong to .36 for the AIR Test for Selecting Research Personnel. All correlations except for the Strong and Concept Mastery are significant at .05 level. The group at NOTS were also given the AIR, and correlations of +.31 were obtained with both originality and quality of work.[67] This test is essentially a work-sample test; Sprecher also found a work sample the best predictor.[66]

At NEL, ninety-four men filled out a biographical questionnaire. Of the fifty items, seven showed a significant relation to creativity, but these results did not hold when the questionnaire was given to the physicists at NOTS. Some further checking would seem desirable, since it is highly probable that the scoring developed for the electronics engineers might not be appropriate for the physicists. In addition, the smaller number of the latter reduced the sensitivity of the significance test.

Smith has reported an extensive study on favorable and unfavorable working conditions for scientists at two government research centers. The concern was with the total contribution of the scientist, not specifically with his creativity. The most frequent and apparently most significant statements made in long, unstructured interviews are the following:[66]

Unfavorable conditions:

Instability of the budget.

Conflict between demands of management and research activities.

Inadequacies in supportive groups and procedures.

Inadequacies in compensation and other attractions.

Lack of professional internship for young scientists.

Poor communication with scientists working elsewhere on related problems.

Inadequacy of physical facilities.

Dearth of suitable recognition.

Insufficient long-range planning in the total scientific program.

Interference between contract monitoring and regular research activity.

Inefficiency in selection and placement programs.

Lack of personnel counseling for scientists.

Favorable conditions:

Certain individual freedoms in the conduct of their research.

Intellectual challenges of the work.

Location and certain facilities.

Relative stability of civil service employment.

Encouragement of continual training.

Studies of Individuals Discussions of the situations within which one individual may do better or poorer work or be more or less creative have not, to my knowledge, rested upon any controlled experiments. They are observational, reportorial, or speculative, which is not to say that they are negligible. It does, however, at the very least suggest the considerable need for more controlled observation.

Among theoretical discussions, one by Carl Rogers is based on his experiences as a therapist. He believes that all persons have creative potential, and the motivation for it is man's tendency to actualize himself, conceiving of this tendency, in effect, as a basic drive. Conditions within an individual which are conducive to constructive creativity are openness to experience, an internal locus of evaluation, and the ability to toy with elements and concepts. These are fostered by external conditions which provide psychological safety and psychological freedom.[54]

Mooney suggests that there are three cultural blocks to our acceptance of ourselves as creative beings: the increasing interdependencies of human beings; the shift to man of primary control, resulting in his concentration upon outside enemies because he cannot yet face himself as his primary controlling agent; and the higher cultural evaluation of outward directedness.[44]

More concretely, the American Psychological Association report on psychologists suggests that while some persons would produce regardless of the requirements of the job and others would not produce under almost any circumstances, probably the largest group are persons described as follows:

[They] may be expected to make substantial research contributions when environmental factors are optimal, but to make little contribution when pressures are toward service or administrative activities. As we examine what the factors are that have this kind of differential influence, it is interesting to note how important the activities of colleagues are, and the availability of time, apparatus, and subjects, and how relatively unimportant financial support is as a factor related to research productivity.[11]

On an even more concrete level, I have gone through the records of my interviews with scientists and culled their comments on situations, both internal and external, which seemed to affect their creative productiveness. For the most part, they seem to do somewhat better under very moderate degrees of pressure of rather impersonal kinds. Such things as a date by which a certain paper has to be ready, for example, may be helpful. But very few of them could work well under any serious degree of pressure without great effort. The most common group of comments have to do with the necessity for time and privacy.

All of this implies that they work as individuals, not as members of groups, and although a number of them feel that talking things over with colleagues may be helpful, in the sense that it forces better organization of their thinking, this is not seriously important to any of this group. All of them said that they did not find teamwork effective.

THE CREATIVE PROCESS

From all of the foregoing it would appear that this process is not unique to a few individuals possessing only one or a limited number of specific capacities. Rather, it would seem that this is one of the ways in which humans interact with their environment, perhaps the most intricate way of all. It would appear to be a form of behavior of which all normal humans are capable to some degree, but one which is clearly manifested more often and more effectively by some persons than by others and more easily under some circumstances than under others. Such sources of variation as are known to us have been discussed. But what is the process itself?

Certainly it is akin to other modes of thought—indeed to speak of different modes of thought is probably marking off arbitrary boundaries on a natural continuum. This is a necessary procedure in analysis, however, and it introduces serious difficulties only when the categories become conceptually reified.[67] The creative process is probably closest to problem solving, but it differs from it in a number of ways. In problem solving, the immediate goal is a specific one, and logical and orderly modes of approach are appropriate—if not always used. In the creative process there is no such clear goal as a rule, and illogical modes of thought are common. Newell, Shaw, and Simon consider that "creative activity appears simply to be a special class of problem-solving activity characterized by novelty, unconventionality, persistence, and difficulty in problem formulation." [46] A major differentiation is the extent of the involvement of the whole person; in the creative process this is very great, and noncognitive and emotional elements loom large, but they are a barrier to effective problem solving. (The whole range of scientific thinking embraces both of these, of course, but we are here concerned with discovery and invention rather than with elaboration.)

Some studies of the process have analyzed it into a series of more or less discrete steps, but perhaps more advance can be made if it is considered as essentially a single action. Among artists, scientists, and others for whom creative production is a way of life, it emerges from a background of absorption in a topic and begins in a state of "imaginative muddled suspense." As

Ghiselin has put it, "the first stirrings and advances of even the most strictly intellectual creative achievements appear to be realized primarily in sensory or passional terms, or in both." [64] There seems to be a vague sort of manipulative play with incommunicable entities—visual, muscular, rarely if at all verbal—in this stage. There is no known technique for speeding up or calling forth the coalescence of all this into a new configuration. It usually comes without an immediate voluntary effort and almost invariably during a moment of dispersed attention, but conscious efforts to disperse attention to permit or facilitate this resolution have not been successful. Too intensive a concentration of conscious attention upon the problem seems to prevent that recourse to the depths of the person that is required. The apprehension of this new configuration, often called the moment of insight, typically comes suddenly and quite completely, although not necessarily so. The experience of insight may be a profoundly moving one, with a sense of great self-realization and intense aesthetic gratification. It is usually accompanied by feelings of certainty which may or may not prove to be valid. In science, insights must be subjected to verification.

Since the activities preceding the emergence of this new configuration are largely not fully conscious, study of them directly is remarkably difficult. Psychoanalytic theory distinguishes between primary and secondary processes of thinking and assigns the inventive phase largely to the primary process, elaboration and verification to the secondary process. Primary-process thinking is nonlogical, and makes use of such mechanisms as are common in dreaming—condensation, displacement, symbolization, and so on. When such ideas first arise in consciousness, they may take various forms—fragments of words or visual images, schematic patterns, a sense of relationship. The secondary process is logical and rational and under voluntary control. [47]

The very creative person is one who can permit himself indulgence in the primitive modes of thought of the primary process, and who has the ability to return easily to rational thought. Persons who are able to do this, who come up with many original ideas, may not also be equally interested in, or capable of, the disciplined and critical procedures required for logical development or evaluation of their ideas. They are "idea men," leaving the sometimes slow and laborious procedures of verification to others. There are also those whose chief contributions in science—and these contributions can be major—are seldom tinged by primary-process activities, but who have spent great effort and much time on the arduous work of elaboration. Finally, there are those who are capable of both to a high degree. These are very few and very precious.

If it is true, however, as I believe, that there is real creative potential in all human beings and that our cultural institutions, rooted in ancient misconceptions of the nature of man and his place in the universe, are enormously more effective in repressing it than encouraging it, our problem is not just to find the people who have somehow been able to resist these pressures. It is also to find ways to change the cultural climate.

REFERENCES

1. Allen, M. S., Guilford, J. P., and Merrifield, P. R. *Rep. Psychol. Lab.*, 25 (1960).

2. Apperly, F. L. "A Study of American Rhodes Scholars," *Journal of Heredity*, 30:493–95 (1939).

3. Barron, F. "Originality in Relation to Personality and Intellect," *Journal of Personality*, 25:730–42 (1957).

4. Bartlett, R. J. "Does the Psychogalvanic Phenomenon Indicate Emotion?" *British Journal of Psychology*, 18:23 (1927).

5. Bell, E. T. *Men of Mathematics*. New York: Simon & Schuster, 1937.

6. Bellak, L. "Creativity: Some Random Notes to a Systematic Consideration," *Journal of Projective Techniques*, 22:363–80 (1958).

7. Brandwein, P. F. *The Gifted Student as Future Scientist*. New York: Harcourt, Brace & Co., 1955.

8. Castore, G. F. *A Screening and Selection Battery for Prospective Physicists and Chemical Engineers*. Unpublished doctoral dissertation. Pennsylvania State College, 1948.

9. Cattell, J. M., and Brimhall, D. R. *American Men of Science*. Third edition. Garrison, N.Y.: Science, 1921.

10. Cattell, R. B., and Drevdahl, J. E. "A Comparison of the Personality Profile (16 P. F.) of Eminent Researchers with that of Eminent Teachers and Administrators, and of the General Population," *British Journal of Psychology*, 46:248–61 (1955).

11. Clark, K. *America's Psychologists*. Washington, D.C.: American Psychological Association, 1957.

12. Cole, C. C., Jr. *Encouraging Scientific Talent*. College Entrance Examination Board (mimeographed), 1955.

13. Coppersmith, S., Church, C., and Markowitz, J. EPA (mimeographed), 1960.

14. Cox, C. S. *Genetic Studies of Genius. (Early Mental Traits of Three Hundred Geniuses. Vol. II.)* Stanford: Stanford University Press, 1926.

15. Davis, B. "Eminence and Level of Social Origin," *American Journal of Sociology*, 59:11–18 (1953).

16. Dennis, W. "Bibliographies of Eminent Scientists," *Scientific Monthly*, 79:180–83 (1954).

17. Drews, E. M. Yearbook of Education. In press.

18. Edgerton, H. A., and Britt, S. H. "Sex Differences in the Science Talent Test," *Science*, 100:192–93 (1944).

19. ———. "Science Talent Search in Relation to Education and Economic Indices," *School and Society,* 63:172–75 (1946).

20. Fenichel, O. *The Psychoanalytic Theory of Neurosis.* New York: W. W. Norton & Company, Inc., 1945.

21. Friend, J. G., and Haggard, E. A. "Work Adjustment in Relation to Family Background," *Applied Psychology Monographs,* 16 (1948).

22. Galton, F. *English Men of Science, Their Nature and Nurture.* London: The Macmillan Co., 1874.

23. Guilford, J. P., Christensen, P. R., Frick, J. W., and Merrifield, P. R. *Rep. Psychol. Lab.,* 20 (1957).

24. Guilford, J. P., and Merrifield, P. R. *Rep. Psychol. Lab.,* 24 (1960).

25. Harmon, L. R. *Ability Patterns in Seven Science Fields.* Technical Report No. 10, Washington: National Research Council, 1955.

26. Holland, J. L. "Undergraduate Origins of American Students," *Science,* 126:433–37 (1957).

27. Hulbeck, C. R. *American Journal of Psychoanalysis,* 5:49 (1945).

28. Jex, F. B., and Merrill, R. M. *An Evaluation of the Joint Academic-Year Institute, University of Utah, 1957–58.* University of Utah Research Monograph. Education, Vol. I and II. Salt Lake City: University of Utah Press, 1958.

29. Knapp, R. H. *The Non-Intellective Determinants of Scientific Interest.* Unpublished mimeographed report. Wesleyan University. No date.

30. Knapp, R. H., and Greenbaum, J. J. *The Younger American Scholar, His Collegiate Origins.* Chicago: University of Chicago Press, 1953.

31. Knapp, R. H., and Goodrich, J. B. *Origins of American Scientists.* Chicago: University of Chicago Press, 1952.

32. Kriss, E. *Psychoanalytic Explorations in Art.* New York: International University Press, 1952.

33. Kroeber, A. L. *Configurations of Culture Growth.* Berkeley: University of California Press, 1944.

34. Kubie, L. S. "Some Unsolved Problems of the Scientific Career," *American Scientist,* 41:596–613 (1953).

35. ———. "Some Unsolved Problems of the Scientific Career II," *American Scientist,* 42:104–12 (1954).

36. ———. *Neurotic Distortion of the Creative Process.* Lawrence, Kans.: University of Kansas Press, 1958.

37. Kuder, G. F. *Manual to the Kuder Preference Record.* Chicago: Science Research Associates, 1946.

38. Lehman, H. C., and Witty, P. A. "Scientific Eminence and Church Membership," *Scientific Monographs,* 33:544–49 (1931).

39. McArthur, C. "Personalities of First and Second Children." *Psychiatry,* 19:47 (1956).

40. McClelland, D. C., Atkinson, J. W., Clark, R. A., and Lowell, E. L. *The Achievement Motive.* New York: Appleton-Century-Crofts, 1953.

41. MacCurdy, R. D. "Characteristics of Superior Science Students and Their Own Sub-groups," *Science Education,* 40:3–24 (1956).

42. MacKinnon, D. W. Colloquium on Problems and Responsibilities of U.S. Colleges in the Research for Talented Students, College Entrance Examination Board, New York, N. Y. (1959).

43. Martin, A. M. *The Oldest and the Youngest Child.* New York: Auxiliary Council to the Association for the Advancement of Psychoanalysis, 1945.

44. Mooney, R. L. "Cultural Blocks and Creative Possibilities," *Educational Leadership,* 13:273–78 (1956).

45. Mundy-Castle, A. C. "Electrophysicological Correlates of Intelligence," *Journal of Personality,* 26:184–99 (1958).

46. Newell, A., Shaw, J. C., and Simon, H. A. *The Processes of Creative Thinking.* Santa Monica, Calif.: Rand Corporation, 1958.

47. Rapaport, D. *Organization and Pathology of Thought*. New York: Columbia University Press, 1951.

48. Raskin, E. "Comparison of Scientific and Literary Ability: A Bibliographical Study of Eminent Scientists and Men of Letters of the Nineteenth Century," *Journal of Abnormal and Social Psychology*, **31**:20–35 (1936).

49. Roe, A. "A Psychological Study of Eminent Biologists," *Psychological Monographs*, **65** (No. 14, 1951).

50. ———. "A Study of Imagery in Research Scientists," *Journal of Personality*, **19**:459–70 (1951).

51. ———. "A Psychologist Examines 64 Eminent Scientists," *Scientific American*, **187**(5):21–25 (1952).

52. ———. *The Making of a Scientist*. New York: Dodd, Mead & Co., 1952.

53. ———. "A Psychological Study of Eminent Psychologists and Anthropologists, and a Comparison with Biological and Physical Scientists," *Psychological Monographs*, **67** (No. 2, 1953).

54. Rogers, C. R. "Toward a Theory of Creativity," *ETC: A Review of General Semantics*, **11**:249–60 (1954).

55. Schultz, M., and Angoff, W. H. Educational Testing Service Research Bulletin RB, 54–15 (May 25, 1954).

56. Shachter, S. *The Psychology of Affiliation: Experimental Studies of the Sources of Gregariousness*. Stanford, Calif.: Stanford University Press, 1959.

57. Shepard, H. A. "Creativity in R/D Teams," *Research & Engineering*, **11**:10–12 (1956).

58. Smith, M. "The Racial Origins of Eminent Personages," *Journal of Abnormal and Social Psychology*, **32**:63–73 (1937).

59. ———. "Eminent Men," *Scientific Monthly*, **48**:554–62 (1939).

60. Stein, M. I. "Creativity and Culture," *Journal of Psychology*, **36**:311–22 (1953).

61. Stringham, E. J. D. *Outline of Patent Law and Guide to Digests*. Madison, Wis.: Pacot Publications, 1937.

62. Strong, E. K. *Vocational Interests of Men and Women*. Stanford, Calif.: Stanford University Press, 1943.

63. Super, D., and Bachrach, P. *Scientific Careers and Vocational Development Theory*. New York: Teachers College, Columbia University, 1957.

64. Taylor, C. W. (ed.) *The 1955 University of Utah Research Conference on the Identification of Creative Scientific Talent*. Salt Lake City: University of Utah Press, 1956. Includes: Bloom, S., "Report on Creativity Research at the University of Utah," p. 182; Ghiselin, B., "The Creative Process and Its Relation to the Identification of Creative Talent," p. 195; Guilford, J. P., "The Relation of Intellectual Factors to Creative Thinking in Science," p. 69; Knapp, R. H., "Demographic Cultural and Personality Attributes of Scientists," p. 204; McClelland, D. C., "The Calculated Risk: An Aspect of Scientific Performance," p. 96; McPherson, J. H., "A Proposal for Establishing Ultimate Criteria for Measuring Creative Output," p. 62; Pelz, D. C., "Relationships Between Measures of Scientific Performance and Other Variables," p. 53; Stein, M. I., "A Transactional Approach to Creativity," p. 171.

65. ———. *The Second (1957) University of Utah Research Conference on the Identification of Creative Scientific Talent*. Salt Lake City: University of Utah Press, 1958. Includes: Harmon, L. R., "Development of a Criterion of Science Competence," p. 82; Taylor, D. W., "Variables Related to Creativity and Productivity Among Men in Two Research Laboratories," p. 20.

66. ———. *The Third (1959) University of Utah Research Conference on the Identification of Creative Scientific Talent*. Salt Lake City: Uni-

versity of Utah Press, 1959. Includes: Getzels, J. W., and Jackson, P. W., "The Highly Intelligent and the Highly Creative Adolescent: A Summary of Some Research Findings"; Guilford, J. P., "Intellectual Resources and Their Value as Seen by Creative Scientists," p. 128; Smith, W. R., "Favorable and Unfavorable Working Conditions Reported by Scientists at Two Research Centers," p. 250; Sprecher, T. B., "A Proposal for Identifying the Meaning of Creativity," p. 29; Sprecher, T. B. (Chairman) Committee Report on Criteria of Creativity; Taylor, C. M., and Ghiselin, B., "Analyses of Multiple Criteria of Creativity and Productivity of Scientists," p. 5.

67. Taylor, D. W. "Thinking and Creativity" in Har E. Ed. *Fundamentals of Psychology: The Psychology of Thinking.* New York: New York Academy of Science, Vol. 91, 1960.

68. Terman, L. M. "The Discovery and Encouragement of Exceptional Talent," *American Psychologist, 9:* 221–30 (1954).

69. ———. "Scientists and Non-Scientists in a Group of 800 Gifted Men," *Psychological Monographs,* 68 (No. 7, 1954).

70. Terman, L. M., and Miles, C. C. *Sex and Personality.* New York: McGraw-Hill, 1936.

71. Thorndike, E. L. *Annals of the New York Academy of Science, 39:* 213 (1939).

72. Thurber, J. *Let Your Mind Alone.* New York: Grosset and Dunlap, 1935.

73. Torrance, E. P. Research Memo BER–60–18. Bureau of Educational Research, College of Education, University of Minnesota (1960).

74. Torrance, E. P. (ed.) *Creativity Proceedings of the Second Minnesota Conference on Gifted Children.* Center for Continuation Study, University of Minnesota, 1959.

75. Tyler, L. E. "The Relationship of Interest to Abilities and Reputation Among First-grade Children," *Educational and Psychological Measurement, 11:*255 (1951).

76. Visher, S. S. *Scientists Starred in 1903–43 American Men of Science.* Baltimore: Johns Hopkins University Press, 1947.

77. ———. "Environmental Backgrounds of Leading American Scientists," *American Sociological Review,* 13:65–72 (1948).

78. Warner, W. L., Havighurst, R. J., and Loeb, M. G. *Who Shall Be Educated?* New York: Harper & Bros., 1944.

79. West, S. S. "The Hypothesis of Slow Cyclical Variation of Creativity," *American Journal of Sociology,* 63:143–51 (1957).

80. Westbrook, J. H. "Identifying Significant Research," *Science, 132:* 1229–34 (1960).

81. Wolfle, D., and Oxtoby, T. "Distributions of Ability of Students Specializing in Different Fields," *Science,* 116:311–14 (1952).

CREATIVE SCIENCE

Ellis Blade

INTRODUCTION

In thinking about creativity in science, and the way scientific ideas are produced, I found myself faced with several related questions, typified by, What is creativity? What is science? and, How is science related to other human endeavors? Without supposing that any of these questions could be answered very completely in a few pages, I have recorded here some of my thoughts. Science, I find, has gone through an evolution, whose traceable history goes back at least twenty-five centuries to ancient Greece, and each epoch has contributed something to it. Against this background one can surmise that the nature of science is in a state of change today just as it has been in the past. I am not speaking here of the subject matter of science, whose change over this period is quite apparent, but of the methods of science and the attitude of society toward it, and the relations of scientists to the people at large and with power figures in society. I presume that science in this fundamental respect will continue to evolve, responsive to political-social-economic forces, which themselves are rushing headlong toward new configurations.

In this discussion I have found it convenient to regard science in two aspects. Viewed as a compendium of information about the world, increasing and changing with time, science is a part of recorded history. On the other hand, science is an ongoing process, dispersed among the peoples and places of the earth. This aspect of science is very large, and we are too close to it to see it at all clearly. We can know only a small part of it intimately. Hence it may be presumptuous to attempt any hard and fast conclusions about it.

One of the tests of science as an ongoing process in any epoch, it seems to me, is its relation to, and treatment of, its minority groups, and for this reason I am glad of the opportunity to say a few words about a very controversial subject, extra-sensory perception. The status of this subject in science is puzzling, and there is no dearth of strong opinion both for and against it. My purpose here is neither to support nor to oppose it, but to examine certain of its features, and I conclude, in view of the record, if objectivity is to be retained, statements about it should be held as tentative.

Science as we know it today grew out of philosophy, and philosophers have always retained a lively interest in the doings of science. Indeed, it is they who have contributed much of the writing about science, including very much written in philosophy's role as self-appointed critic. The part of science that has particularly fascinated philosophers is the so-called "scientific method." The philosophical attitude toward the source of knowledge about the world has oscillated back and forth between the extremes of *rationalism,* in which reason plays the dominant role, and *empiricism,* in which the evidence of the senses is considered to be paramount. Current science seems to employ these two streams intermingled, and the force that holds them together is the creative genius of the scientist.

Creativity, whether in science or out of it, can be discussed in relation to its products, which are its outward manifestations. This aspect must indeed be considered when we have practical applications in mind, for it is only by the products of creativity that we can know of its existence and can thereby appraise it, measure it, and discover it. On the other hand, creativity arises as a process of some kind, a very private one, and it is this process that has to be thought of if we want at all to understand creativity. Various authorities seem to regard creativity in different ways, so one has a certain amount of choice of definitions. In my own view, I like to think of it as a universal phenomenon, certainly not confined to eminent people, but something shared by everyone—even broader than that, by all living creatures and, of course, in highly varying degree. It is linked, it seems to me, to the general variability which is the property of all behavior, as I shall try to show in the following pages.

THE NATURE OF SCIENCE

There is, of course, a close relation between science and knowledge, but in the sense I use here, science is concerned solely with the kinds of knowledge that can be derived by observation of the world in which we are immersed. More important, such observations must be capable of consensual validation by people everywhere, and any ideas derived therefrom are held always subject to test by further observation of the world. In this sense science can have little, if anything, to do with matters of religion, ethics, or morals, nor with any philosophical speculation for which there is not an ostensible possibility of testing by observation.

In its most obvious aspect, therefore, science consists in a compendium of knowledge, which includes statements, "natural laws," theories, speculations, hypotheses—in short, all ideas of whatever character. It includes also the methods and procedures by which these ideas are obtained, tested, and extended; and finally, the actual data of observation themselves. This is an ever-growing collection which is the result of the indirect and often competitive collaboration of a very large number of investigators situated all over the world. This collaboration is possible only because science belongs to the public domain.

The uniquely distinguishing characteristic of knowledge earmarked as scientific is its eternal liability to further testing against human experience. This is well illustrated by the history of two famous ideas whose final disposition has been the work of many centuries.

Starting as far back in time as mankind had any effective experience with the different metals, a distinction was recognized between base metals such as zinc and iron, which are subject to corrosion and disintegration under the action of the weather; and noble metals like silver, copper, and gold, which not only resist tarnishing but are readily workable into useful articles. Men had long hoped that by some process, magic or otherwise, the less desirable base metals might be changed into the more desirable noble ones. In particular, there came to be a belief in an object called the philosopher's stone, by which people might transmute certain metals into gold.

This belief stirred men into experimental activity to discover the coveted stone, but, of course, subsequent history shows that, after innumerable unsuccessful attempts, the quest had to be abandoned for want of any material encouragement whatever. Under the test of experience, the idea of transmutation had been found wanting. Moreover, with the growth of chemistry out of alchemy, followed later by the insight obtained from discovery of the periodic system of the elements, such a large heap of theoretical evidence was added to the practical experience that the very concept of the philosopher's stone came to be regarded as silly. Ironically, in mid-twentieth century the transmutation secret has become known, but of course, under very adverse conditions of cost and rate of conversion.

My second example is the history of perpetual motion. Almost anyone can think up an energy-producing machine which, after once being started, feeds back energy into itself in such a way as to keep itself going. Then a small fraction of the total energy might be taken off to do useful work. This very attractive idea, in which one gets something for nothing or very nearly so, has appealed to thousands of mechanically minded men ever since the beginning of the industrial revolution, with hardly anyone so bold as to deny its feasibility.

Nevertheless, by 1775 the Paris Academy of Sciences had received so many claims for perpetual-motion machines, none of which had ever worked out, that they decided not to consider any more. Then, one after the other, Carnot (1796–1832), Clapeyron (1799–1864), and Helmholtz (1821–1894), each working independently, boldly denied the possibility of perpetual motion as a principle, and from axioms based on the denial, they derived the principle of the conservation of energy. All subsequent experiments in energy transformations, from those days to this, have uniformly upheld the conservation principle as consistent with experience. Even more, this principle has been so fertile in fostering ideas and practical devices that it has been given the very highest status in our thinking, and is now known everywhere as the First Law of Thermodynamics. Thus, an idea that could not withstand the test of experience was thrown out, but its inverse was able to survive, and today is accorded the highest regard.

Despite these developments in the learned world of science, practical inventors have continued to come forward, even to the present day, with the most varied proposals for perpetual-motion machines; but so far not one of them has demonstrated his invention successfully before a knowledgeable audience. Not only has no one produced a machine that would keep on delivering energy out of nothing, but no one has ever been able even to make a machine that would continue running indefinitely by itself. Indeed, Clausius (1822–1888) showed that part of the energy associated with every self-acting process is always dissipated as heat; and, moreover, hot objects always tend to cool to the temperature of their surroundings. Both the dissipation and the cooling are these irreversible processes; hence, as Clausius showed, all natural processes exhibit the characteristic of "running down." Expressed in common language, all naturally occurring processes are subject to energy dissipation of the kind typified by friction, so merely to keep anything running for very long requires a constant input of energy just to balance the dissipation. These statements amount to a theoretical description of the impossibility of any man-made perpetual-motion machine.

The theoretical demonstration would not stand very long, however, had any inventor ever actually demonstrated just one perpetual-motion device. It is the *practical*, or empirical, demonstration by the enormous number of unsuccessful attempts either to produce perpetual motion or to overthrow first Carnot's principle, and later Clausius' principle, that is so impressive. As Polya would say, the failure of each such attempt has rendered the principles a little more plausible.[1] Taken all together, the evidence from these thousands of failures is overwhelming. Clausius' principle, known as the Second Law of Thermodynamics, has become a pillar of modern science. Eddington enthusiastically dubbed it "time's arrow."

These two dramatic examples illustrate both the negative and positive aspects of the testing of ideas in science. The philosopher's stone and perpetual motion, after a tenacious struggle lasting centuries, were rejected because of an overwhelming failure of anyone to find support for them. Their long tenure was made possible only by the lack of adequate observational materials. Both ideas were sterile, except in the negative sense that the rejection of one led to chemistry, and of the other, thermodynamics. On the other hand, the ideas of both chemistry and thermodynamics have stood the test of experience and have been enormously fruitful.

The foregoing examples indicate that among the many ideas in science, some have not yet settled down into their final resting place, but have an insecure status. They are still in the process of being examined, criticized, and tested. The vast majority of these are the relative newcomers. It is these ideas in flux, as it were, that fill the scientific journals from month to month, appear in scientific monographs, and provide topics of active discussion. This flurry of activity belongs to another aspect of science, that of an *ongoing process*, of making observations, producing ideas, and getting ideas tested. This aspect, a dynamic one, stands in contradistinction to science's compendium aspect as data, ideas, and methods, the relatively static aspect discussed so far.

The ideas of science first emerge into the public domain upon being published, which exposes them to criticism, both partisan and impartial. The test is likely to be severe in direct proportion to the novelty of the idea, and if sufficiently bizarre, the idea is likely to be rejected outright by the scientific community. It was this violent reaction to new ideas which prompted Max Planck to the bitter remark that a new idea does not win over opposition by convincing its opponents, but by waiting for its opponents to die off and the young generation of scientists, growing up without the prejudice of their elders, to accept it.

Hence the process of getting scientific ideas launched is an ordeal of testing, and only ideas that are solidly based on observation can stand the onslaught. The struggle may take, as Planck said, a generation. On the other hand, a new idea is a great stimulus to other workers in its special field of interest, for they will build on it and apply it to their own particular projects. In this way, through the joint efforts of many workers, known to each other primarily only through the journals, a new idea becomes firmly established. Because these people work under a wide variety of conditions, use strange apparatus, and apply a host of different techniques, a new idea, after "making the rounds," receives considerable broadening and often some modification. It is this public aspect of the methods, data, and conclusions of experiment which gives science its special character not possessed by other forms of knowledge. Although the individual introduces ideas, it is the whole scientific community's function to appraise them.

As a result of this public testing and modification of the ideas of science, any bias ascribable to an individual, to his methods, or to his special situation is eventually washed out. In the place of the personal experience of the individual is put the consensual experience of the whole community. What guarantee is there, then, that there may not remain a residual bias which reflects a systematic error common to all the members of the community? There is, of course, no such guarantee, but it is the role of philosophy to reflect on such matters.

EXTRASENSORY PERCEPTION

The public nature of science is nowhere better illustrated, it seems to me, than in the case of paranormal behavior, or psi phenomena, of which the most studied aspect is extrasensory perception (ESP). The researchers into ESP (principally J. B. Rhine and coworkers in the United States) have relied chiefly on card-guessing experiments for their data. In one form of experiment there are five kinds of cards, each of which bears on its face a characteristic symbol. The five symbols occur five times each in a standard deck of twenty-five cards. After someone shuffles the deck, an "agent" of the experimenter turns the cards face up one by one, while the "percipient" tries to guess each symbol as it appears. If the percipient has no ESP ability whatever, he would be expected, by pure chance, to guess correctly about five out of every twenty-five; hence, any substantial margin over the five "hits" allotted by chance may be taken as evidence of a "non-chance" cause. Under the special conditions and precautions of the experiment, such evidence points to the operation of ESP.

S. G. Soal, a mathematician at the University of London, made his initial studies of ESP in a spirit of skepticism, as an appraisal of some previous work of Rhine. Over several years' time Soal accumulated well over 100,000 guesses, made by 160 persons, and the results were declared negative. In 1939, however, while reviewing his data, Soal discovered a remarkable correlation among the guesses made by two of the 160 percipients.

In each case there was an excessively large number of hits on the cards immediately *preceding* and *following* the target card! Hits on the target card itself were seen to fall off as the experiment proceeded, which was considered normal, but hits on the adjacent cards continued throughout.

Soal estimated the probability of this streak of guesses occurring by chance alone to be of the order of 10^{-4} for each of the two percipients separately, leading to a very strong presumption in favor of the occurrence of a phenomenon called "precognition," or sensing an event prior to its occurrence. The extreme care with which the experiments had been conducted appeared to rule out any other causal explanation.

As pointed out by G. Evelyn Hutchinson, it is not just the unexpected nature of these results which makes them noteworthy, but the extreme probabilities by which they have been established. In most fields of science, says Hutchinson, when the probability of an event attributable to chance has been reduced to 0.001 or even to 0.01, workers, and editors too, feel their conclusions are well established beyond reasonable doubt, although of course, a certain number of these conclusions may later prove to have been accepted too hastily. Hence, the experiments of Soal raise "questions of extraordinary importance to all scientific workers, *irrespective of whether or not they accept the conclusion that the future can influence the past.*"[2] (The italics are Hutchinson's.)

So far, I have told only half the story. At the time Soal was reviewing the results mentioned, the war in England was in full course, but he again approached his two successful percipients and was able to persuade one of them to return for a continuation of the experiments. According to Hutchinson, the long series of experiments which ensued can hardly be equaled in psychological investigation for rigor and variety of approach. The results again were notable. In one experiment there were 1,101 precognitive hits, against 776 expected. Calculations indicated the probability of these hits occurring by chance alone would be only about $5 \cdot 10^{-35}$. In another experiment there were 439 precognitive hits, against 322 expected, giving a probability of these hits occurring by chance, of only $1.3 \cdot 10^{-11}$. These probabilities are even more extreme than the ones obtained in the earlier experiments, and it would seem that, as far as data are concerned, the phenomenon of precognition ought to be firmly established.

Although ESP data, in one form or another, have been collected for about fifty years in the United States, it is clear that this work has gone relatively unnoticed, and it is safe to say that, with the exception of a few scattered individuals, the scientific community the world over has not been impressed. Indeed, it seems likely that few scientists not actually engaged in the work have any belief in it. This raises a question about what the scientific world really considers acceptable data, and whether or not data are, in fact, our primary basis for belief in phenomena. Next, if data are not our primary basis for belief, what is the basis? Are the criteria actually used in the establishment of scientific ideas really different from what we suppose? These shocking questions deserve the attention of all of us.

In an attempt to resolve these questions I have cast about for other plausible criteria, and I list below the ones I have thought of. There are no doubt others, but let the reader decide.

1. The experiments must be meaningful rather than irrelevant or farfetched. (There are no clearly authenticated reports of nontrivial applications of the ESP faculty.)

2. There must be a possible mechanism, and preferably a plausible one. (No generally acceptable mechanism has been proposed for ESP.)

3. The phenomena must have meaningful relation to existing knowledge. (There is no apparent relation between ESP and any known biological need or function.)

4. The materials of study, even though rare, must be available generally. (ESP percipients are exceptionally rare, and they cannot be recognized without considerable effort.)

5. The outcome of experiments must be systematic and must have a reasonable degree of reliability. (ESP experiments are exceptionally uncertain and unpredictable. They cannot be performed at the experimenter's pleasure, nor can they be demonstrated before a public audience.)

Items (1), (2), and (3) propose the requirement that a part of science must have a consistent theoretical structure. Items (4) and (5) propose additional conditions of testability. All the items, (1) to (5), express additional restrictions on that part of science which may be said to exist in the *public mode*. Now, which of these criteria (or others not mentioned) are actually being applied against ESP? Or should we concede that in exceptional cases, at our own option, we are justified in applying extrascientific criteria?

I shall now digress for a moment to explain what I mean by the public and private mode of science. If I perform some experiments which lead me to some excellent conclusions about a certain phenomenon, and if I keep these experiments and conclusions to myself, I can hardly claim that what I have done belongs to science. It obviously belongs to me, and to me alone, because I have not shared it with anyone. To the extent that this work can be considered to be science, it can only be called science in the *private mode*. Now, suppose I communicate what I have done, and it receives wide distribution in a scientific journal. As I have already pointed out, this act exposes my work to the appraisal of others. The appraisal may be accomplished by others repeating parts of my work, or by carrying out supplementary experiments which take my conclusions as a presupposition. In this way my work becomes the property of all those who repeat it, extend it, utilize it, or modify it, so it is then science in the ordinary sense of the word, or, as I say, science in the *public mode*.

On the other hand, suppose my journal article lies there unnoticed, as for example, once happened to the great work of Willard Gibbs, which was published in a relatively obscure journal. In this case the work can be said to exist in a *quasi-public mode*, for although it is really public, yet the effect is the same as if it were still private.

Now, ESP, if it really exists, has terribly important implications for all of us, the whole human race. The ESP results, however, have been available mostly in the special journals devoted to psychic research, whose small readership consists of those with a special personal interest in such phenomena. This readership is small in relation to the whole scientific community, just as the scientific community itself is small compared to the whole literate public. Thus, the ESP work exists in the world's scientific literature only in the quasi-public mode. There are, in addition, some popular descriptions in print. Therefore, one might argue, ESP must not be a true phenomenon, for if it were it would certainly cause more stir. Here seems to be an argument against ESP, but is it a scientific one?

The opponents of ESP have brought every conceivable argument against it, from careless experimentation to fraud. For example, George R. Price of the University of Minnesota alleged that ESP findings "are dependent on clerical and statistical errors and unintentional use of sensory clues, and that all extrachance results not so explicable are dependent on deliberate fraud or mildly abnormal conditions." [3] These are strong charges, but in reply I would urge that the experiments in most cases have been surrounded with such excessive precautions that unintentional errors and clues must be ruled out at once.

I am reminded that in the 1920's the forerunner of the present *Scientific American*, the original possessor of the name, underwrote a prize competition among spiritualistic mediums for the demonstration of genuine psychic phenomena. A medium whose pseudonym was Martha, as I recall, had passed all the preliminaries and the semifinals. She would undoubtedly have been awarded the prize if her demonstration could have convinced the *Scientific American's* committee of prominent citizens, which included some well-known scientists. During the final séance the committee, duly impressed, was about to conclude the affair with a favorable report, when Harry Houdini, the magician, who was one of the committee members, caught the medium manipulating a string which operated some of the manifestations. At that moment the prize competition ended.

This example does not suggest that ESP may be tainted with fraud, but points out that reputable men of science have been known to miss the obvious, and may give credence to a wisp that is not there at all. The prize committee, fortunately, contained a scattering of people with widely differing training, and in each case these people observed what they had come mentally prepared to observe. I have further remarks on this topic, which I shall have to defer until later.

The ESP puzzle indicates that the ongoing process of science as we like to think of it may not *necessarily* be its true nature. At least it seems that, for the fullest effectiveness, science has to be in the public mode. Conversely, it may be reasonable to say that any data and conclusions which exist only in the quasi-public mode, for whatever reason, do not belong to science in the full meaning of the word "belong."

THE PHILOSOPHERS

Francis Bacon (1561–1626) was the first modern philosopher to break with the ancient tradition of seeking knowledge by appeal to pure reason. He went to the opposite extreme of insisting on the use of observation alone, called the method of induction. Bacon had great faith in *system*. The proper scientific method, he thought, was to accumulate as large a number as possible of particular examples of the "nature" to be investigated. These examples were to be distributed among three great lists, titled the Affirmative, the Negative, and the Comparative, accordingly as the nature appeared, or failed to appear where expected, or appeared in variable degree. Next, the investigator was to cast his eye over the lists and pick out the common element. As an aid in this endeavor, he was to prepare a fourth list, titled Rejections, in which to enter his trial generalizations and reasons for rejecting them. At some point in this sifting procedure the final "complete affirmation" would make itself known almost automatically. The whole process was so direct and obvious that men of little wit could be employed to carry on the work.[4] Had mass production been known at the time, Bacon would have adopted it as an ideal medium for the prosecution of scientific research. The defect in Bacon's proposal lies in his assumption that induction can be reduced to a mere mechanical process which does not require inventive thought.

Bacon's principle of induction did not prove so easy of application, however. Subsequent writers tried to clarify the method by showing that induction was an extension of formal logic. To some it seemed that induction and deduction were merely inverse forms, like the two sides of a coin. Others viewed induction as a special case of deduction. J. M. Keynes credited Stanley Jevons (1835–1882) with relating induction to the theory of probability.[5] Subsequent writers, including Keynes himself, have tried to fit the theory of probability itself into formal logic. This trend of the philosophers to concern themselves about the logical aspects of induction and its relations to deduction and probability has persisted to the present day.

Science as we know it started out as a branch of philosophy, so the early scientists were, of course, philosophers. The relation of philosophy to science will be clarified by a brief consideration of what philosophy is supposed to do. According to C. D. Broad there are two principal divisions, critical and speculative. The aim of critical philosophy is the examination and criticism of beliefs. Its first duty is therefore to isolate each belief from all others and to state it clearly. Next, it must test each belief by exposing it resolutely and honestly to all the objections that one can think of.[6] To this I remark that if such an attack be prosecuted to its logical conclusion, hardly any belief will remain, as we know from Descartes' experience. At the end of his doubting spree, Descartes was left with only two unassailable beliefs: "I think" and "I am." One can only conclude that this process is not suitable for the purpose of overthrowing untenable beliefs, but only for understanding them better, perhaps better to appreciate their relation to the beliefs of others.

The object of the second division of philosophy, the speculative, according to Broad, is to reflect upon the scientific, religious, and ethical experience of mankind, in the hope of reaching some general conclusion about the nature of the universe and man's prospects in it. Insofar as speculation is based on observation and is capable of being tested thereby, the aims of science and philosophy seem to coincide, but for practical purposes philosophy has long ago relinquished this role in favor of science. Philosophy holds itself aloof from actual participation in the work of science, but retains its role as critic. In this role, philosophy examines the methods and results of science in an attempt to understand and justify them. If they could, the philosophers would be glad to show that scientific induction is an application of the principles of formal logic. The difficulty they have had with this problem in more than three hundred years indicates the futility of the attempt and offers an interesting parallel to my examples of testing ideas in science.

The failure of this approach, however, has had no noticeable effect on the actual production and development of scientific ideas. While Bacon was theorizing about induction and the "scientific method," Galileo (1564–1642) was already making observations and experiments in the modern way, using *hypothesis and test*. In this he was following an earlier experimenter, Archimedes (287–212 B.C.), who in turn was only one of a long series of observers going back into prehistory. I shall try to show in subsequent pages that these observers must all have used the same general method.

The widespread use of the method of hypothesis and test is revealed by the writings of the experimenters themselves. Jevons observes that Robert Hooke (1635–1703), in his posthumous works, asserted that the first requisite of the natural philosopher is readiness at guessing the solution of phenomena and making queries. Jeremiah Horrocks (1617–1641), "than whom no one was more filled with the scientific spirit" according to Jevons, told how he tried theory after theory in order to discover one which was in accordance with the motions of Mars.[7]

Even Newton (1642–1727), whose remark "I don't frame hypotheses" has been so widely quoted, actually was forever framing them, and according to Jevons, Newton's genius lay just in the exhaustiveness of his treatment and the unbounded power of his insight.

If he treats of central forces, it is not one law of force which he discusses, but many, or almost all imaginable laws, the results of each of which he sketches out in a few pregnant words.

. . . .

Newton's work was really that of developing the methods of *deductive reasoning and experimental verification* [italics mine], by which alone great hypotheses can be brought to the touchstone of fact.[7]

Jevons urges that Newton's work, rather than Bacon's, is the true Novum Organum of science. The philosophers have been slow to recognize that the real scientific method, since the time of Galileo at least, has been that of *hypothesis and test,* and induction in the strict Baconian sense has never existed.

The part of induction that was left untouched by philosophy, and which could never be fitted into logic, is the making of hypotheses, which is a *creative endeavor* characterized by groping, forgetting, remembering, testing, discarding, reusing, and so on. This is the area of prescience, or science in the *private mode,* in which ideas are in a state of violent ferment, conjecture is rampant, and methods are predominantly *ad hoc.* The watchwords are "try and see." To any member of the lay public who regards science as the epitome of cold logic, the private mode of science would be a shock. J. S. Mill (1806–1873) may have been the first philosopher to recognize that the generation of scientific ideas is an extralogical matter, for he stated that the purpose of logic is to ascertain whether inferences have been correctly drawn rather than to discover them.[7]

CREATIVITY

The best concise description I know for creative action is that it achieves increased unity or order in some situation. The creative person is one who works with relations, and who selects and organizes them in such a way as to reveal one or more of their essential aspects. The degree of condensation achieved is one measure of creative excellence. Creative action seems to be the result of a self-motivated urge to resolve complexity and express its essence.

In this respect, the work of the research scientist is to discover order in our manifestly chaotic world, using observation coupled with the method of hypothesis and test. His raw material is the kind of information obtainable from observation, aided where appropriate by experiment. The creative part of this work is to devise theoretical relations or hypotheses which are consistent with the widest possible assortment of pertinent data and which have predictive value for data as yet unobtained.

The aspect of creativity of interest here is the process by which new scientific ideas are produced. Inasmuch as the producers of scientific ideas range from our greatest thinkers down to rather plain men and women, the faculty to be discussed must be one that is common to all. This faculty I shall call *chi*, the Greek letter, mnemonic for the words "creativity" and "creative," but not necessarily identical with any of the many existing usages of these words. (I choose chi rather than psi, because psi has already been taken by others as a symbol for paranormal behavior.) My definition is *Chi is a purposive psychological process leading to novel behavior.*

It may seem odd that I begin by mentioning relations and ideas, but frame the definition in terms of behavior. The anomaly disappears, though, when it is understood that conscious mental activity can be construed as a particular form of behavior. Now, it may be seen that, under this definition, chi automatically includes all the categories commonly thought of as belonging to creativity, invention, discovery of ideas, and every type of purposive innovation. The definition is therefore considerably broader than is necessary for its application solely to science, and, indeed, is quite general. The word "purposive" is included in the definition to rule out purely accidental conditions which frequently lead to novel behavior. This inclusion, however, is by no means intended as a deprecation of the role of accident in scientific discovery, for accident is one of the most prolific sources of new ideas. Nevertheless, these fortunate accidents almost always occur in the course of intensive searching, so the process which leads to them is properly labeled purposive.

Any one of the kinds of behavior mentioned that is new to the person himself or which marks a noticeable change from his previous behavior is chi behavior under the definition, even though it may be familiar already to others or even well known throughout society in general. The matter of utility or appraisal by others, as well as the timeliness of an innovation or discovery from the viewpoint of society, are all left out of the definition, even though these are important considerations and even practical necessities for formal recognition and evaluation of creative behavior. These remarks should serve to relate my usage of the word "chi" to various other current usages of the words "creativity," "innovation," and so on.

In order to discuss the nature of the chi process, I shall begin with a description of the variability of behavior which is merely ordinary. I have chosen a very simple example to illustrate this. It is the kind of example that anyone can easily corroborate by some close observation of himself or a friend. One need only choose some allegedly repetitive routine operation like the following:

> *Ritual for Old-Fashioned Boiled Coffee Every Morning*
> Enter kitchen; open hot-water faucet; light stove; take down saucepan; take out coffee and milk containers; fill saucepan if water is running hot; place on fire; add two heaping teaspoons of coffee; stir thoroughly; perform other chores while keeping one eye on the coffee. Stir vigorously from time to time until boiling is imminent; stir again; remove from fire and tilt saucepan against drainboard so grounds will collect; allow to stand a few minutes for settling; decant coffee into cup; add milk; serve.

I have found that this routine, which I have been performing daily for many years, never repeats itself exactly from one day to the next; hence any description of it, like the one above, is little more than an approximation. For one thing, neither times nor quantities have been mentioned, both matters of personal judgment, and both subject to variation.

The daily variations are usually small, but occasionally everything may turn out differently. The explanation of the variability is both personal and environmental. Typical of the personal reasons might be that I have been out most of the night, I am preoccupied with the work of the day, I am ill, and so on. Because of these things I may stub my toe, hit my head on the sharp cabinet corner, or make some gross mistake in procedure. One thing leads to another, and the result is variability. Typical of the environmental reasons might be ingredients missing or misplaced, the pan in need of washing, water not hot, and so on. That is, even in a simple daily situation, neither the person nor the surrounding conditions can be expected to remain the same, but differences intrude to alter the procedure or change its order. In more formal language, the continual changes in both internal and external stimuli result in variable behavior. The saying of Heraclitus the Naturalist (*ca.* 500 B.C.) is indeed still true after twenty-five centuries: "No man ever steps into the same river twice."

Another example, of considerable economic significance and which many of us have had occasion to observe, is the behavior of workers in a factory. Specifications may call for 10,000 product units, all exactly alike, but experience shows that they always come out all different. Sometimes it seems to be largely a matter of luck whether or not a substantial number of produced units have exceeded the tolerance limits of the specifications and are therefore unacceptable for shipment to the customer. The cause of this situation is to be found primarily in the workers: it is not in the nature of a human being to repeat.

In a situation where a large amount of repetitive behavior is demanded, people always like to introduce variations, for the pleasure it gives them or, as they say, to reduce boredom and make the time pass quickly. The story is told of a Mexican artist who had produced a very attractive ceramic piece, his price being twenty pesos. His California customer liked the article so well that he had in mind to obtain ten more exactly like the first. He also hoped for a more favorable price because he was buying in quantity, but to his astonishment the artist's price for the lot was thirty pesos each, the reason being the burdensome repetition that had to be compensated at a higher rate.

These examples characterize, on a small scale, the behavioral variability that is in each of us, which can be observed under suitably controlled conditions. It is the outward expression of an inner restlessness, traceable perhaps to the "irritability" exhibited by all protoplasm, the kind of random homeostatic activity which was pointed out by Ross Ashby.[8] At the opposite extreme, on a scale far vaster then the individual, this variability plays a fundamental role in the development and modification of whole cultures, through the occurrence of innovations. These are more or less permanent changes in behavior patterns.[9] These simple examples, therefore, far from being trivial, are prototypes of a universal phenomenon.

One can explain this variability by starting from the assumption that in a behavioral sense a human life can be construed as a continuous succession of personal situations calling for responses. By a personal situation I mean the moment by moment interaction between the individual and his environment. As the situation changes, so must also the response. In the presence of other people, or even sometimes merely in the presence of other living creatures or inanimate matter, a person's response, triggered by the current situation, in turn initiates a new situation. This calls for a new response, which again initiates another new situation, and so forth. Therefore the successive situations and their responses have a cyclic quality which may be influenced by the occurrence of feedback.

In this succession of personal situations, no two of them are ever exactly alike, each containing something novel which distinguishes it from those previously encountered. One novel aspect, for example, which is nontrivial and always present in the situation, is the memory of previous situations. This discussion therefore shows how the variability of situations carries with it a corresponding variability of behavior, which can be seen to be inevitable.

Now, to return to the coffee-making, I must mention that, plain though it is, it has undergone development over the years through the occasional incorporation of improvements. This is innovation, and it is often brought about as the result of some accident such as the emergency substitution of one kind of utensil for another, hot water for cold or cold for hot, fine grind for coarse, brand A for brand B, and the like. Something irregular occurs which interferes with the standard procedure, and the resulting product may turn out better. In other cases there may be a complaint about the product, which precipitates inquiry.

Insofar as such interruptions stimulate deliberate action, the resulting innovations can be taken as chi behavior, the result of a conscious and purposive search for something better. To the extent that the process of finding the improvement arises from a deliberate use of observation combined with a search for a better understanding of the physics and chemistry of the operation, as in the coffee, the grains, the fire, the convections, the extraction rates, or whatever, the process is also characteristically scientific. Thus, the improvement in a coffee-making operation can epitomize the whole scientific process in miniature: peculiarity noted, hypothesis thought of, deduction made, experiments tried, results noted, and, finally, revision adopted.

To sum up thus far, I have stated that behavior is inherently variable; variable behavior may lead to innovation; innovation is a chi process if purposively directed; and a chi process is part of a scientific induction if observations lead to hypotheses capable of being tested.

These statements suggest an interesting, if unusual, view of science, the ongoing process. As far back as the dim reaches of prehistory, ancient man had to learn by trial and success, for indeed, there was no other way. Much of our own daily learning is also done this way. It is the way animals and children learn. Even in learning by imitation, trial and success may be the method. If we examine the method of hypothesis and test, which I submit is the method of science, we see that it, too, is a special application of the method of trial and success.

In other words, it seems to me that, except for refinements of technique, superior knowledge, and a high degree of sophistication, there is no essential difference in kind between a research scientist's efforts in discovering a new scientific relation, on the one hand, and, on the other hand, the efforts of any person, or a child, animal, or any living creature, in getting acquainted with and interpreting the ordinary facts of life by which we all exist from day to day. Each in his own way appeals to observation, interpretation, and test. The farther up the scale we go, the greater is the potentiality for creative effort in the interpretive aspect of this process.

THE ART OF DISCOVERY

The nourishing source from which all science begins is the figurative laboratory bench where man is in intimate contact with some aspect of nature, just as the sensitive growing root tip of a plant is in contact with its nourishing soil. It is here that the facts of nature are absorbed into science through observation, and here that new ideas about the physical world have their inception. The really important question about these new ideas is not, Which hypothesis to accept? but, Which hypothesis? Given certain facts of observation, how does one find a useful interpretation of them? In this lies the art of discovery.

I turn now to procedure. What does the research scientist actually do? The answer, it seem to me, is deceptively simple and not very startling. I think it can be summed up in *observe, think, formulate*. As I look back on this statement it strikes me as verging on the trivial unless these things are done with a certain spirit, perhaps the spirit that the astronomer Horrocks was supposed to have had. Certainly the words as they stand can mean anything or nothing. Hence I had better expand on them.

By *observe*, I mean a great deal more than just "taking a look." I have in mind an intense concentration on the subject of inquiry, coupled with a singleness of purpose and the persistence to overcome difficulties. This requires a high degree of "inner direction." We are so constituted that, although we have eyes that see, they often see not. Perception takes a lot of looking, which is likely to be very tedious. Often only a consummate curiosity can carry one through. The best word I have ever heard for it is *passion*.

I remember spending a summer in a spruce woods on the Maine coast, where I became intrigued with learning to distinguish all the different species of spruce trees. After a number of days of looking, without seeming to see very much, I felt confused and considerably annoyed, but I persisted until I began to recognize the presence of patterns which had completely escaped me at first. I should explain that botanical material poses a special problem for observation because of its frequent high variability from specimen to specimen, which may demand examination of hundreds of specimens before the underlying pattern is revealed. My most important gain from this experience came unexpectedly: I realized that observing is a complex process which demands a surprising amount of time and patience, but if a person persists he is sure to learn something new. An unexpected lesson of a different kind came later when I discovered the reason for my slow progress in distinguishing the different species: All the trees accessible to me were members of the same species.

One of the occupational difficulties of observing is that one tends to notice only those things toward which his mind happens to be directed, and he is relatively insensitive to all other matters. W. H. George illustrates this point by citing the tired laboratory worker who hears the clock's chimes, decides it is late, and goes home. On another occasion, at the same hour, he is engrossed in some task that occupies his whole attention, so he misses the chimes, and as far as he is concerned the clock has not struck.[10]

W. I. B. Beveridge cites another well-known phenomenon. The botanist in a country scene notices the plants, the zoologist the animals, the geologist the terrain, the farmer the crops, and so on. We see the things that we are most familiar with and that occupy our principal attention; other objects may completely escape notice. The "canals" on Mars are a famous example: Observers were divided into two sharply defined camps, accordingly as they perceived canal-like structures or they did not. Those that were led to expect such structures apparently "saw" them, while those who did not "saw" something else.[11]

A beautiful example was quoted by W. H. George borrowing from A. Gennep. During a meeting of the Congress of Psychologists in Göttingen, a man rushed into the hall pursued by another, shots were fired, and after twenty seconds the commotion ended with the two men rushing out of the room. The chairman, explaining that an inquiry was sure to follow, pleaded that each man present immediately write out an exact description of what they had just witnessed.[10]

When the forty reports had been compared with the photographic record of the incident, which had been secretly staged in advance, the most complete of them was found to contain 20 percent inaccuracies, and most of the others contained substantial amounts of purely fictitious material. These psychologists, all trained observers, had been taken by surprise. At the time of the interruption, their minds had been directed toward some academic matter, and could not be brought to bear on anything so different in the brief time allotted. This example demonstrates clearly that mere seeing cannot be called observation in any meaningful scientific sense.

An observation is a transaction between the mind and the environment to which each contributes a part, so that a certain prior conditioning of the mind is essential. The situation is analogous to that of a key and a lock. The lock is the environment, whose opening constitutes the observation; the key is the mind, which can perform its part only when properly prepared. Perception takes place when the key fits the lock. Like other analogies, this one is not quite true, or wholly new experience would be impossible. It must therefore be postulated further that the key need not be an *exact* fit in order to turn the lock, and moreover, the key must possess the power of gradual adaptation which may eventually enable it to fit. This is learning.

My second item of the list is to *think,* a vague word for which I would gratefully accept a substitute, but at present a more descriptive term does not occur to me. I mean by it that, whether engaged in passive observation or in active experimentation, a person's mind must be busily wondering, comparing, planning, all the time. Observation, to get anywhere, must be done *intelligently* and with a spirit of curiosity. It is only the anticipation of ultimately satisfied curiosity that can drive a scientist day and night through masses of otherwise dry detail. Without intelligence and curiosity, little can be accomplished.

In an experimental investigation, as a result of manipulating the material in various ways, one accumulates all sorts of facts which together or separately may seem to make little sense at all. At this stage each experimental result, instead of clarifying anything, merely piques the curiosity in a new direction and raises additional questions whose answering demands further experimentation. The more copious the data become, the less meaning they may seem to have. A wonderful example is the vast accumulation of spectroscopic data in the early years of the twentieth century, the significance of which became more and more puzzling with each new report.

At such a point great imagination is needed. The approach must, of course, vary greatly with the individual. One has to immerse himself in the data, manipulate them in every conceivable way, rearrange them, combine them, invert them, twist and turn them. For example, the numerical parts of the data may be added, subtracted, multiplied, or integrated; or each variable plotted graphically against every other, in various different co-ordinate systems. This activity, guided always by the intense spirit of inquisitiveness, may lead one to the spark of an idea which will resolve the chaos. On the other hand, the unifying idea sometimes comes from without, as happened when the new quantum theory suddenly gave meaning to whole volumes of collected spectroscopic data.

The foregoing is also a part of my third item, to *formulate*, which is not at all a separate stage of the process. There is no clear distinction between to *formulate* and to *think*; rather, they are aspects of the same thing, the creative process of integrating the data into hypotheses as fast and as frequently as possible. At all stages of the investigation there should be conscious attempts to formulate workable hypotheses, to think of possible mechanisms which might account for the observed phenomena, and to structure the information in every way possible. Hypotheses are cheap. They are easy to come by and easy to discard. The vast majority of them will prove obviously wrong because of conflict with certain of the data, and therefore free generation of hypotheses is encouraged. There is far too much fear in some quarters that one may inadvertently "rediscover the wheel." In my opinion, if the wheel happens to be the best answer to the situation, then let us, by all means, rediscover it. To do anything else is to avoid the obvious for the sake of false pride. The only sin in rediscovering the wheel is perhaps in failing to recognize it as such.

A hypothesis can be retained if it fits the data, is self-consistent, and is in reasonable accord with previously accepted ideas. The last of these is desirable, but by no means mandatory. In the course of digging up more and more hypotheses only to discard each one because of failure in some important respect, one tends to reach for tentative explanations that are "farther and farther out." I am sure Max Planck was in this position when he postulated the existence of quanta as a means of deriving the radiation equation.

EPILOGUE

In these few pages I have tried to present the aspect of science as a *public* phenomenon, the product ultimately not of individuals working alone or in small groups, but in a worldwide "competitive cooperation." I have indicated that it is this public aspect that gives science its special character. It is also characterized by a particular method, employing the cycle: observe and hypothesize, then test the hypothesis against further observation. No idea in science can ever be secure against exposure to the test of fresh observation, with the consequent threat of being modified or supplanted.

There are, of course, other human disciplines that undergo modification under the influence of experience, such, perhaps, as the law, and these disciplines thereby possess a partially scientific character. In this connection it is interesting to note that one of the law degrees is called "Doctor of the Science of Law."

The hypothesis-framing step in the development of new science is *of the essence*, and this step demands *creative action*. Creative action, however, is not reserved for the great and near great, but is a regular ingredient in the mentality of all persons. The great inventor, scientist, or artist undoubtedly possess enhanced creative capacity, but their difference from the common man is one of degree, not of kind.

REFERENCES

1. Pólya, György. *Mathematics and Plausible Reasoning.* Vol. II. Princeton: Princeton University Press, 1954.

2. Hutchinson, G. Evelyn. "Marginalia," *American Scientist* (April 1948).

3. Price, George R. "Science and the Supernatural," *Science*, 122:359–670 (August 26, 1955).

4. Mott-Smith, Morton C. *The Story of Energy.* New York: D. Appleton-Century, 1934, p. 87.

5. Keynes, J. M. *Treatise on Probability.* New York: St. Martins Press, 1952.

6. Broad, C. D. *Scientific Thought.* New York: The Humanities Press, 1952.

7. Jevons, W. Stanley. *The Principles of Science.* London: Macmillan, 1924.

8. Ashby, W. Ross. *Design for a Brain.* New York: John Wiley & Sons, 1952.

9. Barnett, H. G. *Innovation, the Basis of Cultural Change.* Oxford: Clarendon Press, 1953.

10. George, W. H. *The Scientist in Action.* New York: Emerson Books, 1938.

11. Beveridge, William I. B. *The Art of Scientific Investigation.* New York: W. W. Norton & Company, Inc., 1957.

THE DELIBERATE INDUCTION
OF NEW IDEAS

Russell F. W. Smith

A MAN FROM PORLOCK interrupts Coleridge, who in a post-opium hypnotic daze stops dashing "Xanadu" down on paper, and so one of the most haunting and lovely lyrics in English can never be finished.* In an early issue of the *Atlantic Monthly*, Oliver Wendell Holmes, physician-poet-professor-autocrat of the breakfast table, gives a clinical description and decrial of the romantic picture of the writer in the throes of composition. A. E. Housman in the *Name and Nature of English Poetry* denies that he can define poetry any better than a terrier can a rat but defines it by implication by saying that poetry is something he may not safely think of when he's shaving because it makes his beard bristle so that he is likely to cut himself. Emily Dickinson testifies to being smitten over the head and speared through the middle by the nonrational components of poetry. Horace recognizes the need for "aesthetic distance" when he writes, "A poem is like a picture: one will please you more if you stand near, and another if you stand afar." [2] He argues for the virtues of careful, painstaking revision and warns against rushing into print: "Still if you do write some day, let it come first to the ears of the critic Maecius and of your father and myself; then put the parchment away in your desk and store it up for nine years." [3]

At the other extreme, some of the Greek rhapsodists ap-

* So at least the legend. Lowes tries to unravel the connections between Coleridge's reading, his interests, and his writing and presents a longer, more complicated explanation of Coleridge's creativity that is less romantic, though scarcely unromantic.[1]

parently improvised (composed in public) and believed in the permanence of each stammered syllable as the product of gods-given inspiration; in their wake stream the jazz-accompanied beat poets of "the hungry i" and other coffeeshops and nightclubs from San Francisco to Greenwich Village, people like Allen Ginsberg [3] who have no patience for, or belief in, the studied line.*
Even though Archibald MacLeish tells us, "a poem should not mean, but be," many poets have talked interestingly, if not always convincingly, about how their poems have come to be, and still more have left in the palimpsests of their manuscripts tangled traces of their poems' geneses. The librarian who brought together the unique collection of poets' manuscripts in the library of the University of Buffalo (now part of the State University of New York) edited and in part wrote *Poets at Work*, which spells out some examples of what can be seen by examining the poets' revisings.[4] All in all, it is very easy for a teacher of literature to become fascinated by, and uneasy about, the problem of creativity even if he never encounters the exploding technical and semitechnical literature of creativity. This seems proper enough. My experience in the seminar suggests the following:

1. That so far whereas the investigations of the psychologists underpin and prompt speculation, they have discovered neither great nor firm truths showing the way to better identification or exploitation of creative ability.

2. That further speculation may point the way to more successful investigation.

3. That, to put it briefly and immodestly, our speculation is likely to be as useful as that of any other interdisciplinary group. (Compare, for example, one of the best in print, Anderson's,[5] which is interesting and suggestive, but by no means conclusive.)

4. That introspective narratives, no matter how widely cited and how intrinsically interesting, do not take one very far because they are introspective and personal.†

---

* Horace had a word to say about the Beats, too: "Democritus believes that genius is more successful than wretched art, and would fain exclude from Helicon all sane poets. Therefore a large number of would-be poets refuse to pare their nails and trim their beards, seek solitude, and shun the baths." [1]

† Most widely cited surely is Henri Poincaré's account of how in 1913, sleepless after black coffee, he suddenly struck upon the transformations from which he developed the Fuchsian function and of how, on a later occasion, foot raised to board a bus, he suddenly realized that these transformations were the same as those of non-Euclidean geometry. For an example of how this is cited,

The Creative Science Seminar has largely limited the scope of its discussion to speculation about creativity in the sciences, particularly the "hard" sciences, in the not unreasonable hope of avoiding overgenerality and in fear of the faddish wide use of the term "creativity" to cover not only the invention and discovery of devices, techniques, principles, and laws and the writing of poems, the painting of pictures, etc., but also the brainwashing successes in finding advertising gimmicks and slogans or the writing of articles for popular magazines on "creative cookery" or "creative tips for the homemaker." It is certainly possible that the popularity of the term "creativity" has led to its use to describe many activities that have little in common.

Long before I encountered the technical literature of creativity and before we organized the Creative Science Seminar, I had a number of experiences as a reader, as a student of linguistics, and as an English teacher that resulted * in my experimenting with what might be called the random juxtaposition of topics in order to hunt for so-called original or fruitful "new ideas." My experience and my experimentation, if I can call it that, have not been with the sciences, of course, but I was encouraged to write this paper for inclusion in this collection not only by my heretical suspicion that "new ideas" in any field have much the same nature, but by learning that several members of the seminar have begun to play with their own variations upon the random-juxtaposition notion that I shall describe. I have called the paper "The Deliberate Induction of New Ideas" out of only slightly ironic respect for the company it keeps. It might perhaps have been titled "First Aid for the Creative Process, or What to Do Until Inspiration Comes."

I am no judge of the adequacy of Barnett's popularized explanation of Einstein's constributions,[8] but I remember how I

---

see Sinnott in Anderson [5] or Hadamard,[6] who cites other examples as well. Interesting as they are, these accounts build up a mystique of creativity by emphasizing "flashes of genius" and the "activity of the unconscious mind" and by emphasizing the private and the inexplicable. This mystique is no more relevant to identifying creative talent than the equally interesting accounts by poets and other writers, or to providing it with an optimal environment for its development and exercise and seeing what education can do to create, foster, or release creativity if any of these activities is practicable. For the most inclusive collection of introspective accounts, see Ghiselin.[7]

* Perhaps sufficient introspection might discover an irrelevant moment at which the unconscious bubbled up and mixed metaphors by producing a flash of insight.

was struck by what I may paraphrase as his assertion that Einstein would not have developed the theories he did if he had not, unlike others who had thought of them separately, thought of gravity and of inertia at the same time. Was it possible that some "new ideas," at least, are the result of thinking at the same time about two or more things that have been presumed to be unrelated? Dr. Johnson's description of the novelty of some of John Donne's figures of speech suggested this. So did the accident of studying both historical Germanic linguistics and historical Romance linguistics at the same time in graduate school and so suspecting that some of the commonplaces of Germanic linguistics explain some of the puzzling phenomena of northern French dialects and some of the commonplaces of Romance linguistics explain some of the problems in southern German dialects.

An English teacher who has taught freshman composition courses and advanced courses in creative writing suffers not only from, but also with, the students whose plaint is, "What can I write about?" The plaint is the most severe in courses that require daily or weekly themes. Anyone who has had to write or even to read the themes knows that is a real problem, related to the problem of the student looking for a semester-paper topic that is sufficiently original and practicable, the graduate student looking for a dissertation subject, the faculty member doomed to publish or perish, and the professional writer faced with "writer's block" and starvation. "What can I write about?"

If the answers to this question given in classrooms are well reflected in the textbooks for freshman composition and advanced writing classes, it is no wonder the question persists. In general they ring changes on such Polonian advice as this: "Look in your heart and write. Write about what you know about. Write about what interests you. Narrow your subject down. Be specific. And above all, be original." Here is an example from a standard freshman composition textbook.

In the bewilderment of the first few weeks in college, the student will often say, "But I have nothing to write about!" He has only to open his eyes, for there is a world around him so full of interest and tragedy and comedy that he can see and hear enough to provide himself with more material than he can ever use. He may look back into his own experiences and from them write an autobiography which is unique; he may secure good material from a campus bulletin board or from the talk of football-players; he may watch a group of students in bright-colored raincoats, scurrying through the slanting rain of an April shower, and then record this picture in a description; or he may listen to some of his own crowd disagreeing on some points of student government and thereby find material for a classroom debate. Carlyle once said, "It is not the material but the workman that is wanting." [9]

This is not irrelevant advice, but it is inadequate. It may help a floundering freshman to turn out themes indistinguishable from those turned in by most of his classmates, but the intention of a textbook should be to help him do better than that. It suggests, but not very clearly, that it is easier to write well about something that is both personal and timely, but it fails to recognize that many autobiographical fragments, as they are written, are neither unique nor interesting, and it does not point out the problems in dealing with the timely. The subject does have to be delimited to be practicable. It is sad to think of the many acres of woodland that will this year be the vehicle for high school and freshman themes telling the teacher, with aplomb exceeding de Gaulle's, how the world's problems are to be solved. Perhaps the worst consequence is that such misdirected energy is not merely wasted, but *trains* a student to be incapable of hard, rational, consecutive thought.

Here is an excerpt from a freshman composition book that has gone through more editions and contains better advice, perhaps because its author has also been a professional novelist:

Our hero, then, decides to take the afternoon off and go to the movies. He strolls across the campus, says to half a dozen acquaintances, "Hi, fella!" or "How's the boy?" or whatever happens to be the accepted campus greeting at the moment. As he approaches Soldiers' Gate, a memorial arch commemorating the sons of the college killed in the World War, he pauses briefly to watch a woman who is making a sketch of it. "I could do better myself," he thinks contemptuously, and goes on his way.

He starts down the hill. He notices a girl sitting in an expensive automobile parked by the curb. As he passes, she says to the young man who is leaning against the door, "But Bart, you *promised!*" Our hero does not hear Bart's reply, but he does notice that the girl is very urgent, seemingly distressed. He thinks briefly about Bart, a senior known to everyone on the campus, and he thinks of a friend's remark, "If Bart weren't so handsome, he wouldn't have so many chances to show that he's just a pup."

Bart fades from his mind as he passes a girl he knows. They

exchange pleasant greetings, and he naturally considers her for a minute or two. She isn't very bright, she's not at all pretty, and she has no style. "She's nice, though," he thinks generously. "She'll make some fellow a good wife—if she gets the fellow."

At the foot of the hill, the tempting odor of popcorn stops him. The vendor is an Italian, swarthy, unshaven, dirty, and stupid-looking, but his eyes are magnificently large and dark, and he is humming "Celeste Aida" softly to himself.

"A bag of popcorn, Tony," he says, "and put lots of butter and salt on it!" The Italian opens the glass door, and the smell of popcorn increases tenfold. Instantly the student is home. He is ten years old. He and his sister are popping corn over the coals in the fireplace. His face is hot and his hands are burning.

"You betcha," says Tony. "Lotsa da but'."

The student pays for the popcorn, stuffs the bag into his pocket, crosses the street, and pauses to listen to a policeman berating a motorist loudly and profanely.

"Boloney!" the officer replies nastily. "Tell it to the judge."

On the student goes. A little old woman bumps into him and apologizes so profusely that he feels ashamed.

"It was my fault," he lies generously. "I was dreaming." Her shy smile of gratitude makes him feel warm and happy. He is glad he lied.

Let us leave our hero there. We need not take him any further, because he has already collected theme subjects galore:

The Subjects

1. The pleasure of avoiding work.
2. College slang.
3. Soldiers' Gate—what it stands for, what it looks like, or—if the student hates war—what such symbols glorify and perpetuate.
4. Amateur artists.
5. The responsibility charm brings.
6. A good wife.
7. Music and Italians.
8. Dialects.
9. Popcorn memories.
10. A popcorn machine.
11. Italian eyes.
12. The power of smell to evoke memories.
13. Police manners.
14. The timidity of Americans.
15. The pitifulness of old age.
16. Is lying ever justified? [10]

This advice is more likely to assist in the production of better themes. Despite the dated clumsiness of dialogue that often afflicts professors writing about students and the resultant stuffiness of the central figure (it is hard to like "our hero" as he wanders across the campus), this is rather good writing, and it sets a good example of the relationship between generalization and particulars and between experience and writing. It is a good statement of one of the most widely quoted rules for writers. According to Sir Philip Sidney, it was said to him by the muse of poetry, who ordered him to give up posing. He finished his sonnet by her admonition: " 'Fool,' said my muse to me, 'look in thy heart and write.' "

Like mostly widely quoted rules, the look-in-thy-heart dictum is at least a half-truth, if no more than that, especially if it is taken, as it usually is, to mean that one should write only out of real and direct experience. The advice, too, is often vulgarized into a principle of practicality: write only about what you know directly, are enthusiastic about, and know will sell. The evidence runs too strong against so simple-minded a rule. If Herman Melville, Joseph Conrad, and Somerset Maugham wrote about the Far East and the South Seas on the basis of their experience, Stevenson, who sometimes wrote better and sometimes worse than they, wrote about the South Seas before he went there and only went there because he became enthusiastic in the course of his writing. The truest part of the look-into-thy-heart prescription is that people often write most vividly and think most originally as the result of strong interests that awaken their imaginations. Stevenson tells in letters of three things that captured his imagination as a child—the sound of a pegleg tapping, an account of a leper with his bell, the thought of a blind man armed with a pistol. From these, in part, came the imagination of *Treasure Island, Black Arrow,* and *Kidnapped.* But it may be wanting an experience (Stevenson and the South Seas), hating an experience (Sinclair Lewis and the small town or Stephen Crane and what he saw of war as a journalist), and even determination to write what people know will not sell (Lewis and *Main Street,* written as an expected commercial failure to make up for having written five mildly successful potboilers) that captures the imagination and gives rise to the idea from which a new piece of writing can come.

Thomas Uzzell, in discussing how experience must pass through feeling to come into writing, quotes from a private communication from Irvin S. Cobb, telling how he came to write *The Belled Buzzard.*

One morning I was returning in a motor-boat to my father-in-law's summer cottage on Tybee Island, Georgia, after a fishing trip to the mouth of the Savannah River. On a sandspit a flock of buzzards fed on a dead shark. The sight of them, with their ungainly, flipping movements, their naked heads and their unwholesome contours, set me to thinking. My mind went back to the stories I had heard in a country newspaper-office in Kentucky of that hardy animal of rural correspondents, the belled buzzard. To myself I said that here a man might find material for a short story.

That same day I got the notion for my beginning and picked on a name and personality for my principal character. The following day, I think it was, my climax came to me, all in a flash.

I was busied for the moment with other work but when I returned North, a fortnight later, and went up to the Adirondacks, I sat down and wrote the yarn in about four days of fairly steady grinding. The Post printed it and it became perhaps the best known of all my serious stories.[11]

This passage from Cobb not only parallels the classic accounts right down to the Poincaréan "all in a flash," but it makes clearly the additional point already mentioned in referring to Stevenson's *Treasure Island, Black Arrow,* and *Kidnapped*—the importance to the artist of a central image (frequently visual) or symbol or emotion around which the imagination mulls and elaborates, consciously and unconsciously, a complete new construct. This notion of the genesis of a poem or story is frequent enough in the introspective accounts of writers that it may correspond to a kind of motivating force, a kind of imaginative focus, similarly at work in the course of the creative activity of people working in the sciences as well.

Perrin quotes a student's description of her methods of work in completing an assignment for a composition course. Her account closely parallels the classic accounts of the creative process as perceived by scientists: *

1. General interest in some subject.
2. Collecting and reading material or concentrated thinking—expansion.
3. Rest.
4. Deducing some idea.

* Compare H. L. F. Helmholtz's three principal stages of thinking: examination and consideration of a problem; incubation period during which the subconscious gets involved; solution to problem, frequently appearing apparently spontaneously to the conscious mind.

5. Attacking it any way, some way—to get a start.
6. First draft. Bad, very bad. All sorts of irrelevant ideas crop up. No sense to anything. Despair absolute.
7. Dutifully hanging on to some thread.
8. A sudden inspiration. New viewpoint of the whole thing.
9. Shaping an outline.
10. With outline in mind and in sight, beginning fresh copy.
11. Gradual and painful progress. Matter of discrimination. Pulling in all relevant material. Arranging material so that it will bear upon a POINT. Translating my deductions.
12. Finally an end.

Am in habit of thinking slow (perhaps chaotically)—writing slow—usually get stuck at points 5 and 6 and very often cut the whole process off right there—result: all sorts of blasphemous statements.[12]

The trouble with this as a kindly guide to writers is much the same as the trouble with Helmholtz's, John Dewey's, or James Harvey Robinson's descriptions of the creative process, rational thought, or idle curiosity. The unconscious is presumably to be stoked by packing in all sorts and bits of information that may or may not be relevant to the problem. Then, presumably, after having sweated hard for a while, one waits to see whether the underground was ignited and, after smoldering a while, will leap up with a flame that rises to the conscious mind and, in a flash, illuminates the problem and suggests an answer that can then be tried out in an orderly workaday fashion. This is a gratifying way to perceive the creative process from the vantage point of hindsight. It is stupefying to a person faced with a difficult problem and depending upon this way of looking at problem solving, a way that tells him, in effect, "Look up everything you can think of, think hard about everything, tear up your hair a bit, then relax or work on something else and leave it up to your unconscious; if you're lucky you'll get an idea after a while."

The problem, then, is what kind of first aid to offer the creative process, what to do that will make the lightning—the good lightning—more likely to strike. The best kind of rude first aid for the writer in search of an idea has already been cited in discussing what the textbooks have to say: hunt, in effect, for the subject that really involves and kindles your imagination and try to narrow the subject down enough and in such a way that it becomes manageable—and original.

A number of the textbooks devote quite a bit of space to

the notion of narrowing the subject down, though they also treat of this process as something to be done by starting with a general subject (say the Anglo-Norman period in English history), dividing (as into Anglo-Norman literature, Anglo-Norman law, Anglo-Norman architecture, and the like), subdividing (literature: lyrics, allegories, religious, romances, chronicles, and on and on!), and further subdividing (chronicles: Geoffrey of Monmouth and Wace; treatment of Lear in Geoffrey vs. treatment of Lear in Shakespeare). This is to continue until one arrives at a topic that sounds interesting to oneself and presumably satisfactory to a teacher or reader or publisher—both in terms of being related to what he already knows or thinks or believes and in terms of seeming new or different because of bringing a new light to the problem.

Walter S. Campbell, a professor better known to the writing magazines and the readers of Western and Southwestern adventure stories under his pseudonym "Stanley Vestal," has a number of suggestions both in his *Professional Writing* and in his *Writing Non-Fiction*. Talking in the latter about the problem of involving the imagination in landing upon an appropriate subject, he says:

In writing non-fiction, the choice of the subject is of the first importance. . . . There is a valid distinction, not always understood, between subject and subject-matter. . . . By subject-matter we mean the things and people about which an author writes: for example . . . the French Revolution. . . . Thus, if a man were to write of France, he would probably meet with most success if he chose the period of the French Revolution since (in addition to its dramatic events and its connection with American history) it has been written about so often that readers are all prepared. . . . Of course, not every writer can pick and choose at will. He must use what rouses his own imagination. . . . So much for *subject-matter* and your *intimate subject*.[13]

At the end of the chapter from which the preceding quotation is taken, Campbell gives a number of exercises for a student to go through in trying to discover what he will do best to write about:

List ten general subjects in which the public is now keenly interested. Underscore any of these ten which interest you.
List ten general subjects in which few people are now interested. Underscore any of these ten which interest you.
List here general subjects in which you are keenly interested. Which one interests you most?

List here general subjects in which you are not interested.
What are your intimate subjects?
Now suggest several articles or other pieces of non-fiction in which you might combine or express *both* your *subject-matter* and your *intimate subject*.[13]

This is very useful not merely in showing the relationship between the interests of the public or readers and those of the writer and in suggesting the nature of emotional involvement in subject, but also in suggesting some sort of crossing of interests ("combine or express *both* your subject-matter and your intimate subject").*

On the basis, then, of reading such things and worrying about students worrying about what they were going to write about, I experimented with ways of getting them to do two basic things with what seemed to them possible subjects: narrow them down and cross them with each other in the belief that hybrids are likely to be new and larger.

For a first assignment each person in a composition class was asked to turn in a list of at least ten subjects that he thought might be appropriate for him to write about. The assumption that the subjects would be overgeneral ones of the kind that would be likely to result in dull, commonplace pieces that the students would not enjoy writing and no one would enjoy reading was borne out. One example, turned in by a good student, was this:

Occupations	Customs
Hobbies	Home
Reading	Friends
Travel	Nature
Education	Pets
Sports	Organizations
Morals	Amusements
Manners	

For a second assignment each student was asked to take ten of the topics he had turned in for his first assignment, write each at the head of a separate page, and subdivide each into at

---

* This seems to be true despite the end-of-the-volume note on the passages already quoted. It cites as an example of determining both *subject matter* and *intimate subject* a student who read Seger's *I Become a Medicine Man* and decided that he would in writing use "Problems of a Pioneer Teacher" as his "general subject matter" and "Love of Indians" as his "intimate subject." A reasonable inference is that Professor Campbell developed a better idea than he understood.

least ten more specific topics. An example from the same student
who turned in the list already quoted shows how he subdivided
under the heading "Occupations":

Applying for jobs
Lure of aviation
Why I want to teach
Washing dishes in a fraternity house
Summer lifeguard
Picking hops
Running a paper route
Growing prize-winning roses
Summer hotel waiter
I want to be an engineer
The lobster watch
Country doctor
House-furnishing
Is marriage a career?
Caddying
Does society owe me a job?

To be sure, some of these would be better topics than others,
and some people made better lists than others, but the second, or
subdivided, lists did regularly show an improvement over the
first lists, not only because they were more specific and so more
manageable within the compass of a short composition, but because the student's real or desired experience, his life and his
imagination, began to be involved in his subject so that he would
be more likely to write out of his own experience and interest
and so produce something that would seem new, different, or
"interesting" to a reader.

Students were then asked to put each of the topics on the
subdivided, or second, list onto a separate three-by-five-inch
card. They were encouraged to keep notes, in the course of their
ordinary daily routines, on such things as facts, attitudes, phrases,
titles they encountered in books, articles, editorials, movies, radio
programs, lectures, conversations, dreams, and the like—anything
that strongly attracted or repelled them, filled them with enthusiasm, made them shudder, or made them think of something
apparently unrelated or surprising. These notes at intervals were
to be converted into additional topic cards. Once a week for
several months the students were asked to go through their cards,

stopping at each one to see whether they could think of a still more specific subject that deserved being committed to a new card. This was the first, or narrow, stage.

The second, or cross, stage is a free-floating game of random juxtaposition. You are confronted with the need to write and no subject comes insistently to mind? Go through the pack of cards until you come to one, no matter which one, that seems at least generally appropriate. Put it in front of you. Then slowly and painfully, one at a time, put the other cards alongside it. As you look at each pair of randomly juxtaposed topics, see how many topics or notions or ideas you can list that come from putting these two topics together, working out a relation between them, or narrowing one of them down under the influence of the other.*

Students seldom found it necessary to go very far through the pack before finding a subject that got them started, writing or researching, at a paper they were interested in trying to write. Of course, if someone had run through his pack once unsuccessfully, he would have pulled out a new card to replace the first card and then started through his pack a second time.

It is by no means possible to guarantee that the game of random juxtapositions will produce a new general field theory, not even that it can help a student produce a marketable article. I can, however, happily testify that it greatly reduced, almost eliminated, the familiar tedium of the English teacher facing a pile of themes that nobody wanted to write and nobody wants to read.

REFERENCES

1. Lowes, John Livingston. *The Road to Xanadu*. New York: Vantage Press, 1959.

2. Horace. *The Art of Poetry* in Moxon, T. A., editor. *Poetics of Aristotle; On Style by Demetrius; etc.* (Everyman 901.) London: J. M. Dent, 1934.

3. Ginsberg, Allen. *Howl and Other Poems*. San Francisco: City Lights, 1956.

4. Arnheim, Rudolf *et al. Poets at Work*. New York: Harcourt Brace & Co., 1948.

5. Anderson, Harold H. *Creativity and Its Cultivation*. New York: Harper & Bros., 1959.

6. Hadamard, Jacques. *Psychol-*

* One student, for example, who had written "French Revolution" on one card and "practical inventions" on another, after looking at the cards side by side, wrote a fine paper on "Discovery and Invention during the French Revolution," an original idea and paper clearly owing its origin to the random-juxtaposition game.

ogy of Invention in the Mathematical Field. New York: Dover Press, 1954.

7. Ghiselin, Brewster. *The Creative Process*. Berkeley: University of California Press, 1952.

8. Barnett, Lincoln. *The Universe and Mr. Einstein*. New York: William Sloane, 1948.

9. Caskey, John Homer *et al*. *College Composition*. Boston: Ginn & Company, 1943.

10. Marks, Percy. *Better Themes*. New York: Harcourt Brace & Co., 1936.

11. Uzzell, Thomas H. *Narrative Technique*. New York: Harcourt Brace & Co., 1936.

12. Perrin, Porter G. *Writer's Guide and Index to English*. Chicago: Scott Foresman & Co., 1942.

13. Campbell, Walter S. *Writing Non-Fiction*. Boston: The Writer, 1944.

CREATIVITY AND THE SCIENTIFIC PAPER

Myron A. Coler

INTRODUCTION

This essay covers a portion of a larger study with which I have been concerned for a number of years and which now appears to be ripe for delineation of patterns and synthesis.

The larger study relates to methods of dealing with creativity in the sciences. Within that vast area ostensible simplification has been secured at least temporarily by focusing on mathematics, the "natural sciences," and their consequents. Further ostensible simplification has been secured by emphasizing those methods which are manifest in the creative product or contribution rather than those methods which are attributed to the mental processes of the creative person.

Even within these nominal confines, the larger study is an ambitious one which tends to branch and cross-link rather than terminate. One important derivative may be the elimination of the dichotomy between so-called "intuitive" and "logical" methods.

The purpose of the present essay is to provide a first step in the communication of the larger study in such a way as to establish a convenient basis for future reference and cumulative building. Because of this foundation-laying aspect, certain points and concepts have been introduced but not pursued at this time. In the interest of reasonable self-sufficiency and condensation, rigor has yielded to informality in a number of instances. However, again because of the foundation-laying requirements, the overall presentation is rather more formal and structured than a first reading might indicate.

The entire study is not designed ultimately to produce a formula approach to scientific creativity, but rather to develop a way of "talking" systematically and operationally about scientific contributions and particularly about creative ones in a discriminating manner. The present essay indicates one approach and a few of the implications of that approach.

It may be interesting to point out that, despite the tentative flavor of some of the preceding remarks and the abstract nature of the following sections, we are not dealing with something which is purely imaginary or arbitrary. Precursor variants of the abstracted operations have been effectively utilized by such dissimilar workers as Mendeléeff in establishing the periodic table and Hollerith in developing indispensable antecedents of certain modern computing and data-processing techniques. In a small and personal way, I have employed other variants to good advantage in connection with such diverse problems as steering an engineering company through public issue, developing a new nontrivial plastic product for a governmental agency, and devising an improved chemical-separation process.

Although the title refers to "the scientific paper," the term is intended to be regarded broadly and is roughly synonymous with the term "scientific literature." The more representative type of scientific paper has served as a prototype, but the reasoning does not depend on whether or not the "paper" is a conventional article, a book, a patent, or trade literature with some technical content, and so forth. Many of the observations will obviously apply to nonscientific literature and to scientific papers which are not creative.

In view of the longer range purpose of the entire study, an attempt to define "creativity" precisely might not only prove useless but also circuitously self-defeating. Nevertheless, for introductory purposes it may be helpful to associate "creativity" with a product or contribution which is at least partially new, useful, and unexpected. In the case of tangible processes and products, these attributes approximate the requirements for an "invention" in the sense of the patent law and the currently prevalent interpretations.

Perhaps one of the most useful contributions of the present essay is the explicit recognition of the value of the scientific literature, not only as prime and neglected source material but also as the most promising area of attack in attempting to develop scientific methods of coping with the subject of creativity in the sciences.

To be sure, there has always been an established procedure of referral to the prior literature in the supplementing and bolstering of subsequent scientific literature. However, the interest has usually been in the specific technical content and not related to methods in creativity. Apart from the meager and scattered literature bearing on such methods per se, the exploitation of the scientific literature as a self-revealing source of information on methods seems to have been limited to a few anecdotal accounts of dubious general applicability and the marginal use of the literature for assigning productivity ratings to authors. This seems strange in view of the fact that the scientific literature is the best and only source of information regarding most creative scientific contributions since the beginnings of recorded history.

An effort has been made to keep the present essay as simple as possible. However, I do not believe that necessary progress is attainable in this field without the use of symbolic techniques. For simplicity, the use of such symbols has therefore been somewhat restricted, and for convenience a Summary of Symbols has been provided at the end of this essay.

TRANSFORMATION OF A PAPER

Consider an investigator or worker in a scientific field who decides to write a paper on the subject. For convenience let us refer to the writer as **W**, the subject as **S**, and the paper as **P**. We assume that **W** is competent and that **S** is neither trivial nor dead-ended.

In the course of preparing **P**, there is an infinite number of thoughts which might be entertained. However, **W** is a single human being working in a finite period of time and can therefore entertain only a finite number of these thoughts. For a variety of reasons he will express only a portion of them in **P**.

P will be made up of a finite sequence (ordered denumerable set) of symbols on paper. The symbols may be ordinary letters and words, hieroglyphs, chemical formulae, and the like.

If we assume that **W** behaves in a conventional way, most if not all of these symbols will be collected in assemblages which constitute *statements*. Since the symbols of **P** must perforce be ordered, it is convenient to think of **P** as a finite sequence of statements.

We shall now consider a seemingly innocent stepwise transformation of **P**. The transformation is not innocent. In fact, it is not only not unique in a mathematical sense but in instances may prove to be readily conceivable but not formally or practically operable.

We assume, as indicated above, that **W** has prepared **P** and that it can be represented as a sequence of statements. This is not a very restrictive assumption; it gives **W** enormous latitude and license. We now proceed to seek a useful metamorphosis of **P**.

It is possible that **P** includes demonstrative sketches, graphs, and the like. We recall the classic lesson of mathematics in which the foundations of analysis were established by men such as Weierstrass and Cauchy. Needed mathematical rigor, among other things, was gained by requiring algebraic methods, or methods depending on limiting processes in contradistinction to visual demonstrations. As a first step, and possibly with an excess of nonapplicable imitative zeal, we ask **W** to replace all of his graphs and visual aids with corresponding words or analytic expressions. We shall denote the revised manuscript as **P′**. It will consist of a sequence of statements which can presumably be represented in word or symbol-for-word analytic form.

We proceed to have each statement written on a separate card so that **P′** is replaced by a set of cards which we denote as $C_1, C_2, C_3, \ldots, C_M$, and collectively as the set $\{\,C\,\}$.

The word "statement" is now a bit too loose for our purpose. Let us introduce as a device the oversimplified concept of what we shall call a *unit statement*. This is a statement which **W** believes corresponds to a single point or comment which **W** intended to make in his paper. The statements of **P** and hence ultimately those of the cards $\{\,C\,\}$ may be strongly influenced by considerations of syntax, conventions, and literary effects. Many scientific papers have an almost stereotyped form based on the editorial requirements of the journal in which they appear; the form may not be particularly suited to the subject. Again, for ease of reading, a single ordinary statement of **P′** may correspond to several distinct unit statements. Thus, for example, the introduction to an article on "The Dielectric Properties of Organic Compounds" might state, "The aryl ethers, aldehydes, and alcohols have been previously studied by Jones, Smith, and Tompkins." The corresponding unit statements might be: "Jones has studied the aryl ethers," "Smith has studied the aryl aldehydes," and "Tompkins has studied the aryl alcohols." On the other hand, the same intended unit statement might appear in **P′** as a number of scattered and overlapping related statements for purposes of emphasis. For instance, the unit statement "concentrated perchloric acid should be handled with great care" might be covered in the same laboratory manual by the somewhat repetitive statements, "perchloric acid can be dangerously explosive," "the student should discuss the handling of perchloric acid personally with the laboratory assistant on duty before requisitioning it from the stockroom," "students working in the laboratory alone may not use concentrated perchloric acid," and so on.

We now ask **W** to produce a new set of cards by recasting the set $\{\, C \,\}$ into unit statements with only one unit statement on a card. We denote the new cards as $U_1, U_2, U_3, \ldots, U_N$, and the set collectively as $\{\, U \,\}$.

The average paper contains many statements which are peripheral or even irrelevant to the subject proper. Such statements include acknowledgments, name of the author and his affiliation, historical footnotes in nonhistorical papers, parenthetic conversion data from British into metric units, and so forth. There may be statements which on review are considered to be unclear or in error.

Similarly, there may be included statements designed primarily to show how able or thorough the author is or how important the subject is. These statements may actually contribute little or nothing to the subject itself, even though they may serve such pedagogic purposes as helping to hold the reader's attention. Many illustrative examples included in technical papers have more to do with the presentation than with **S** per se.

Again, the peripheral material may include apparently necessary statements which may still not be part of the ultimate subject. Electrical engineering texts often contain significant sections on Laplace transforms and Fourier analysis which are of a purely mathematical nature. Similarly, many scientific papers contain a significant number of statements relating to sign conventions, the use of superscripts and subscripts, standardized nomenclature, and the like.

We next ask **W** to select from the unit statement cards $\{ U \}$ those cards which he believes are central to what **P** presents regarding **S**. We denote this subset $\{ U \}$ by $\{ E \}$ and refer to the corresponding unit statements $E_1, E_2, E_3, \ldots, E_n$ as the *elements* of **P**.

Now, a paper deals with a subject not only through the content of its statements but also by the clustering and ordering of these statements. Even the cards of $C_1, C_2, \ldots, C_M$ which carry the original statements cannot be arbitrarily shuffled and still be regarded as simply representing **P'**. To go from a shuffled $\{ C \}$ to the original ordered $\{ C \}$, and hence **P'**, would require a decoding operation. The situation may become more confused if we shuffle the $\{ U \}$ cards, since as indicated previously there will usually not be a one-to-one correspondence: a single $\{ C \}$ card may result in several $\{ U \}$ cards and several other $\{ C \}$ cards may result in a single $\{ U \}$ card. The apparent economy in replacing several $\{ C \}$ cards by a single $\{ U \}$ card will often tend to be more in the area of uniformity of statement rather than in the elimination of repetition. Thus, for example, in a text on Euclidian geometry, the same postulate is referred to in connection with many proofs even though it may always occur in the same (unit statement) form.

The transition to shuffled $\{ E \}$ cards may involve a simplification in that there may be fewer cards to deal with, but it also may lead to a complication in decoding due to the lack of peripheral hints and clues.

We therefore ask **W** to arrange the $\{ E \}$ cards in a sequence of subsets, each subset consisting of a designated sequence of element cards, so as to best cover what **P** was intended to present. As noted, elements may be repeated.

It is convenient to use a matrix representation in which the rows correspond to the subsequences and the numbers, written in element columns, correspond to the order which the particular element is to assume in the subset.

By way of a somewhat oversimplified example, suppose that $\{ E \}$ consists of just five elements E_1, E_2, E_3, E_4, E_5 and the sequence of subsets happens to be $\{ E_1, E_4 \}, \{ E_2, E_5 \}, \{ E_3 \},$ $\{ E_2, E_1, E_3 \}, \{ E_5, E_1 \},$ and $\{ E_4, E_2, E_3 \},$ respectively. The corresponding matrix would be as follows, with the understanding that the corresponding cards are to be read a row at a time:

SUBSEQUENCE ORDER	E_1	E_2	E_3	E_4	E_5
1	1			2	
2		1			2
3			1		
4	2	1	3		
5	2				1
6		2	3	1	

It is also convenient to adopt a canonical form and rewrite the matrix simply as follows:

$$\begin{Vmatrix} 1 & 0 & 0 & 2 & 0 \\ 0 & 1 & 0 & 0 & 2 \\ 0 & 0 & 1 & 0 & 0 \\ 2 & 1 & 3 & 0 & 0 \\ 2 & 0 & 0 & 0 & 1 \\ 0 & 2 & 3 & 1 & 0 \end{Vmatrix}$$

The corresponding two-dimensional arrangement of cards (elements) for the general case $E_1, E_2, \ldots, E_n$ will be denoted by $M(\{E\})$.

P has thus been transformed, at least in concept, to a doubly ordered sequence of elementary statements believed by W to be central to S. We designate this transformation, mentioned at the outset, as $T(P)$.

If we use an arrow to mean something like "leads to," the steps in the overall transformation may be conveniently recapitulated.

$$T(P) : P \to P' \to \{C\} \to \{U\} \to \{E\} \to M(\{E\})$$

SORTING OF THE ELEMENTS

Quite apart from considerations of order and arrangement, we might also ask W to sort the elements $\{E\}$ into categories which reflect the extent to which P is intended to convey a questioning attitude toward the corresponding statements.

Imagine that **W** is provided with three boxes (set categories) denoted as { Q }, { A }, and { J }, respectively. He is asked to take each card of { E } and place it in the particular box which best approximates the degree of doubt or questioning entertained.

If a statement represents a real open-ended *question* arising in **P**, the corresponding card is to be placed in { Q }.

If a statement is one which is considered to be *accepted* without question, the corresponding card is to be placed in { A }. It does not matter if the statement is accepted on knowledge, faith, hearsay, or even unchallenged assertion. Axioms and so-called "self-evident truths," such as "equals added to equals are equal," will go into { A }.

If **W** considers a statement as presented in **P** to be speculative, the corresponding card is to be placed in { J }, the *conjecture* box. Without further refinement the { J } category may cover an enormous gamut of statements ranging from frankly labeled unabashed guesses to the most elaborately supported theories or hypotheses.

W may object to having just these three categories for disposition of the entire { E } set. He may feel that there are cards which do not properly belong in the { Q }, { A }, or { J } categories. Again, he may feel that he is not quite ready to make the decision as to whether or not certain statements are best classified as { J } or { A } statements for purposes of **P**. He may encounter similar decision problems in assigning marginal { J } or { Q } classifications. **W** may believe that nothing is gained by forcing these decisions. **W** may also object to the lack of resolution in { J } and feel that the category is so broad as to preclude useful discrimination.

Nevertheless, at the risk of some oversimplification, we shall, for present purposes, force these decision problems and insist on the { Q }–{ A }–{ J } sorting procedure. It should be remembered that the criteria for selecting the { E } statements preclude knowing duplication on the part of **W**.

Before considering some of the implications, it is important to observe that the sorting of the { E } statements is not determined by the particular phrasing or punctuation of the statements. A word statement may be cast or recast to "sound" like one which is questioned, accepted, or conjectured, but the intent rather than the form is determining. Consider the three following statements:

1.   Is the visible universe expanding?
2.   The visible universe is expanding.
3.   The visible universe seems to be expanding.

On the basis of mere wording and punctuation, these statements could be classified as { Q }, { A }, and { J } statements, respectively.

If, however, we consider the intent to be an unquestioned assertion that the universe is expanding, then they are all { A } statements with (1) in the form of a rhetorical question and (3) in the form of an underplayed assertion.

If the intent is to offer a hypothesis that the universe is expanding, then they are all { J } statements with (1) in the form of a somewhat underplayed conjecture and (2) in the form of a rhetorical conjecture.

Similarly, the sorting does not depend upon whether or not the statement is cast in positive or negative form. Consider the two statements.

1.   The square of the hypotenuse of a right triangle is equal to the sum of the squares of the two sides.
2.   The square of the hypotenuse of a right triangle is not less nor greater than the sum of the squares of the two sides.

Both of these statements are substantially equivalent from the standpoint of { E } sorting. Technically, (2) might be better covered by two { E } statements.

Many such examples and variations might be adduced. We shall again invoke a simplifying assumption and postulate that **P** is sufficiently well written to permit reasonable sorting of the statements into the { Q }, { A }, and { J } categories.

However, apart from form, there is an important aspect of intent to which we have not yet given necessary consideration. It stems from the almost definitive phenomenon that, in the course of any worthwhile paper which is not a mere catalog, some developments or "action" must take place. Conjectured statements may be validated and become accepted statements. Accepted statements may be challenged and reduced to conjectures and possible open questions. If an accepted statement is shown to be invalid, it may even be replaced by an accepted statement which is the negative of the original. The Pythagorean Theorem cited above corresponds to a { J } statement in advance of demonstration and an { A } statement after demonstration. Pythagoras or his contemporaries at one time might have considered the possibility of a simple relation between the sides of a right triangle to be a { Q } statement.

Again, the number of examples and variations may be very great. A subtle source of confusion arises from the fact that in order to achieve economy of form, all equivalent { C } cards were replaced by a single { U } and hence a single { E } card. But when it comes to sorting the { E } cards according to intent, the same { E } statement may be an { A } statement in one section of **P** and a { J } statement in another, and so on.

If we regard the successive sections as corresponding to the successive rows of $M(\{ E \})$, then we require as many cards carrying the identical { E } statement as the number of rows in which the statement occurs, and for each row the statement is sorted into the appropriate { Q }–{ A }–{ J } category.

The additional sorting information may be conveniently incorporated into the matrix $M(\{ E \})$ resulting in a more informative matrix which we shall designate as $M'(\{ E \})$. Thus, suppose in the previous example the sorting of the elements had yielded the pattern:

SUBSEQUENCE ORDER	E_1	E_2	E_3	E_4	E_5
1	{ Q }			{ J }	
2		{ A }			{ A }
3			{ J }		
4	{ J }	{ A }	{ A }		
5	{ A }				{ J }
6		{ A }	{ A }	{ J }	

For brevity, let us use the simple letters Q, A, or J to indicate that the corresponding element belongs to the subsets { Q }, { A }, or { J }, respectively. $M'(\{ E \})$ may then be conveniently written:

$$
\begin{Vmatrix}
Q1 & 0 & 0 & J2 & 0 \\
0 & A1 & 0 & 0 & A2 \\
0 & 0 & J1 & 0 & 0 \\
J2 & A1 & A3 & 0 & 0 \\
A2 & 0 & 0 & 0 & J1 \\
0 & A2 & A3 & J1 & 0
\end{Vmatrix}
$$

Let M'({ Q }) correspond to M'({ E }) with all of the A and J members replaced by zeros. Similarly, let M'({ A }) and M'({ J }) correspond to M'({ E }) with corresponding Q-J and Q-A replacements. Then it is interesting to note that, in general,

$$M'(\{ E \}) = M'(\{ Q \}) + M'(\{ A \}) + M'(\{ J \})$$

SOME IMPLICATIONS AND OBSERVATIONS

Thus far we have been concerned with an analytic resolution of P *as written.* Considerations of intent have been further reflected in recasting, ordering, and sorting of the statements of P. However, before P can come into existence, W must decide what shall be *included,* directly or by reference. We have mentioned that within the inclusion area, certain statements may be regarded as central and others as peripheral or even irrelevant to S.

It is also important to note that there are usually many statements which are central to S and which could be made but which are perforce just tacitly assumed. A paper on an organic synthesis may state without further elaboration that a particular compound was prepared by a Diels-Alder or a Friedel-Crafts reaction. A paper on quantum mechanics may state that a certain relation "follows from the wave equation" without stating the equation or deriving the relation.

We are not attempting to deal here with such problems as those arising from careless omissions or poorly written papers. We are recognizing the fact that W must deliberately rely upon the cumulative nature of S and the assumption that the reader has some knowledge of S or its antecedents. It is convenient for such discussions to introduce a technical concept of the "reader," which we shall denote by R.

R may or may not coincide with any actual reader of P. R is an image in the mind of W, the imaginary person or persons for whom the paper is written. If W is a competent and aware worker in the field, the resemblance between R and actual readers will obviously be more than fortuitous. Yet the distinction is an essential one and should be preserved. Even when W maintains a scientific notebook or diary solely for his future personal use, there is room for offset and discrepancy. Those of us who have tried to recapture the intent and details of old notes are often reminded of the transformations of time.

Much of the substance and tone of **P** is determined by the **R** image. If **W** conceives of **R** as having very little knowledge of **S**, **P** will tend to be spelled out in great detail. If **W** conceives of **R** as having highly specialized knowledge of **S**, **P** may exhibit a catering tendency with respect to the assumed area of specialization. If **W** holds mixed images regarding **R**, this may also be reflected in **P** by oscillation of emphasis, unevenness, and other similar tendencies.

From the standpoint of observations regarding creativity, it is expedient to introduce the concept of the "encyclopedic reader," denoted here as $\mathscr{R}$. $\mathscr{R}$ personified is to be regarded as the reader who has all prior existing knowledge regarding **S** at his command. $\mathscr{R}$ is not a mere personified catalog or information-retrieval system; his knowledge is "at command," not just "on file." $\mathscr{R}$ corresponds in patent parlance to "one skilled in the art."

Unlike **R**, $\mathscr{R}$ is not limited to conception by **W**. **W** may underestimate or overestimate the knowledge possessed by $\mathscr{R}$ according to the extent of **W**'s own knowledge of the field.

$\mathscr{R}$ now assumes a quasi-judicial role. We can say that **P** is a creative contribution to **S** if $\mathscr{R}$ considers it to be creative. In terms of the oversimplified introductory limning of a creative product, **P** is a creative product if $\mathscr{R}$ considers it to be at least partially new, useful, and unexpected. (These attributes should, of course, characterize the same parts simultaneously.) As an approximating example, we may contemplate the case in which **P** is a patent application and $\mathscr{R}$ is an extremely competent patent examiner.

We can now render the approach somewhat more objective by introducing another conceptual device. We imagine that $\mathscr{R}$ turns author and writes the encyclopedic paper on **S** covering the period from the beginnings of **S** to the appearance of **P**. We designate this paper as $\mathscr{P}$. $\mathscr{P}$ is roughly approximated by the aggregate of all of the literature on **S** which has appeared prior to **P**. We denote the augmented literature by $\mathscr{P}$ + **P**. We offer for future exploitation the possibility of evaluating the contribution of **P** to **S** by comparing $\mathscr{P}$ with $\mathscr{P}$ + **P**.

It is most interesting and important to note for future reference that we can probably show that **S** may be so adequately represented by $\mathscr{P}$ or a formally augmented $\mathscr{P}$ as to permit interchangeable usage in most relations between $\mathscr{P}$ and **S**.

Since emphasis is on the contribution, we shall usually be concerned with the difference between certain functions of $\mathscr{P}$ and $\mathscr{P} + \mathbf{P}$ rather than the individual absolute functions. Thus, for example, if, with some temporary begging of the definition, we let $G(\mathscr{P})$ represent the gist of $\mathscr{P}$ and its direct implications, then we may be particularly interested in ΔG where $\Delta G \equiv G(\mathscr{P} + \mathbf{P}) - G(\mathscr{P})$. Obviously, a necessary condition for **P** to be a material contribution is that $\Delta G > 0$. This is not a sufficient condition for a creative contribution.

If we involve the Q–A–J sorting scheme, then ΔG may be characterized by changes in the Q–A–J pattern of $\mathscr{P}$ resulting from the addition of **P**. Typical, though not definitive, effects of a creative **P** would include:

1.   Establishing new A entities.
2.   Reducing Q's to J's.
3.   Reducing J's to A's.
4.   Replacing many A's by a single J.
5.   Establishing new Q entities.

There are indications that creative scientific contributions may be characterizable by distinctive algorithms of the Q–A–J shift patterns corresponding to ΔG.

The significant number of possible oversimplifications and conceptual operations introduced in this essay may be a source of concern. However, much progress has been made in science by the use of such mental devices. Many practical problems have been solved by analyses based on nonexistent ideal gases. We manipulate symbols assigned infinite values even though we may only conceive of infinity as the result of finite trending processes. We have even learned to distinguish different types of infinities such as $\aleph_0$ and c. We do not hesitate to write and familiarly calculate with a number like 10^{23} although we are not able or interested in actually executing the implied counting process. No one has ever built a "Turing machine."

Yet we are not committed to particular oversimplifications and devices. They will be modified or replaced if necessary as the subject reveals itself.

SUMMARY OF SYMBOLS

W   Writer

S   Subject

P   Paper written by **W** on **S**.

P′   **P** rewritten by **W** to eliminate dependence on visual aids.

$\{C\}$ The set of statements of **P′** written as separate cards corresponding to $C_1, C_2, C_3, \ldots, C_M$.

$\{U\}$ The set of *unit statements* of **P′** recast from $\{C\}$ by **W** corresponding to $U_1, U_2, U_3, \ldots, U_N$.

$\{E\}$ The set of *elements* of **P′** selected from $\{U\}$ by **W** corresponding to $E_1, E_2, E_3, \ldots, E_n$ and believed to be central to **S**.

$M(\{E\})$ Arrangement of $\{E\}$ by **W** into a matrix so that when the rows are read sequentially the intent of **P** (with respect to matters central to **S**) will be best represented.

T(P)   The overall transformation of **P** into $M(\{E\})$.

→   "Leads to" as applied to the steps or subtransformations of T(P). May also be applied to the overall transformation.

$\{Q\}$ The subset of $\{E\}$ corresponding to a question intended to be raised by **P** as sorted out by **W**.

$\{A\}$ The subset of $\{E\}$ corresponding to statements intended to be accepted by **P** as sorted out by **W**.

$\{J\}$ The subset of $\{E\}$ corresponding to statements intended as conjectures by **P** as sorted out by **W**.

$M'(\{E\})$ The matrix $M(\{E\})$ incorporating the additional information derived from sorting of $\{E\}$ by **W**. (Wherever a column element occurs its priority number in the row is prefixed by a Q, A, or J to indicate that in that row the column element belongs to the subsets $\{Q\}$, $\{A\}$, or $\{J\}$, respectively.)

$M'(\{Q\})$ Matrix resulting from the replacement of all A and J members of $M'(\{E\})$ by zeros.

$M'(\{A\})$ Matrix resulting from the replacement of all Q and J members of $M'(\{E\})$ by zeros.

$M'(\{\ J\ \})$ Matrix resulting from the replacement of all Q and A members of $M'(\{\ E\ \})$ by zeros.

R   The "reader" of **P** as conceived by **W**.

$\mathscr{R}$ "Reader" having encyclopedic knowledge with respect to **S**.

$\mathscr{P}$ Encyclopedic paper on **S** written by $\mathscr{R}$ prior to reading **P**.

$\mathscr{P}+$ **P** $\mathscr{P}$ augmented by **P**.

$G(\mathscr{P})$ Gist of $\mathscr{P}$ and its direct implications.

ΔG $G(\mathscr{P}+$ **P** $) - G(\mathscr{P})$.

REFERENCES

It may have been noted that there are no specific references included in the text of this essay. This arises, on the one hand, from the consideration that, to my knowledge, the direct material is substantially original. On the other hand, my indebtedness for indirect material is so extensive and diffuse that any annotated selection would be arbitrary or overburdening.

Nevertheless, I would like to cite a few references which I have found to be especially helpful or provocative, even though I may have made no visible use of them. In fact, in certain cases I have developed a seemingly, or actually, incompatible approach.

1. Boole, George. *An Investigation of the Laws of Thought* (1854). New York: Dover Publications, 1951.

2. Cohen, John, and Hansel, Mark. *Risk and Gambling.* New York: Philosophical Library, 1956.

3. Jaffe, Bernard. *Mendeléeff.* (*The World of Mathematics,* ed. James R. Newman, II, 919–31.) New York: Simon & Schuster, 1956.

4. Mendeléeff, Dmitri. *Periodic Laws of the Chemical Elements.* (*The World of Mathematics,* ed. James R. Newman, II, 913–18.) New York: Simon & Schuster, 1956.

5. Nagel, Ernest, and Newman, James R. *Gödel's Proof.* New York: New York University Press, 1958.

6. Pólya, George. *Mathematics and Plausible Reasoning.* 2 vols. Princeton: Princeton University Press, 1954.

7. Shockley, William. "On the Statistics of Individual Variations of Productivity in Research Laboratories," *Proceedings of the IRE,* 45:279–90 (1957).

8. Turing, A. M. *Can a Machine Think?* (*The World of Mathematics,* ed. James R. Newman, IV, 2099–2123.) New York: Simon & Schuster, 1956.

9. Von Neumann, John, and Morgenstern, Oskar. *Theory of Games and Economic Behavior.* Princeton: Princeton University Press, 1953.

1892